TARGET AMERICA

The Influence of Communist Propaganda on U.S. Media

James L. Tyson

REGNERY GATEWAY
CHICAGO

Published by Regnery Gatewav
360 West Superior Street
Chicago, Illinois 60610

Manufactured in the United States of America

Library of Congress Catalog Card Number: 80-54762
International Standard Book Number: 0-89526-671-7

CONTENTS

PREFACE

Since 1950, the United States has fought two wars, both against countries vastly inferior to us militarily, economically, and in terms of population and resources. Our enemies, North Korea and North Vietnam, were third or fourth rate countries, but against one the best we could do was fight to a draw. In Vietnam, we suffered a humiliating and costly defeat.

How could this have happened?

It is important that Americans understand the answer to that question, lest they go on repeating the mistakes that have already cost us so dearly. As we embark—and rightly so—on an expensive effort to reconstitute our military might, we must recognize that the best weapons systems in the world will do us no good if we continue to disregard our vulnerability on the battlefield of words.

It was with words and ideas that our enemies frustrated our military might in Korea and Vietnam. They demonstrated the continuing validity of the old adage, "The pen is mightier than the sword." Their target was the morale of both our troops in the field and our civilian population, but especially the latter.

In World War I and World War II, we were well aware of the importance of using words and ideas to sap the morale of our foes. We also knew that it was important to defend ourselves against similar efforts by the Germans and Japanese directed against our military forces and the civilians who were backing them up.

Ironically, when we were confronted with enemies affiliated with the international communist network in the years following World War II we neglected the power of words and ideas even though we knew that the communists were masters of propaganda and disinformation. In this vital area, we literally practiced unilateral disarmament, abandoning all defense and gutting our offensive capabilities, leaving only a hollow shell.

Needless to say, the communists have used their own agents of influence, propaganda and disinformation to encourage this process, just as they encouraged us to neglect our military defenses. Despite a wealth of incontrovertible evidence to the contrary, our people are constantly bombarded with assurances that defenses against the enemy's war of words and ideas are not only unnecessary but damaging to our cause. Occasionally, a man of wisdom, who has taken the trouble to study the real world, has tried to warn us against this folly. One of the most eloquent was the longshoreman philosopher, Eric Hoffer, who in his *Ordeal of Change*, published in 1952, wrote:

> We know that words cannot move mountains, but they can move the multitude; and men are more ready to fight and die for a word than for anything else. Words shape thought, stir feeling and beget action; they kill and revive, corrupt and cure. The "men of words"—priests, prophets, intellectuals—have played a more decisive role in history than military leaders, statesmen, and businessmen.

No less important than the priests, prophets, and intellectuals are those who staff and control the mass communications media. It was they, after all, who determined to set all America awash on a sea of guilt over the killing by American troops of some 100 civilians at My Lai while virtually ignoring the communist massacre of 5,000 civilians at Hue in February 1968. It was they who decided that we lost the battles known as the Tet Offensive, even though the enemy failed to achieve his goal of capturing the major population centers of Vietnam and we virtually destroyed the Viet Cong as a fighting force.

Such anomalies are perplexing and seemingly irrational if we make the standard assumption that all Americans share a common interest in preserving and expanding freedom and defeating the efforts of the communists to extend their totalitarian dominion.

They make sense only if they are viewed as part of the effort of the enemies of freedom to confuse its defenders and undermine their morale. That is a jarring notion. Those who advance it are almost certain to be accused of "McCarthyism," a convenient term invented by the communists to smear anyone who endeavors to call attention to their very real machinations. Two respected world-class journalists, Arnaud de Borchgrave and Robert Moss, performed an immense service in calling attention to the worldwide disinformation operations of the Soviet KGB in their novel, *The Spike*.

That was fiction, although it was not entirely divorced from reality. Now James Tyson has tackled this very serious problem in a nonfiction work, *Target America*. Tyson documents what so many have only surmised. This country is the target of a massive and frighteningly successful war of words inspired by governments that despise and fear freedom and aided by a host of witting and unwitting helpers. As a long-time media critic, I have been appalled to observe the ease with which important media organs in this country have been enlisted to assist in this campaign.

Truth in labeling is enforced for goods on the shelves of grocery stores, but not for what you see in the newspapers or on television. Communist writers are published in such prestigious and influential papers as The New York *Times* without being properly identified. Communist propaganda is not only aired over our public broadcasting facilities, but is even financed with grants from the taxpayer-funded Corporation for Public Broadcasting. It is not, of course, so labeled. The "most trusted man in America," Walter Cronkite gives Soviet disinformation experts a national platform—the CBS television network—to lie about the Soviet military build-up and to claim non-involvement in communist-led coups in other countries. Cronkite does not contradict them.

James Tyson has performed a valuable service in documenting the baleful record and showing why the United States is frighteningly vulnerable. It should alert the American people to the fact that wars are fought and won with words and ideas as much as with missiles, planes, tanks and ships. And those wars go on even when we think we are at peace.

Reed Irvine

INTRODUCTION

During 1980 the American people displayed several signs of growing anger and alarm at continuing Soviet aggression and American reversals abroad. In November this concern was a major factor in the defeat of the Carter Administration and several appeasement-minded senators.

But anxiety about America's position in the world continues. The trends of the past decade cannot be reversed overnight, and in recent years many of the ablest observers of our defense situation went so far as to declare that if these trends persisted, the U.S. could be defeated by the Soviet Union within the next ten years. Brian Crozier, one of Great Britain's leading students of strategy, published a study of the peril of the West entitled *Strategy of Survival* in 1978, in which he says the democracies face defeat in the near future. "Unless the West reacts *now*," he concludes, "meaning by 1980, the chances are that the tide of retreat will be irreversible."[1]

Several American defense experts are equally concerned but reluctant to be so frank for publication. The closer the observer is to the facts of Soviet preparations, the more worried he is. The most worried of all are those Russian emigres *who have seen Communist preparations from the inside*. Dr. Igor S. Glagolev was a member of the Soviet Academy of Sciences and an adviser to the Russian SALT I negotiators. After the treaty was signed, he recommended some logical armaments cuts. He was shocked to be told by his superiors that they had no intention of reducing their arms, but instead planned to increase them until they had overwhelming superiority. In disillusionment he defected to the West in 1976, settled in Washington, and has been waging a one-man warning campaign ever since.

Another better known émigré, of course, is Alexander Solzhenit-

1

syn, who has also been a tireless Jeremiah, warning America of probable defeat if we do not regain our courage. "Will you wait until the Communists are beating at your gates and your sons will have to defend your borders with their breasts?" he cried in one of his most dramatic appeals.

A third prominent Russian refugee is Lev Navrozov, formerly a leading translator of English in Russia who worked frequently with propaganda organs. He emigrated to the U.S. in 1972 via Israel and published a best-selling autobiography, *The Education of Lev Navrozov*, in 1975. Navrozov says the main Communist propaganda goal is to lull the West into complacency and hide the facts of the Soviet military build-up until their superiority is so vast that they can impose Communism on the democracies without having to fire a shot.[2]

The Soviets are following a three-part strategy: (1) the enormous arms buildup, as Glagolev and Navrozov warn, hidden under the smoke screen of detente and the SALT negotiations; (2) a gradual take-over of other weaker countries by pro-Communist regimes, leading to the eventual encirclement of the U.S. on the outside; and (3) a massive, secret propaganda campaign designed to weaken and demoralize America from the inside.

The first two threats are recognized by some of the public and many of our leaders, particularly in the new Reagan administration. But the third is virtually unknown except to a few specialists. And it may be as dangerous as the first two because of the fact that the public is not even aware of it.

This propaganda campaign has been going on with increasing vigor and long-range planning ever since the Bolshevik Revolution. It is designed to undermine our confidence in our own democratic system and our leaders, to destroy our trust in our security agencies (the FBI, CIA, and police forces) so that the Communists can operate more freely against us in this country and abroad, and to undermine our foreign policy so that we fail to support our allies in the fight against Communism and allow the encirclement to continue almost unopposed.

If this forecast of encirclement sounds alarmist, just consider the history of the past 40 years. In 1939 there was only one Communist country, the Soviet Union, accounting for about 7% of the earth's population. In 1940 the Soviets swallowed up the three Baltic Republics. Within a year after VJ Day they had forced Communist governments on Poland, Rumania, Hungary, Bulgaria, Yu-

2

goslavia, East Germany, and North Korea. In succeeding years we have seen the communization of Czechoslovakia, China, North Viet Nam, Cuba, South Viet Nam, Cambodia, Laos, Mozambique, Angola, South Yemen, Ethiopia, and Afghanistan. As a result, Communist governments now control more than a third of the world's population. The Communists prepared for every one of these conquests by a massive campaign of propaganda and subversion before taking any military action. In most of their victim countries they directed the softening up against the local governments, but in addition, for all of Eastern Europe, China, Cuba, South Viet Nam, Cambodia, and Angola, they also waged clever propaganda campaigns in the U.S. and Western Europe to confuse the democracies and undermine our resolve to resist this Communist imperialism.

While the American people are waking up to the Communist political and military threat, it is time they were awakened to this propaganda threat. Only if we become aware of it can we neutralize it. In its present largely undercover form, it represents one of the most serious dangers facing the country today.

How is it possible to illustrate the effects of such Communist propaganda in the United States? It has become difficult in recent years to identify Communist agents in the media or other influential organizations. The FBI has been ordered not to investigate subversive activity unless there is *already evidence of criminal behaviour*. This restriction has literally wrecked the Bureau's ability to monitor Communist subversion. (How can you get evidence of criminal behaviour until you have first conducted an investigation?) The FBI's number of open cases of security investigations dropped from 21,414 in 1973 to 50 in 1979.

Investigation of Communist *propaganda* activities in the U.S. is considered even further outside the FBI's present charter. This was made clear in an exchange of correspondence between the Bureau and Senator Gordon Humphrey of the Senate Armed Service Committee in late 1979. Several senators on this Committee were concerned that the Soviets were attempting to manipulate American media and public opinion to obtain a SALT II Treaty favorable to the USSR and damaging to U.S. security.

Humphrey's first letter to the FBI was prompted by the CIA's large study of Soviet propaganda *in other countries* released on July 3, 1978 (See page 264). In the covering letter for this study, CIA Director Admiral Turner said that it did not cover propaganda activities within the U.S. since that was outside the CIA's purview, but he recommended that Congress request such a study from "the appropriate agency" since the CIA had "indications that Soviet propaganda activities against the United States will increase in the future." On August 22, 1979, Humphrey wrote William Webster, director of the FBI, recommending such a study as being of benefit to several matters of Armed Services Committee concern. After several oral exchanges with Bureau personnel, Humphrey received a letter from Webster on November 19 saying, *"This Bureau does not have a data base upon which to predicate a study or discussion of such issues, since we do not dedicate personnel to tracking the sources of news articles bearing on U.S.-USSR relations to see if they were Soviet inspired.... In view of the foregoing, the unclassified study requested in your letter of August 22 cannot be undertaken....* The FBI's foreign counter-intelligence mission is narrowly focused on the clandestine intelligence and terrorist activities of foreign powers in this country. In that regard, the FBI does possess considerable classified information pertaining to clandestine efforts on the part of Soviet intelligence operatives in the United States to use, or rather manipulate, the American media and/or influence policymakers ...."

The last sentence seems to indicate that the Bureau has *some* information on clandestine Soviet propaganda efforts, but evidently this was not gathered as a result of a systematic investigation of the matter, since that is beyond the Bureau's present charter. In subsequent correspondence and conversations with the Bureau and the Justice Department, Senator Humphrey was unable to arrange for a briefing or a public report on this subject.[3]

Not only the FBI's counter-subversion efforts, but the congressional committees that used to investigate Communist (as well as right-wing) subversion, have all been dismantled, including the Senate Internal Securities Subcommittee, the Senate Subcommittee on Criminal Laws and Procedures, and the House Internal Security Committee. The Subversive Activities Control Board has also been abolished, all under the theory that the Cold War is an outdated concept.

As a result the only media personalities who can be positively identified as present or former Communists today are those of the *older generation*, whose careers extend back into the years when there were active investigations of subversives.

But there are two techniques we can use to provide at least strong circumstantial evidence of Communist influence:

The "Balance Sheet" method

Draw up a balance sheet listing all the major stories, articles, or broadcasts of the media personality in question. These can be listed under two major headings: (a) debits—those that appear to follow the current Communist line, or (b) credits—those written from a position harmful to the Communist line. It may be that many of the articles under (a) are based somewhat on true facts. The Communists frequently select their propaganda campaigns in areas where there is a large element of truth (for example, corruption or lack of ideal democracy in a small country under attack by the Communists—as we shall see below for Cambodia). But if the writer in question shows a balance sheet with all his articles on the debit— pro-Communist—side, and *none* on the credit side, this may not be firm proof that he is an agent, but it is certainly strong evidence that he is being useful to the USSR. Six such balance sheets are presented in the Appendix for four individuals and two think-tanks, whose activities are described more fully in later chapters.[4]

The Case History method

Prepare a brief case history of media treatment of a major subject whose treatment can now be shown to have been based so clearly on *false information* and at the same time to have *followed the Communist line so closely* that it must have been the work either of agents or of Communist manipulation.

Later chapters employ this technique. They present seven case histories illustrating how major issues in American foreign or defense policies were the subject of Communist propaganda that can now be shown to have been based on *falsehoods*. These chapters will also describe how such campaigns affected public opinion, and in some cases, government policy as well.

5

COMMUNIST PROPAGANDA - HISTORY, PRESENT TECHNIQUES, AND ORGANIZATION

Since the United States and most of the Soviet Union's other major targets are democracies, since democracies are ruled by public opinion, and since the function of propaganda is to sway public opinion, the importance of propaganda to the Soviets is obvious. The Soviet Union has many ways of swaying public opinion. But none is so devastatingly effective as covert propaganda, that is a stream of thoughts, arguments, and positions designed to favor Soviet goals, which do not appear to come from the Soviet Union, but rather to emanate from the Western body politic itself. The distinguishing feature of democracies is that they believe themselves to be ruled by their own public opinion. When a democracy listens to the open declarations and appeals from a foreign nation, it in fact grants that foreign nation something like the most precious political privilege it grants its own citizens: the right to be heard. But when a nation succeeds in clandestinely introducing ideas into a democracy's public discourse, then it succeeds in gaining for itself an important share in that democracy's own government. When the Soviet Union succeeds in planting clandestine propaganda in any democratic country, it in effect diminishes the importance of that country's genuinely domestic opinion. This is the very definition of subversion. And this is what the Soviet Union is well practiced at doing.

Since the most effective propaganda is clandestine, the means by which it is spread are quite indistinguishable from those of covert political action and very close indeed to those of clandestine intelligence collection. All these means involve finding persons in the target country who, for whatever reason, wittingly, semi-wittingly, or unwittingly, are willing to promote the line of argument favored by the communists or to insure that the opposing points of view are killed ("spiked," in newspaper parlance).

Countries affected by successful covert propaganda may suffer internal demoralization, controversy, and eventual surrender, and in the end blame it on "divisions within our society" "selfish corporations" "big labor unions," and the agents we hear falsely blamed so often when democracies criticize themselves.

Propaganda as a Communist Weapon

We can begin to glimpse the scope of Soviet covert propaganda in the life history of one notably successful Russian propagandist: General Ivan Ivanovitch Agayants. Details of his background are hidden (even the name may be an alias), but by the latest account he was an Armenian Communist who climbed rapidly through the ranks of the KGB to become a senior officer of the KGB and first director of its Department D, or Disinformation Department (sometimes called the Demolition Department), a vital organ in the Soviets' propaganda apparatus.[1] But it is known that he was the brains behind the "Swastika Operation" that swept Western Germany and many other countries in 1959 and 1960. On Christmas Eve in 1959 swastikas were painted on a synagogue in Cologne. During the next few weeks, other synagogues and Jewish tombstones and memorials were defaced with swastikas all across West Germany. Jews in Germany and Britain received threatening phone calls, and one Jewish member of Parliament had to have a body guard. Over the following months, similar incidents occured in twenty cities in Europe, the U.S., Latin America, and Australia. A great reaction against West Germany took place: some companies cancelled orders for German goods, and Germans working abroad were fired from their jobs. It was not until later in the 1960s that evidence from Russian defectors was pieced together to show that the entire affair was a "disinformation operation," designed to embitter relations between West Germany and the other democracies. It had been conducted not by resurgent Nazis, but by Agayants' Department D.[2]

By 1961 Agayants was stationed in France under another pseudonym, Ivan Ivanovitch Avalov. There his work seems to have been as much involved with espionage as with propaganda, showing the close association between these two types of undercover work in the Soviet scheme of things. Among his other accomplishments in

Paris, Agayants was the "Control" for George Pacques, a French Communist agent who had held top positions in the French military establishment. In 1961, during the Berlin crisis, Pacques gave the KGB a copy of the Allied plans for the defense of the city which revealed that if the Communists built a barrier to seal off East Berlin, the Allies would not stop them by force. This enabled the Communists to erect the Berlin Wall with impunity, virtually eliminating the great flow of defectors from East to West Germany. In 1963 Pacques was a senior official in the NATO command with the highest ("cosmic") security clearance. His work for the Russians was discovered and after a long investigation and trial, he was sentenced to life imprisonment in the most sensational French spy scandal since Mata Hari.[3]

The skills that brought General Agayants the Soviet Union's dark and secret equivalents of fame and fortune are encouraged by the Soviet system but not at all encouraged in the United States. There are no schools in the U.S. for propagandists in democratic priniciples. Of the 1.8 million young people who graduate from American colleges every year, none are trained specifically to promote democracy or free enterprise abroad or in the U.S. Those who have studied politics and make careers in that field are concerned mainly with promoting the fortunes of the Democratic Party versus the Republicans, or vice versa. None are educated for careers in propaganda for democracy.

In the USSR the situation could not be more different. It has been estimated that there are more than 3 million people inside the country with the job of agitation and propaganda (agitprop) among the Russian people themselves. Some of these agiprop cadres are assigned to as few as three other people only, with the task of keeping in touch with them full-time to make sure they are toeing the party line (and, incidentally, reporting them if they stray).

But in addition to the millions of domestic propagandists, thousands of young people are being trained every year for careers in agitation and propaganda overseas. The Lenin School in Moscow, founded in 1926, is devoted exclusively to training Communist cadres from other Western countries. This and similar revolutionary academies have graduated more than 120,000 foreign students since 1926, including many who later became well known Communists like Gus Hall in the United States, Maurice Thorez in France, Ernst Thaelman of Germany, and Chou En Lai of China.

Furthermore, large numbers of additional bureaucrats are busy with general internal propaganda duties in the information media; in newspapers, magazines, and broadcasting services; and in the propaganda ministry. And hundreds of thousands are engaged in propaganda work abroad.

Size of the Effort

How much money does the Soviet Union spend on propaganda? How successful has the Soviet Union been in placing propaganda agents in the U.S.? It is impossible to get exact figures, but all reasonable estimates are so huge that, even discounting for error, they provide an astonishing picture of the size of the Soviet effort.

Suzanne Labin, a French expert on Communism, estimated in 1967 that the Communists were spending about $2 billion annually and were supporting at least a half million people on propaganda outside the USSR as agents, fellow travellers, or active sympathizers. The U.S. Information Agency *twenty years ago* made estimates ranging from $1.5 to $2 billion. This was judged to be about 2% of the entire Soviet GNP and more than twenty times what the U.S. was spending on propaganda or "information" at the time.[4] The CIA now puts the figure at more than $3 billion and says this estimate is probably conservative.[5] These figures can be compared with estimates from an even more direct source on the number of people engaged in propaganda *within the Soviet Union itself.* On September 11, 1970, Pravda said that 1.1 million people are engaged in propaganda inside the Soviet Union. The Eastern European Bible Mission, which monitors Soviet media and Free World commentary on the Soviets, has assembled the following estimates:

> 1,200,000 active propagandists
> 80,000 atheist lecturers
> 1,800,000 political informers
> 3,700,000 agitators who specialize in working with teachers and students, youth organizations, and labor unions

Total: 6,780,000 (part time and full time—There may be some duplication in these figures.)[6]

The Economist estimates that there are 9 million agit-props working within the USSR![7] It is difficult to judge such figures, except to note, once again, that they are very large, and that even if only a fraction of these numbers are engaged in propaganda, the effort is awesome.

The position of propagandist or agitprop is a prestigious one in the Soviet apparatus, considered to be as respectable a profession in Communist countries as accountancy or civil engineering in the United States. Present day Communist periodicals make frequent and matter-of-fact reference to "Propagandists" within the Soviet Union as offhandedly as American newspapers would refer to an attorney or a surgeon. The Russian people themselves are washed in a continuing shower of propaganda, not only in the newspapers and on radio and TV, but also from bill-boards in the streets and factories and by streetcorner speakers and even speakers on soap-boxes in theatre lobbies during intermissions.[8]

Another indication of the size and dignity of this profession is that there are no less than six professional journals for agitprops in the Soviet Union, which we could compare to the *Journal of Accountancy* or *Engineering News-Record*[f] in the U.S. One of these journals, *Agitator,* is used mainly for training foreigners in the techniques of propaganda and agitation. Lee Harvey Oswald read it regularly during his years in the Soviet Union, though he was refused when he tried to subscribe to it after his return to the U.S.[9] Another is *The Agitator's Notebook,* a small hand-held periodical with flip-over binding like a stenographer's pad, summarizing the latest party line. (An issue in early 1980 summarized the line the propagandists should use to demonstrate how the Olympics will show the superiority of the Communist way of life.) Every political unit in the USSR from provinces down to cities and villages has a Communist Party organization with at least three top officials: the chairman, the secretary, *and the agitprop.* There is a similar party structure, including the agit-prop, within most other major organizations such as labor unions.

If one considers that the Communist Party has assigned these millions of people to carry out propaganda *against their own citizens* within the Soviet Union, the estimate of a half million agents outside the country does not seem far-fetched. According to figures quoted earlier, the various universities and schools for Communist cadres have graduated more than 120,000 people *from foreign countries* since 1926. These are the top experts, the full time professional cadres. They do not include the less fully trained: the fellow travellers and sympathizers who may have never even visited the Soviet Union.

How many of these are operating in the United States? Again there are no official figures, but it is possible to arrive at maximum and minimum estimates, and even the minimums are surprising. Let us disregard the half million world total for a moment and start with the $3 billion annual expenditures worldwide. Allowing one quarter of this for personnel costs would be $750 million. We might in turn allow $15,000 per average person. This is only perhaps one fifth of the cost of a senior agent, but it is several times the cost of the large number of part-time sympathizers with other full-time paying jobs. Dividing $750 million by $15,000 equals 50,000 agents around the world.

Let us assume that the Soviets have allocated the effort roughly in proportion to the population of target countries. The United States has about 8% of the world's population outside the Communist bloc. Eight percent of 50,000 equals 4,000 active propagandists in the United States! This estimate assumes that the Communists have planned their effort simply on population, *i.e.*, that they consider the U.S. less important than, for example, India, which is certainly not true. If, however, we took the world-wide total estimate of 500,000 rather than our 50,000, the figure for the U.S. would be 40,000! Let us simply say that there is presumptive evidence that there are something more than 4,000 agents, fellow travellers, or sympathizers actively supporting Communist propaganda efforts in the U.S.

Finally we can get another fix on the size of the campaign in the U.S. by applying the 8% population ratio to the figure of $3 billion of world-wide propaganda expenditures. *Eight percent of $3 billion equals $240 million*, a large sum to be devoted annually to an effort most Americans do not realize even exists.

Partial corroboration comes from the best source the FBI ever had in the U.S. Communist Party. Herbert Philbrick, a young pacifist who became disillusioned with the cynicism of the Communists in first opposing and then supporting the war against Hitler, offered to work undercover for the FBI in the 1940s. He estimated that in the late 1940s there were more than 2,000 members of Communist "Pro-Cells" in the United States. Pro-Cell members were American professionals—doctors, lawyers, journalists, advertising agency executives, and other opinion leaders—organized into ultra-secret cells. They were ordered to destroy their party cards, and their membership was unknown even to most regular party members. These were the vanguard of the vanguard, the intelligentsia, who were assigned special tasks of long-term propaganda and espionage.[10] Today the roll of formal party members is about one fourth what it was in the 1940s, but we have lost the ability even to estimate the size of the corps of secret "non-member" sympathizers such as the ones in the old Pro-Cells. Of course, one would expect that only a fraction of the Soviet propaganda effort in the U.S. would be conducted by such long-term assets.

So in summary it seems conservative to hypothesize, for lack of better data, that there are probably a few thousand Communist propaganda agents working within the United States today, and that over $240 million is being spent annually on such efforts.

Organization

How is this broad activity organized? Again the evidence is sketchy. Responsibility for Soviet propaganda rests not with any government department but *with the Communist Party*, which directs a huge Department of Propaganda and Agitation responsible for both foreign and domestic efforts. This is housed in a massive building in Moscow. Alexander Kasnacheev, a KGB agent who defected to the Americans in Burma, describes occasional visits to this headquarters where he was awed by the military discipline, elaborate security, and extreme secrecy.[11]

The man in charge is M. A. Suslov, one of the senior members of the Politburo. Suslov is considered to be the Soviet's leading theoretician on Communism. Second in command is Boris Ponomarev, head of the International Department and responsible for operations in non-Communist countries. This International Department has taken over the work formerly performed by the notorious Comintern which in the days of operators like Grigory Zinoviev and the Hungarian, Bela Kun, was responsible for the control of Communist parties in other countries and the planning and execution of foreign propaganda and subversion. These now fall under Ponomarev's department. Suslov is responsible for setting overall propaganda policies, while Ponomarev is in charge of carrying out these policies around the free world.

Under Ponomarev's International Department is the International Information Department responsible for such overt activities as the news services (*Tass* and *Novostii*), foreign work of *Pravda*, *Izvestiya*, and Radio Moscow, and the voluminous activities of Embassy Information Departments. While these operations are ostensibly public, they also include a large amount of undercover propaganda. Head of this International Information Department is Leonid M. Zamyatin, formerly director of *Tass*.

The KGB's Department of Disinformation mentioned earlier is

13

another important center of power in propaganda. General Agay-ants' old Disinformation Department D was expanded from a "De-partment" to a "Service" when Yuri Andropov became chief of the KGB, and is now known as Directorate A, responsible for an in-creased level of psychological warfare around the world, consisting of the floating of forgeries, planting mendacious articles in friendly media, and similar deceptions. While other Soviet organs are re-sponsible for more subtle propaganda, the Disinformation Direc-torate specializes in "outright lies," to quote Dr. Glagolev. Accord-ing to Glagolev's estimate, they are now executing more than 500 such disinformation operations per year around the world. A further symptom of the Soviets' high regard for propaganda and espionage is that the KGB's Director, General Yuri Andropov, like Suslov, is a member of the Politburo. (Contrast that with the U.S. where the heads of the FBI, CIA and the International Communications Agency are well below Cabinet rank.)

Another influential organ in propaganda against the United States is the Institute for the Study of the U.S.A. and Canada, a part of the Soviet Academy, headed by Dr. Georgi Arbatov.

How is the apparatus organized within the United States? Ray Wannall, former chief of the FBI's Counter-Intelligence Service, is of the opinion that since the early 1950s Soviet propaganda against the U.S. has been directed from outside the country. Certainly the Com-munist Party U.S.A. plays only a subsidiary role. Most propaganda direction comes from Ponomarev's International Department of the Central Committee, although often the KGB performs overlapping operations. In order to direct activities in the U.S., Soviet control officers travel in and out of the country. They do so under a variety of identities and pretexts. In this, the large international Communist front groups are useful. The largest of these is the World Peace Council. Other activities are transmitted through a myriad of other fronts, including the World Federation of Trade Unions (WFTU), the International Union of Students, the International Organization of Journalists, the Christian Peace Conference (which despite its name is a Communist front), the Women's International Democratic Federation, and the International Association of Democratic Law-yers. All of these groups maintain relations with contacts in the U.S. and promote continuous intercourse through international con-ferences, periodicals, and other communications. But the U.S. is so open that virtually anyone can come and go on any pretext what-ever. And some of these groups have American counterparts. The

World Peace Council works through the U.S. Peace Council headed by veteran American Communist Pauline Rosen. The American counterpart of the World Federation of Democratic Youth is the Young Workers Liberation League. Other links are less formal, and direct control has not been proven. But for example, the National Lawyers Guild has close ties to the International Association of Democratic Lawyers, while Women Strike for Peace in the U.S. has a long-standing close association with the Women's International Democratic Federation. And the WFTU maintains close relations with an American organization known as Trade Unionists for Action and Democracy.

In addition, within the U.S. there has grown up a large number of study centers, citizens' committees, and public affairs coalitions that maintain close relationships with these international Communist fronts. Only a few of these have been identified by congressional committees or the attorney general as Communist fronts, but all of them have one common characteristic: they consistently back causes that knowingly or unknowingly give aid or comfort to the Communists and have *never* advocated policies that are contrary to the Communist line. As a group they can be classified under one name, "The Far Left Lobby," and will be described in the next chapter. The most important of these and their knowing or unknowing support of the Soviet propaganda organs are also summarized on Chart I on the next page.

Chinese Operations

So far we have been describing mainly the development of techniques by the Soviet Union. But Communist China from its beginnings has also devoted a large amount of resources to propaganda. The late Chou En Lai and hundreds of other Chinese officials spent years studying in Russia and have followed Soviet propaganda practices as well as elaborating on them with their own native skills. The Chinese, in fact, were the first to produce a textbook on military theory containing a clear definition of propaganda. Writing about 600 B.C., the Chinese military genius Sun Tzu said, "Undermine the enemy first, then his army will fall to you. Subvert him, attack his morals, strike at his economy, corrupt him. Sow discord among his leaders. Destroy him without fighting him."[12]

The Chinese Communist government administers a propaganda apparatus within its own borders almost as massive as that of the Soviets. There are a large central propaganda department and agit-

ORGANIZATION OF SOVIET PROPAGANDA AND U.S. GROUPS PROVIDING KNOWING AND UNKNOWING SUPPORT

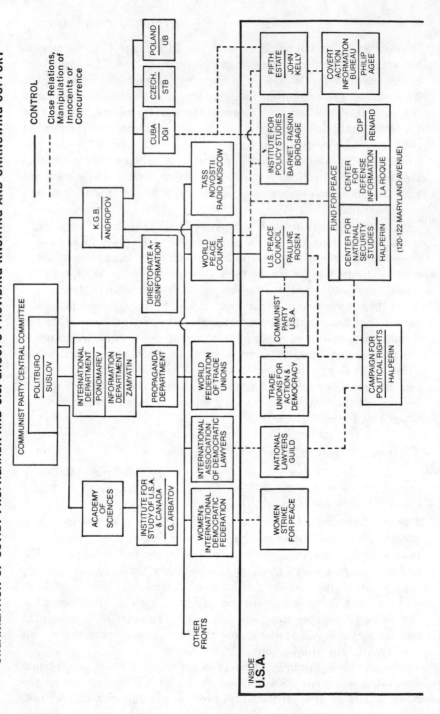

CONTROL ⎯⎯⎯⎯

Close Relations, Manipulation of Innocents or Concurrence - - - - -

COMMUNIST PARTY CENTRAL COMMITTEE

POLITBURO / SUSLOV

ACADEMY OF SCIENCES

INSTITUTE FOR STUDY OF U.S.A. & CANADA / G. ARBATOV

INTERNATIONAL DEPARTMENT / PONOMAREV

INFORMATION DEPARTMENT / ZAMYATIN

PROPAGANDA DEPARTMENT

K.G.B. / ANDROPOV

DIRECTORATE A - DISINFORMATION

TASS NOVOSTII RADIO MOSCOW

CUBA / DGI

CZECH. / STB

POLAND / UB

WOMEN's INTERNATIONAL DEMOCRATIC FEDERATION

INTERNATIONAL ASSOCIATION OF DEMOCRATIC LAWYERS

WORLD FEDERATION OF TRADE UNIONS

WORLD PEACE COUNCIL

WOMEN STRIKE FOR PEACE

NATIONAL LAWYERS GUILD

TRADE UNIONS FOR ACTION & DEMOCRACY

COMMUNIST PARTY U.S.A.

U.S. PEACE COUNCIL / PAULINE ROSEN

INSTITUTE FOR POLICY STUDIES / BARNET RASKIN BOROSAGE

FIFTH ESTATE / JOHN KELLY

COVERT ACTION INFORMATION BUREAU / PHILIP AGEE

FUND FOR PEACE

CENTER FOR NATIONAL SECURITY STUDIES / HALPERIN

CENTER FOR DEFENSE INFORMATION / LA ROQUE

CIP / RENARD

(120-122 MARYLAND AVENUE)

CAMPAIGN FOR POLITICAL RIGHTS / HALPERIN

OTHER FRONTS

INSIDE U.S.A.

prop cadres down through every level of government and other institutions to the lowest echelons.[13] All media are instruments of the central government, and must tailor their editorial policies to the party line. The overseas efforts are not as vast as the Soviets but are substantial and include energetic efforts to manipulate media in other countries.[14] Later chapters show some of the results of these efforts.

The Chinese also work partly through their own agents and partly through local citizens. There are now several legal "Maoist" Communist parties in other countries. In the United States this is the "Communist Party (Marxist-Leninist)" based in Chicago and led by Mike Klonsky, formerly one of the toughest agitators of the Students for a Democratic Society. Klonsky and other CP (ML) officers were welcomed to Peking in 1977, where they were given a massive banquet by Chairman Hua Kuo-feng himself and had several audiences with top leaders where the progress of the revolutionary movement in the U.S. was discussed. Klonsky appeared on the cover of the *Peking Peoples Daily*, in color.[15] But Chinese propaganda, like Soviet propaganda, works only partly through these above-ground parties. Most of the propaganda is carried out by undercover agents and sympathetic *local citizens*.[16]

Although we are now in a period of uneasy rapprochement with the Peoples Republic, there are many areas in recent years where their interests have not coincided with ours. While this book mainly concerns Soviet propaganda, we will see examples in the following pages where pro-Chinese propaganda has affected American media and policy.

Purpose and Methods of Soviet Propaganda

Propaganda has been a principal weapon in the Communist armory from the beginning. Most of the big names in early Socialist history from Marx and Engels down through Herzen, Chernyshevsky, Plekhanov, etc. were voluminous writers possessing varying degrees of skill in promoting the faith. By 1900 Lenin was the Managing Editor of the Communist newspaper, *Iskra* (The Spark), published first in London and then in Geneva.

In 1902 Lenin produced a small pamphlet with a rather clumsy title, "What Is To Be Done?" This dull-sounding little booklet, which is scarcely known today among non-Communists is the first systematic outline of what has since become known as Leninism. It has probably had a more baleful influence than any other publication in twentieth century history. After 1902 Lenin and his followers over the years produced snowstorms of theoretical writings, which have been published and republished in multi-volume editions and pored over by studious Communists. But the major lines of Lenin's theories were all contained in this first grim little pamphlet.

The pamphlet's first main point is that the working class must be led by an elite of dedicated full-time professional revolutionaries, the party faithful, the vanguard. Second, Lenin called for internal discipline, the need to follow a party line agreed to at the highest level. Since then Communist parties have been distinguished from all other political organizations by the practice of "democratic centralism"; i.e., rule by a central elite. Third, Lenin urged the need for propaganda and outlined some of his preliminary ideas on its principles. He stressed the importance of a party newspaper to communicate with the members back in Russia and to help spread the word to others in Russia and elsewhere. Exhorting his followers to "go to all classes of the population as theoreticians, propagandists, agitators, and organizers," he defined agitators as those who would spread a few simple ideas among the mass of the population, and propagandists as those who would promote more sophisticated ideas among the educated elites, who were better equipped to understand.[17]

In the years which followed *What is to be Done?*, Lenin and the Bolsheviks elaborated and refined the methods of propaganda. Lenin became a deep student of mass movements, mass psychology, and the history of revolutionary techniques. While Americans were developing methods of mass production, mass advertising, and market research—techniques for producing and selling goods—the Bolsheviks were devising methods for selling Communism to the world by clandestine propaganda, understood as a method not of intellectual argumentation but of political warfare.

During this period, Lenin developed some important laws of revolutionary propaganda practiced to this day, as we will see in later chapters. Among the most important:

1. *Divide our friends and enemies into clear-cut groups of heroes or villains.* Promote *hate campaigns* against our enemies and even our luke-warm opponents. "The wording [of our press campaigns]," wrote Lenin, "is calculated to provoke in the reader hatred, disgust, contempt. The phrasing must be calculated not to convince but to destroy, not to correct the adversary's mistakes but to annihilate his organization, and wipe it off the face of the earth . . . . It must sow discord and confusion in the ranks and be the opposite of phrasing which would convince and correct." From that time forward, the propaganda of the Communists and even many sympathizers has been characterized by violent language, designed not so much to persuade or convince as it is to shock and dismay. The Radcliffe girls who invade President Pusey's office at Harvard and shout obscenities at him, the Columbia boys who do the same to President Kirk, occupying his office and urinating in his files, the young men and women Viet Nam War protesters marching and chanting

> one, two, three, four,
> we don't want your f - - - - ng war

are all using the same techniques. Opponents of Communist causes are not answered with logical arguments but with accusations of being "fascists," "imperialists," "racists," "war-mongers," "murderers," and so forth. We will see in the following chapters further examples of how these techniques have been applied in practice.

2. Sloganeering. Communist positions should be reduced to simple *slogans*. This technique is one in which Lenin was not ahead of American and European advertising experts and politicians. Slogans had been a lively symptom of the democratic process and commercial life in the United States and Western Europe from early times. But certainly the Communists have been vastly more successful in creating slogans to use against free enterprise and democracy than the latter have been in creating slogans which effectively attack Communism.

3. Transitional Sloganeering, or "Partial Demands." After the Communists gained power in Russia and began to promote world revolution, Lenin and his followers saw that it was time for relaxation of the push and for a consolidation. So they scaled down promotion of the Communist cause itself for a time and instead resorted to promoting all sorts of "partial demands" which they knew would be more acceptable and would gain them followers among people not necessarily sympathetic to Communism.

4. The use of "hooks" to attract sympathizers from all levels of society. This technique was formalized at the Third Communist International in 1921 and in a *Thesis on Tactics* written by Lenin that year. Communist parties around the world were advised to search out and exploit every source of discontent in the masses, every excuse to proselytise and to stir up opposition to existing institutions. Poor wages and working conditions, unemployment, inadequate farm credit, poor teaching in universities, excessive college discipline, poor food in government cafeterias, and every other small excuse could be made a "hook" to attract sympathizers.

This technique was also recommended in *What Is to be Done?*, and was such an important part of Lenin's recommendations that it has been called "Lenin's Law" by some commentators. "There is no segment in the population," Lenin wrote, "without its circle of discontented and maladjusted and alienated individuals, predisposed targets for radical hate propaganda, who can be hooked up to a revolutionary mass movement .... We must use every grain of discontent. We must collect every grain of protest."

5. *The use of mass media to sway mass audiences.* In *What is to be Done?* Lenin stressed the importance of *Iskra* as a party newspaper to spread the word. In his later writings and those of his followers, he continually pounded on the importance of the mass media in propaganda. As radio, movies, and finally TV grew into their present gigantic importance as mass communicators, the Communists were right there to use them. In 1950 Stalin said, "If I could control the movies, I could rule the world." This was before he had any conception of the power of television.

A blunt statement of these objectives was provided by Vyacheslav Molotov, Soviet Foreign Minister, in a report to the Politburo on propaganda: "Who reads the Communist papers? Only a few people who are already Communists. We don't need to propagandize them. What is our object? Who do we have to influence? We have to influence non-Communists if we want to make them Communists or if we want to fool them. So we have to try to infiltrate the big press, to influence millions of people, and not merely thousands."[18]

More recently, John Maury, a senior CIA officer who was head of the Russian section for five years and retired in 1977, quoted a KGB manual obtained by the CIA which gives top priority to recruiting agents not only among the opponents' military and government officials with access to top secret information, but also among *the media.*[19]

6. *The cultivation of satellite organizations and fronts and the enlistment of non-Communist sympathizers and fellow travellers.* These new strategies grew naturally out of the principle enunciated in *What Is To Be Done?* that the Communist Party should be the vanguard leading less sophisticated satellite groups towards a final goal of Communism. As early as 1920, Grigory Zinoviev, president of the Comintern, began to preach the transmission belt method, urging the Comintern members to use every hook to manipulate all groups with any grounds for dissatisfaction: labor unions, veterans organizations, tenants' leagues, and so forth. Of course 'front' groups are useful for many other purposes besides propaganda.

The first master of the art of Communist fronts was Willi Munzenberg. Munzenberg first came to prominence organizing Communist-dominated Youth Groups in Germany after World War I. From there he branched into organizing the International Workers Aid, the first true Communist front—*i.e.*, an organization dominated secretly by the Communists for ostensibly disinterested purposes. The International Workers Aid ran campaigns to raise relief money to help the Russian people who were suffering from a famine in 1921. It was a tremendous success in stimulating assistance and sympathy among non-Communist organizations and opinion leaders in the democracies. After Munzenberg rose to become the (secret) director of the Comintern's Agit-Prop Department in Western Europe, countless organizations of all kinds were created or infiltrated: stamp clubs, hiking clubs, rabbit-raising clubs, workers organizations, peace groups, drama clubs, writers organizations, and so forth. Munzenberg called these his "innocents' clubs."

Munzenberg also masterminded the launching of a number of journals and newspapers, including one picture magazine that reached a circulation of 500,000. He was especially skilled at attracting leading intellectuals to his Communist-inspired functions, including the French writer, Henri Barbusse (who later wrote a flattering biography of Stalin); Britons like Lord Marley and Allen Wilkinson; the American black leader, James W. Ford; and even on some occasions, Albert Einstein. Countless writers, artists, and scholars around the world helped to parrot the party line without in most cases realizing that it was the party line. Munzenberg was the first to use the phrase "fellow traveller" to describe the more dedicated of these collaborators.[20]

Sometimes the innocents are part of the political process. Herbert Philbrick describes a ploy which can be repeated with countless variations.

During the Congressional campaign of 1946, the Communist Party in Massachusetts decided not to run their own candidate but to select someone on the Democratic ticket who could be supported and manipulated into promoting Communist propaganda lines. The party decided on Anthony M. Roche, a liberal pro-labor Democrat. Several Communists wormed their way into Roche's campaign organization. Philbrick was introduced to the candidate by one of them as an "advertising man" who could help him with his publicity and speechwriting, and Roche welcomed this support. As the campaign proceeded, Philbrick and the others had a large part in writing his speeches and setting the tone for campaign rallies and publicity.

On one occasion, when Roche was dragging his feet on the subject of price controls, an important plank in the Communist platform, the Communists organized a fake parade of Massachusetts "housewives" in support of price controls. When the "housewives" just happened to march past Roche's headquarters carrying placards and wheeling baby-carriages, Roche was so impressed with this evidence of "popular support" for price controls that he switched his line to favor them.

In the election Roche polled only 40,000 votes and lost badly, but the Communists had succeeded in using him to promote their own lines and, incidentally, to recruit potential members by means of the meetings and rallies. They dropped him like an old shoe immediately following the election.[21] Such innocents can be played with as long as they remain innocent, in the hope that either they'll never wake up or they'll become committed to the cause.

7. *Planting Stories written in Moscow.* Alexander Kaznecheev, the senior KGB officer specializing in Burmese affairs at the Soviet Embassy in Rangoon who defected to the Americans in 1959, describes the continuing, massive Soviet effort to plant stories in local media around the world. His department of the embassy, secret even to most other Russians in Rangoon, was responsible for receiving drafts of articles from the propaganda headquarters in Moscow, translating them into Burmese, editing them for local consumption, and then seeing that they were placed in local publications to appear as though they had been written by Burmese authors. The final step was to send copies and translations of the Burmese articles back to Moscow. From here they were often quoted in Soviet broadcasts or publications as evidence of "Burmese opinion" that favored the Communist line.[22]

A variant of this technique is to search the Western press for quotations which can be used to support the Soviet line, and then see that they are published. Usually the Soviets don't have to search hard for materials they can use. The open debates which characterize political life in the West generate enough. In the 1970s it was striking to read the Soviet press and broadcast coverage of the Viet Nam War and to note how attacks on U.S. policy are mainly built around quotes from American sources. In other cases the KGB's Disinformation Department relies on outright forgeries. American intelligence has detected innumerable cases over the years of forged documents being used to discredit American agencies or policies. Sometimes these are such obvious fakes as to boomerang on the Communists, but frequently they leave enough smoke to lead people to believe there was some fire. A notable example was the series of Communist forgeries making it appear that the CIA had been behind the efforts by French Generals to overthrow or assassinate President De Gaulle.[23]

8. *Formal Training in Propaganda.* As noted earlier, the U.S.S.R. trains thousands of people a year for careers in agitation and propaganda. Lenin and his followers said early that revolutions do not just happen. Lenin set up a training program in a suburb of Paris in 1907. Other Bolsheviks organized similar schools on Capri; in Bologna, Italy; and in Geneva, with instructors including many of the big names of the Russian Revolution, such as Lenin, Zinoviev, Kamenev, and Lunacharsky. Propaganda was always prominent in the curriculum. And after the revolution Lenin's interest in formal training did not flag. In 1922 he founded the Communist University of Toilers of the East, for Asian students. Soon thereafter the Communist University of Peoples of the West was founded and the Sun-Yat Sen University for Chinese communist students. Revolutionary techniques of propaganda and subversion were important parts of the curriculum at all of these institutions. In 1926, the Director of Agitation and Propaganda of the Comintern, the Hungarian Comunist, Bela Kun, founded the Lenin School in Moscow for the express purpose of training foreign Coummunist functionaries in advanced techniques of agitation and propaganda. Within a few years the student body grew to 900.

A Czech-American graduate of the Lenin School who later renounced Communism has estimated that by 1959 more than 120,000 foreign students had been trained in these Soviet revolutionary academies. This number includes only professional revolutionaries and does not include the much larger number of foreign students who have attended the Soviet Union's more conventional but still propaganda-laden university courses. Moscow State University has a School of Journalism devoted full time to propaganda and Communist journalistic techniques. This institution has *800 day students* taking a five year course and 600 evening and 1,100 correspondence students taking a six year course. There is similar formal training in propaganda at 18 other Soviet universities and Communist Party schools.[15] Furthermore, the institution with the engaging name of the Patrice Lumumba People's Friendship University, founded in 1960, by 1965 had 4,000 students from foreign countries. The courses are mainly technical, with no specific emphasis on subversive techniques. But the vice rector is a major general in the KGB. Many of the promising students are recruited to be trained to engage in political work—including propaganda—when they return home. In 1965 there were an estimated 27,000 foreign students in Russian universities and many more studying in other Eastern European institutions.[24]

Latest Techniques— Propaganda from Within

Since the death of Stalin and the launching of "detente," Soviet propagandists have not abandoned old methods. But they have added new ones. Consider, for example, Dr. Georgi Arbatov, Director of the Institute for the Study of the U.S.A. and Canada, a division of the Soviet Academy of Sciences. Arbatov's principal function is the supervision of studies of American institutions and politics, to advise the Soviet propaganda agencies on the best methods for manipulating American opinion. In *The White House Years*, Henry Kissinger says that Arbatov "knew much about America and was skillful in adjusting his arguments to the prevailing fashion. He was especially subtle in playing to the inexhaustible masochism of American intellectuals, who took it as an article of faith that every difficulty in U.S.-Soviet relations had to be caused by American stupidity or intransigence. He was endlessly ingenious in demonstrating how American rebuffs were frustrating the peaceful, sensitive leaders of the Kremlin, who were being driven reluctantly by our inflexibility into conflicts that offended their inherently gentle natures".[25] Arbatov is regularly welcomed by academic and think-tank scholars in the U.S. and often quoted by CBS, *Newsweek*, the *New York Times*, and other media without comment as to his true motives. For example, in 1977 Dr. J. Kenneth Galbraith was the narrator of a Public Broadcasting System TV series on Socialism and Free Enterprise entitled "The Age of Uncertainty." Georgi Arbatov appeared at a luncheon table seated between Galbraith and Mrs. Katherine Graham, owner of the *Washington Post-Newsweek* enterprise. Late in the program, the camera focussed on Arbatov, who delivered the following statement: "The Russian people love freedom!"[26] Neither Galbraith, Graham, nor PBS pointed out to the audience that while the Russian people may indeed love freedom, Arbatov and his bosses are its enemies.

With people like Arbatov enjoying such prestigious platforms, such respectable company, and such lack of contradiction, older forms of propaganda like Radio Moscow and Russian foreign language magazines have become less significant. Our own media do a better job.

Thus in recent years the Soviets have relied most heavily on *propaganda from within*—i.e., propaganda executed *by citizens of the target countries themselves*, by media personnel, members of public affairs organizations or front groups, and other opinion leaders who have either been recruited as "agents of influence" or are being manipulated without their knowledge. In principle, propaganda from within is the most difficult and least reliable form of the art. To do it successfully one has to stimulate great numbers of people to follow a line simply by giving them cues to which they have accustomed themselves to respond. It is difficult. But when it works, large scale propaganda campaigns can be waged without the target people even being aware that propaganda is taking place or that the Communists are behind it.

Typical Recruits

Since it is far more effective to have one's own line of propaganda written or spoken by people of the same nationality as the target population, the art of propaganda is dependent on the art of inducing persons in the target populations to, in effect, act as agents. The techniques for doing this are not so different from the ones used to recruit agents for espionage or covert action. Yet recruitment for purposes of propaganda is different. The nature of espionage and covert action leaves no doubt in the agent's mind that he *is* an agent. But propaganda is another affair. Some of the best propaganda assets are people who genuinely believe they have a mind of their own, yet follow their cues almost invariably. Also, it is quite normal for people to associate themselves with a propaganda effort through one front organization or another. This means that their association with the effort, effective as it might be at any given time, is only secured by tenuous bonds.

An old example of a front group is the Cambridge Youth Council, which attracted young pacifists in the Boston area to the Communist cause around 1940. Herbert Philbrick was one of those attracted. But when the youth council became pro-war following the Soviet Union's entry into the conflict, Philbrick became disillusioned and began reporting on the group for the FBI.

The modern techniques of propaganda from within requires not so much manipulated front groups as congenial groups encouraged to do their own thing. According to Miles Copeland, a retired CIA officer, the CIA dubbed this technique the "Franchise System" and compared it to the way franchises operate in the field of fast food. The Communists have been encouraging every radical organization around the world that was pushing anything approaching the Communist line or *any line opposed to the United States.* They scaled down their efforts to *control* every such organization, first because it was becoming impossible, and second because it was unnecessary.[27]

Encouragement might take the form of money or advice for smaller organizations (often without such organizations knowing the source), or even manpower and weapons for larger groups.[40]

The Soviets regularly go so far as to give secret support to Trotskyite or Maoist groups that are ostensibly opposed to the Soviet Union or supporting Communist China. The only criterion is that they be *opposed to the United States* on the principle that any enemy of my enemy is my friend.[28] "Let's go after the U.S. now," General Agayants was quoted as saying. 'We can take care of China later." The U.S. is "Glavny Vrag," the main enemy.

Up until 1968 the Soviets had given only lukewarm support to many of the New Left groups, believing them too crazy, irrational, and hard to control. But after 1968, when they saw that the New Left had played a major role in the retirement of Lyndon Johnson and the near downfall of Charles De Gaulle and had put a major crimp in the U.S. Viet Nam effort, they began to take them more seriously and support them actively, even though many such groups were unaware of the support and in some cases continued to attack the Soviet Union.

The recently retired head of the Counter-Intelligence Division of the FBI, Ray Wannall, says that the Communists in recent years are doing more of their recruiting of Americans in foreign countries during international conferences, foreign visits, and other occasions. In the 1920s and 30s, he says, recruiting and "control" of agents were done mainly within the U.S., as in the case of Elizabeth Bentley, Alger Hiss, and others. But since the 1950s this is just as likely to be done abroad, where it is considered safer.[29]

A typical instance is the Venceremos Brigade. From 1968 onwards Cuban and North Vietnamese intelligence agents in the U.S. were active in persuading young radical activists in the U.S. to join this Brigade, which ostensibly was helping with sugar harvests, teaching school, and conducting other peaceful pursuits in Cuba. Many of these young people came from the Weather Underground, an extreme off-shoot of the radical Students for a Democratic Society (SDS). In fact, the Brigade became a pool for the Communists to recruit agents for work in the United States. War protest movement needed not just intellectual protesters but also physically rugged recruits for more violent duty. Such people were trained in guerilla warfare techniques, including the use of arms and explosives. One of the results was the so-called "Days of Rage" in Chicago in 1969 in which several police were injured and at least one permanently crippled.

Another objective of the Cuban Intelligence effort through the Brigade was the recruitment of "individuals who are politically oriented and who someday may obtain a position in the U.S. government, which would provide Cuba with access to political, economic or military intelligence."[30]

Another regular source of recruits is the Soviet educational establishment mentioned above, including the Patrice Lumumba Peoples Friendship University, the Lenin School, etc. All have high KGB officers in their administration.

Journalists, scholars, scientists, and other visitors to Russia are also targets of recruiting efforts.

Yuri Krotkov was a Russian playwright and part-time employee of the KGB on propaganda who defected to the West in 1965. In testimony before the Senate Subcommittee on Internal Security, he described how the KGB was carrying out constant efforts to subvert foreign journalists in Moscow. He cited the KGB's energetic but unsuccessful efforts to subvert two *New York Times* correspondents, Bill Jordan and Jack Raymond. But he says the Soviets were successful in recruiting the Australian journalist, Wilfred Burchett. Krotkov says that Burchett carried out an assignment for Ho Chi

Minh to work with the Pathet Lao communists in Laos, and he has been reported by other sources to have been active in North Korea during the Korean War, attempting to propagandize American prisoners and assisting in interrogation.[31]

Joseph Frolik, a member of the Czech intelligence service for 16 years, defected to the United States in 1975. In November 1975 he testified before the Senate Subcommittee that Czech intelligence in the U.S. was closely controlled by the Russian KGB, and was carrying out an energetic campaign to recruit among the staffs of the U.S. Congress, Government departments, the Republican and Democratic parties, and "mass organizations" like the AFL-CIO, NAACP, and the American Civil Liberties Union. During his tenure in Washington, he said, the Czech embassy devoted considerable time in an attempt to penetrate Ralph Nader's organization, cooperating with Syrian intelligence to gather data on Nader's relatives in Lebanon. He had no knowledge that Nader was recruited but mentioned this activity as typical of Communist efforts to influence opinion leaders.[32]

Recruitment Appeals

Once contact is established, what inducements are used to recruit? In descending order of meritoriousness, following are six typical appeals:

> Idealism
> Ambition
> Money
> Sex
> Alcohol
> Blackmail

Idealism is one of the most common though the success of Communism in recruiting through idealism seems to move in cycles. There are crests when world conditions allow Communists to recruit by the thousands, then troughs when disillusionment sets in and wholesale defections take place.

During the 1930s thousands of idealists in many countries joined the Party because of concern over wide unemployment and hunger during the Depression, followed by the rise of Fascism in Italy and Germany. During this time men joined who later became espionage agents like Kim Philby as well as propaganda "agents of influence" like Hollywood writer Dalton Trumbo and Joseph Barnes of the *Herald Tribune.*

Trumbo claims that all the "finest people" in Hollywood joined the party in protest against Depression conditions in the 1930s. He became so committed that he was even willing to follow the party line and opposed the war against Hitler in 1939 and 1940, during the Hitler-Stalin pact. His novel *Johnny Got His Gun,* written in 1938 about a deaf and blind quadruple amputee, was a brutal attack on all wars, and was widely used in the U.S. by isolationists, Communists, and others opposed to the war. But after Hitler invaded Russia in 1941, Trumbo switched abruptly like other Communists and began to support the war.

Many Hollywood Communists deserted the party after the Hitler-Stalin pact and later Soviet excesses, but Trumbo and others hardlined it and remained party members. They included the "Hollywood Ten," who refused to testify before the House Un-American Activities Committee in 1947, went to jail for contempt and were blacklished by the movie industry. The jailing and blacklishing were later condemned by many, including playwright Lillian Hellman in *Scoundrel Time.* But regardless of the merits of the blacklisting, it is a fact that many members of the Hollywood Ten succeeded in influencing the contents of motion pictures towards a Communist line. Trumbo has boasted that they may not have managed to get pro-Communist films produced by Hollywood, but they did succeed in preventing several outstanding anti-Communist stories from becoming motion pictures, most notably, he said, Arthur Koestler's great novel of the Communist purge trial period, *Darkness at Noon.*[33]

Money is another major appeal. The CIA obtained a top secret KGB training manual, "The Practice of Recruiting Americans in the U.S.A. and the Third World," which states, "Correct use of the factor of material interest requires an understanding of the psychological make-up of the American, who soberly regards money as the sole means of ensuring personal freedom and independence ... to satisfy his material and spiritual needs ... During the process of development, determination of the monetary income of an American is an extremely important matter.[34]

Ambition is frequently used as an appeal. In *Beyond Cloak and Dagger; Inside the CIA,* Miles Copeland, a senior CIA official who retired in 1974, describes a type of American journalist whom the Russians call "maggots." These are reporters who have no strong opinions of their own but believe that in the current climate of opinion they can be most successful by following an anti-anti-Communist line.

Copeland says that the Russians also identify another type they call "termites". These are individuals who are not agents but are so leftist in sympathy that they become anti-anti-Communist. Opposed to efforts to contain Communism, which they believe violate their liberal principles, they aid Communists in passing along their propaganda line.[35]

Sex as a means for recruiting Americans, surprisingly, is rated rather low by the KGB. Their manual says that "promiscuous relationships with women usually cannot serve as convincing compromising material." This is contrary to much popular lore about the KGB, which has used such compromising situations frequently *in Europe*. On the other hand, the manual does say that homosexuality can be grounds for compromising and blackmailing an American, as well as evidence of criminal behavior.

Alcohol is a classic persuader, used more in manipulation than in outright recruiting. Yuri Besmenoff, a recent defector from *Novostii*, the Russian News agency, now living in Canada, testified that during his apprenticeship in Moscow, one of his principal duties was to work on foreign visiting delegations. "As soon as any group got off the plane," he says, "my job was to get them drunk as soon as possible and keep them that way throughout their visit. If I had too much alcohol myself, there were always other comrades to take over from me — but there was no one to replace our delighted guests ... Our first function was to make every foreigner think everything in Russia was just splendid." He adds that he personally "did such a job" on a *Look* photographer in 1967, accompanying him around Russia. He was so successful in maneuvering this American into presenting a favorable picture story of Russia that he was later rewarded with a ticket for a week in Italy.

"If foreign guests showed strong sympathy for the Soviet Union," Besmenoff says, "our job was to prepare them psychologically, and then pass them over to the KGB agents to indoctrinate and recruit them. . . . Such foreign recruits do the dirtiest jobs of all. . . . The KGB trains them to destroy anti-Soviet activists in their own countries through character assassination. The same thing happens to Soviet defectors such as Gouzenko and Solzhenitsyn. . . . Recruits also infiltrate universities, trade unions, and organizations such as the Canadian-Soviet Friendship Society."[36]

Manipulation of well-meaning persons without their knowledge is an important technique. Examples abound.

There are even more subtle forms of manipulation used constantly by the Communist propaganda organizations. Western correspondents and media commentators are targets of continuous efforts. An early example was the Eisenhower-Krushchev Summit Conference of 1955 in Geneva. The Soviets skillfully maneuvered the large crowd of free world journalists into creating an exaggerated atmosphere of hopefulness at the start. When the conference fizzled out with no real progress, the journalists were encouraged to lay much of the blame on Dulles and other democratic statesmen. The Soviet propaganda organs were then able to make it appear that all criticism of Western statesmen was coming from free world sources and the Westerners alone were responsible for the failure of the conference.[37]

And as noted earlier, Soviet attacks on U.S. Vietnam policy in the 1970s, as before were built largely around quotations from American sources.

In summary, there may be little concrete evidence detailing the exact dimensions of the Soviet covert propaganda effort in the U.S. — with our investigative agencies crippled, how could there be? — but there are plenty of indications that the USSR is conducting a massive, deliberate, and highly effective campaign which has had a major impact on our national policy. As indicated above, the overall propaganda *goals* are determined by the Central Committee of the Communist Party in Moscow. (For example, "Get the United States out of Indo-China," "Destroy the CIA," "Kill the Neutron Bomb," etc.) These are implemented by the International Department under Ponomarev and the Information Department under Zamyatin. Their departments get specialized assistance from the KGB, especially its Disinformation Directorate. They work mainly through the local embassies around the world, through Soviet travellers and agents, and through the many international Communist front groups. They also obtain advice from Georgi Arbatov's Institute on the U.S. and Canada.

However, in recent years most of the implementation has been carried out by *agents and sympathisers within the U.S., mainly American citizens*, working in the think tanks, citizens committees, and foundations, and helped by their friends in the media and the government. These are the people primarily responsible for converting the Kremlin's basic goals into specific propaganda campaigns

31

and devising the slogans and tactics that will have most effect on American media, public opinion, and government policy.

A large number of such think tanks, citizens committees, and other organizations have grown up in recent years. Only a few of these have been identified as Communist fronts by the Attorney General or Congressional Committees, but this "Far Left Lobby," which consistently backs causes that help the Communists and *never* advocates policies that contradict the Communist line, will be discussed in detail in the next chapter.

THE FAR LEFT LOBBY

Q. *"Don't you think that some people in the U.S. are always seeing Communists under the bed?"*

Eldridge Cleaver: "But there are Communists under the bed!"

From *Rolling Stone* magazine, 4 September 1976, interview with the former Black Panther leader after his return from being a fugitive in several Communist countries and France.

According to principles developed by Lenin and his associates, front groups are among the finest vehicles for Communist propaganda. The principle of fronts is to employ one or another attraction or "hook" to induce non-Communists to cooperate with Communists or to serve the Communists' objectives. As regards propaganda, fronts are useful because they can pour forth the Communist line, yet give the impression, sometimes correct, that the line is coming from non-Communist sources.

Fronts can conduct research studies, publish books and pamphlets, write letters, conduct seminars, encourage demonstrations, take legal action, and in many similar ways exert influence on the media, on political figures, and on public policy. Kim Philby, the British intelligence officer who was found to be a Communist agent, understood this principle well, having worked for a time in a British propaganda office during World War II. He expressed the principle that if you want to float a propaganda statement, "it is much better to quote an organization than an individual. If the right organizatino doesn't exist, you can invent one." He might have added that it is almost as easy to create real fronts as it is to invent them.

In the affluent society of the United States, "movement" groups have proliferated tremendously. Every man can be Director or

33

Chairman of his own radical pressure group. Francis Watson, an expert on subversion and terrorism now with the Rockford Institute, quotes a figure of no less than 2,400 such movement organizations in the U.S.[1]. Not all can be identified as Communist fronts, but many consistently follow a line favorable to Communist objectives and seldom espouse any cause which the Communists oppose.

This chapter will describe those "movement" groups that wield the greatest influence on the media and public policy and which also show the clearest signs of following a pro-Communist line, knowingly or unknowingly. Some of these organizations have been identified as Communist fronts, and many of the others have Communists sprinkled among their memberships.[2]

Radio Moscow or Peking or the other Iron Curtain countries' broadcasts and print media, quote pronouncements by these groups regularly, almost on a daily basis, in line with the Leninist technique of stimulating comments by supposedly independent sources and then playing them back as evidence of widespread support for Communist objectives.[3] These organizations can be classified under five headings: Legal Organizations, Foundations, Think Tanks, Citizens Committees, and Innocents.

Legal Organizations

It is no accident that the Communists have put a major effort into infiltrating the legal professions in the U.S. In no other country is the Law more influential in politics and even in foreign relations. Overseas observers have commented on our emphasis on the law in our political activities and the almost religious reverence for the details of the Constitution. Any pronouncement by a lawyer or group of lawyers that a given American activity is illegal or that a given Soviet activity is legal can be the starting point for a first class propaganda campaign.

Infiltration of American legal organizations began in 1922 when the Communist International founded an agency known as MOPR (the Russian initials for "International Class War Prisoners Aid Society"). This became known as the International Red Aid (IRA). An American section was set up in 1925 called the International Labor Defense. In 1936 this ILD helped to organize the *National Lawyers Guild (NLG)*, which in 1946 became affiliated with the *International Association of Democratic Lawyers (IADL)*, the world-wide Communist front group for attorneys.[4]

The National Lawyers Guild

Today the Guild has several thousand members, offices in 50 cities, units in most of the leading law schools, and a major operation in Washington. When the League testifies before Congress, its views are accepted as those of strong civil libertarians.

The major media frequently give NLG members a sounding board without identifying their far left tendencies. For example, on May 28, 1978, at the height of the controversy over the indictment of several FBI agents for their investigation of the Weather Underground terrorists, the *New York Times* ran an article on the Op Ed page by Gerald Lefcourt attacking the FBI. Lefcourt was identified only as "an attorney." In fact he is a leading member of the Guild and has a long history of radical activities. In the late 60s and 70s he was attorney for the SDS and the Weather Underground, primary subjects of FBI investigations. So he is hardly a neutral commentator on the FBI.[5]

In December 1978, the AP and UP wire services carried stories on a Middle East report of the NLG accusing Israel of violating the rights of Palestinians and using torture. The Washington *Post* and other papers ran these stories, which failed to mention the pro-Communist leanings of the NLG or that the PLO had initiated the NLG visit to the Middle East and paid the delegates' expenses while there.[6]

Cited several times by HUAC and the Senate Internal Security Committee as a Communist front, the Guild showed its legal clout by mounting a series of hearings and appeals to obtain a dismissal of the listing as a subversive organization on the grounds of "lack of prosecution" by the Government. Nevertheless, it has continued to exhibit unmistakable signs of Communist domination: its continued membership in the IADL, its consistent espousal of Communist causes, the large number of identified Communists in its membership and (a minor but significant point) the singing of "The Internationale" at the conclusion of its 1973 convention in Austin, Texas! And this anthem is not a simple college pep song, as evidenced by the words of its chorus:

Tis the final conflict, let each stand in his place.
The International Soviet shall be the Human Race!

Following is a partial list of present and former NLG officers and members, with their other affiliations:

Paul Harris, President

David Rudovsky, Vice President — also member of National Emergency Civil Liberties Committee (NECLC). Active in several suits against the CIA, FBI, and Selective Service. On Steering Committee of National Conference on Government Spying organized by NLG in Chicago in January 1977, which led to formation of the Campaign to Stop Government Spying. Member of the Center for Constitutional Rights. (For further details on these organizations, see below.)

Catherine Roraback, former President (1972-75) — also a member of the ACLU and Center for Constitutional Rights.

Victor Rabinowitz — member of law firm of Rabinowitz, Boudin, and Standard, which has represented Daniel Ellsberg, Alger Hiss, Communist Cuba, and Soviet spy Judith Coplon. Also member of NECLC. On four occasions refused to answer questions before congressional committees about membership in Communist Party.[7]

Bernardine Dohrn, National Student Organizer, 1967-68 — until recently underground, a fugitive from justice as a member of the Weather Underground.

Doris B. Walker, President, 1971 — member of firm Treuhoff, Walker, and Bernstein, Oakland, California. Treuhoff is a known Communist, married to Jessica Mitford, another admitted Communist.

Jonathan Lubell — member of the firm of Lubell, Lubell, and Schaap. Lubell and his brother were identified as Communists while at Harvard Law School. Schaap is now active with Philip Agee and is Washington representative of Counterwatch, publishers of *Covert Action Information Bulletin,* a magazine that denounces CIA personnel around the world.[8]

Robert Borosage — now Director of the Institute for Policy Studies.

William Kunstler

Arthur Kinoy — law partner of Kunstler's. Counsel for atom spy Martin Sobell, the Southern Conference Education Fund, and the Chicago Seven, etc.

Bella Abzug

The NLG is one of the most influential groups in the Far Left

Lobby and will appear frequently in this volume. It has spawned a number of other radical organizations, including the following:

The National Emergency Civil Liberties Committee

The *National Emergency Civil Liberties Committee*, founded in 1951 by NLG members, was cited as a Communist Front by the House Un-American Activities Committee in 1958 for repeatedly defending Communists in legal proceedings and disseminating Communist propaganda. Recent prominent clients include Alger Hiss, and Ramsey Clark and the "Teheran Ten."

Several members have had close ties with such Communist fronts as the National Council of American-Soviet Friendship, the National Committee Against Repressive Legislation, the People's Coalition for Peace and Justice, and the World Peace Council.[9] Its members will figure prominently in later chapters as active in campaigns against the CIA and a strong American foreign policy.

A partial list of officers and members includes:

Corliss Lamont, Chairman

Leonard Boudin, Counsel — father of Kathy Boudin, another Weather Underground fugitive; registered representative of the Cuban Government.

Sidney Gluck, Secretary

Tom Hayden, former SDS, husband of Jane Fonda.

William Kunstler

Jonathan Lubell

Harvey O'Connor

Eleanor Jackson Piel — wife of Gerard Piel, publisher of *Scientific American;* also Co-chairperson of Lillian Hellman's Committee for Public Justice.

Victor Rabinowitz

Morton Stavis

Peter Weiss — Board Chairman, Institute for Policy Studies; Vice President, Rubin Foundation; Vice President, Center for Constitutional Rights.

Frank Wilkinson

Gerald Lefcourt, Legislative Director

Gluck, O'Connor, and Wilkinson have been identified before Congressional Committees as Communist Party members. Stavis has taken the Fifth Amendment before a Congressional Committee when asked this question.[10]

The Center for Constitutional Rights

The Center for Constitutional Rights was founded in 1966 by three NLG members: William Kunstler, Arthur Kinoy, and Morton Stavis, ostensibly for legitimate purposes such as promoting civil liberties in the South. Soon the Center began to concentrate on far left activities, including

— an attempt to have American support of the Cambodian Government declared unconstitutional;

— a suit to return the orphans brought to the U.S. before the fall of Saigon to the custody of the Communist regime in Viet Nam;

— defense of Puerto Rican terrorists;

— a campaign against the FBI. The Center published a pamphlet entitled *Say "No" to the FBI*. The Center also engaged in other anti-intelligence activities described more fully below.[11]

Here is a partial list of its officers and members:

Arthur Kinoy, Vice President

Morton Stavis, President

William Kunstler, Vice President

Peter Weiss, Vice President

Benjamin E. Smith, Past President (a New Orleans attorney, representing the Castro Government)

William Schaap (an associate of Philip Agee)

Ramsey Clark

David Scribner (identified as a CP member before HUAC in 1955)

Catherine Roraback

David Rudovsky

The Campaign to Stop Government Spying

The Campaign to Stop Government Spying, later re-named the *Campaign for Political Rights*, was founded at a meeting organized by the NLG in Chicago in January, 1977. It has grown to include many radicals other than lawyers, and has drawn in more than eighty far left or well-meaning liberal organizations including:

ACLU

American Friends Service Committee

ADA

Black Panthers

Church of Scientology
Clergy & Laity Concerned
Committee for Public Justice (see below)
Counter Spy (magazine)
Covert Action Information Bureau
Friends of the Earth
National Committee to Reopen the Rosenberg Case
NECLC
Puerto Rican Socialist Party (a Communist organization)
Women's International League for Peace and Freedom
Women Strike for Peace and
several church groups

This coalition has been a leader in the campaign against the CIA, FBI, and local law enforcement agencies and will be described more fully in the CIA chapter. Prominent officers and members include

Morton H. Halperin, Chairperson — also Director of the Center for National Security Studies, an important anti-intelligence group. (See below.)

Eqbal Ahmad — member of IPS.

Robert Borosage — Director, IPS.

John Marks — co-author with Victor Marchetti of *The CIA and the Cult of Intelligence.*

Frank Donner — identified as a Communist before Congressional Committees.

Dorothy Samuels — Committee for Public Justice.

Members of the NLG and of these offshoots have been prominent in the transmission of Communist propaganda lines and have been key initiators in forming other groups that aid in transmitting these lines, as described below. Their activities can be well summed up by a statement of William Kunstler in a speech that aroused the greatest outburst at the NLG 1971 convention in Boulder, Colorado: "I am a double agent," he cried, "I want to use the System to bring down the System."

Foundations

Foundations can be valuable components in any propaganda machine. They can supply large amounts of funds that do not need to be imported. Ever since the time of the German millionaire, Parvus, who helped to finance Lenin (and maintained his secrecy while doing so), Communists have been skillful in persuading the idealistic wealthy to back their cause. Some foundations are established by a pro-Communist or a sympathizer precisely for the purpose of fostering Communist causes. Other foundations have been infiltrated by agents or sympathizers who have since influenced the foundation's decisions. Still other foundations whose officers have nothing to do with Communism have been sold on projects without realizing they are Communist-inspired. Communists have been all too skillful at disguising their projects so that they appear consistent with many of the charitable objectives of foundations: peace, democracy, human needs, poverty, youth, social change, etc.

The following foundations have been notable for sponsoring causes which have resulted in favorable publicity to the Communist line.

Rubin Foundation

The late Samuel Rubin, Chairman of the Board of Fabergé Inc., started the Rubin Foundation. Socialist Carey McWilliams characterized Rubin as "a confirmed Socialist but many times a millionaire in a capitalist society." Rubin started Fabergé as a small perfume company in 1937. His first business coup was a peculiar one, which illustrates his early close association with Communists. With the undercover help of the Communists in Spain, he made a deal with the Spanish Government to buy a large consignment of ambergris (an essential ingredient in many perfumes), which that regime was having trouble selling during the war. Shipped out of the country for him in Communist ships running the blockade, this cut-rate purchase enabled him to produce perfume with a much higher profit margin. It was an early step enabling him to build Fabergé into a multimillion dollar enterprise selling scents with names like "Aphrodisia" and "Tigress." He later sold the company for $25 million and established the Rubin Foundation.[13]

Officers of the foundation include:

Peter Weiss, Vice President — NLG; Center for Constitutional Rights; Board Chairman, Institute for Policy Studies, etc.

Cora Weiss, Secretary — Wife of Peter Weiss and daughter of Samuel Rubin. Active in several other leftist causes including Women Strike for Peace, Clergy and Laity Concerned, and the Disarmament Program of the Riverside Church.

Reed Rubin, Treasurer — Son of Samuel Rubin, named for

John Reed, the American Communist who died in Russia and was buried in the Kremlin wall.

Peter and Cora Weiss are prominent in many other leftist organizations described in this chapter and throughout this volume.

The Rubin Foundation is one of the principal backers of the Institute for Policy Studies, probably the most important far-left think-tank in the U.S., described more fully below. Another more surprising activity is the financial support it gives to Breira Inc. Breira is a group in New York City with a grotesque mission: simply put, it is a Jewish organization opposed to the State of Israel. This opposition has been thinly disguised under a veneer of claims to be working for a "just peace" in the Middle East, but the opposition has surfaced frequently in Breira publications and activities. Prominent in Breira is Arthur Waskow, who was one of the founders of the Institute for Policy Studies. (Breira, like so many other groups in the Far Left Lobby, has some well-meaning humanitarians on its "board" who are probably unaware of its true aims.)

Opposition to Israel and support of the more extreme Arabs have been major elements in Soviet foreign policy since soon after the formation of Israel. Thus the activities of Breira and the Rubin Foundation in this field follow closely the Soviet party line. (One insider account claims there was jubliation in the Breira Washington office during the early days of the 1973 war when it appeared the Egyptians were winning.[24])

The Stern Fund

This Fund has backed the Institute for Policy Studies and other far left groups, including the Peoples' Bicentennial Commission, the Center for Defense Information, the Center for National Security Studies, the National Lawyers Guild and the Campaign to Stop Government Spying. Black politician Channing Phillips has said, "You are most likely to get to Philip Stern if you are doing something that threatens the System.[15]

Philip M. Stern, its President, is associated with a number of far left organizations. He is a trustee of the Institute for Policy Studies, a member of the Committee for Public Justice, and a board member of the Fund for Investigative Journalism.

One of the organizations sparked by Mr. Stern is *The Fund for Investigative Journalism.* When it was founded in 1969 its Board of Directors included many liberals. A number of these have since dropped off. The Fund is now controlled by radicals, including:

41

Richard Barnet, a founder president of IPS

Seymour Hersh, the journalist whose stories began the massive attacks on American intelligence in the mid-1970's

Jim Boyd, who assisted Victor Machetti in preparing "The CIA and the Cult of Intelligence"

Richard Dudman, whose stories in the St. Louis Post-Dispatch have made him perhaps the foremost American apologist for the savage Pol Pot regime in Cambodia

James Ridgeway, a radical writer formerly with IPS, now with the Public Resource Center.[16]

The Fund for Peace

This fund was also founded in 1969 by a combination of leftists and liberals. In recent years most of the well-meaning liberals, including George Ball, Najeeb Halaby, Clark Kerr, and Jacob Javits, have dropped out, and the far left has dominated the Fund. The Fund's principal financial backer today is Stewart R. Mott, probably the largest individual shareholder of General Motors. He has also built a substantial reputation as a supporter of leftist causes, both moderate and radical. One of the main financial backers of Eugene McCarthy in his unsuccessful run for the Presidency in 1968, Mott in the 1980 primary campaign backed John Anderson. But on June 16, 1980, David Garth, Anderson's chief campaign strategist, announced the organization was dropping Mott because he was trying to bring into the Anderson team "the same group that ran McCarthy into the ground in 1968," presumably referring to the far leftists who dominate the organizations financed by his Fund for Peace.[17] These organizations share office space in two houses owned by Mott on Washington's Maryland Avenue within walking distance of the Capitol. They are among the most important think tanks on the far left: the Center for National Security Studies, the Center for Defense Information, and the Center for International Policy. Mr. Mott's complex from time to time has also housed the Women's International League for Peace and Freedom and Women's Strike for Peace.[18]

Other Foundations

Other foundations which regularly back left projects include the *Southern Conference Education Fund,* which at one time was the Communist Party's major front in the South,[19] and the *Youth Project,* a large fund formerly headed by Marge Tabankin between 1972 and 1977. One can gain some perspective on the Project's character and influence from Mrs. Tabankin's activities. In 1972, she visited Hanoi as a representative of the People's Coalition for Peace and Justice, an old Communist front. That same year she attended a Soviet-created World Peace Assembly in France and was elected to its ruling council. In the Carter Administration, Sam Brown, director of ACTION, appointed her to be Director of VISTA (Volunteers in Service to America).[20]

In addition, from time to time many of the large, well known organizations such as the Ford Foundation and the Marshall Field Foundation have been persuaded to finance projects which follow the Communist line. Some of these projects will be described in later chapters.

In August, 1980, an upheaval occurred in the directorship of the Field Foundation, which illustrates two important points: that many such foundations started with worthy humanitarian goals and were later manipulated into more radical policies, and that a gradual reaction has started among some such organizations away from these extremist objectives. The Field Foundation, started forty years ago by Marshall Field, was one of the earliest to support civil rights causes. In the 1960s it actively supported voter registration projects in the South. But in more recent years it turned increasingly from these admirable objectives to funding radical causes and organizations, including the Institute for Policy Studies, the Center for National Security Studies, Lillian Hellman's Committee for Public Justice, and others.

In June 1980 its board decided to review the foundation's grant-making policies. It determined to turn down a proposal of funds for the Committee Against Registration and the Draft, and a grant of $50,000 for studies on armaments "transfers" and human rights by the Institute for Policy Studies. The board questioned some activities of this Institute, including its submission of a human rights complaint to the UN on the treatment of American Indians. The Director of the Foundation, Leslie W. Dunbar, resigned "to make it easier for the Board members to conduct their review". Morris Abram, the foundation's president, said that "Les has increasingly seen international peace as being threatened by what he describes as U.S. militarism. The foundation did not accept his vision that the U.S. is the principle offender in the arms race or the disturber of world peace."[21]

During 1976 there was a heated election for the presidency of the United Steel Workers which also indicates the surprising scope of these foundation's activities. McBride, the official candidate, was opposed by a radical, Ed Sadlowski. Sadlowski's backers were frank in their aims to radicalize the Steelworkers, bring about more direct confrontations with steel management, and incidentally reverse the foreign policy of the Steelworkers and the AFL/CIO, which has been strongly anti-Communist.

Sadlowski received support from a number of liberals and radicals (e.g. John K. Galbraith, Arthur Schlesinger Jr. and Marjorie Tabankin). After McBride had won, George Meany stated that Sadlowski had received financial support from a number of "eastern foundations who had no business interfering in labor affairs." Included in his blast were some of the above.[22]

Think Tanks

We now come to the organizations that are the leading edge of the Far Left Lobby in influencing the media and public policy — the think tanks. These are ostensibly engaged in research and publishing, but they are also highly active in the sponsorship of conferences and seminars. They brief Congress and the executive departments, and in fact they frequently become involved with more activist roles in law suits or even mass demonstrations.

The Institute for Policy Studies

The most important think tank is the Institute for Policy Studies (IPS). Founded in Washington in 1963, it has since grown to have an annual budget of more than $1 million. It is the center of a large web of project groups and other related institutes, which have consistently followed a far left line, including unilateral disarmament for the U.S., withdrawal of support for American allies abroad, and attacks on free enterprise and democratic institutions at home. Paul Dickson in *Think Tanks* says the IPS is "attempting to lay the groundwork for the new society that will replace the present collapsing one. It has not only dedicated itself to ushering in the new society by inquiry and experimentation but is also doing what it can to hasten the demise of the present one."[23]

Following is a summary of the major IPS project groups and leading present and former personalities involved.

> *Robert L. Borosage*, Director — head of NLG Washington Office, former Director of Center for International Policy, a Fund for Peace group. Frequent writer on anti-CIA themes.
>
> *Arthur Waskow* — one of the founders. Formerly associated

with Students for a Democratic Society. Active in disruptions of Chicago Democratic Convention in 1968. Leading member of Breira. Resigned from IPS in 1977 to start another group, the Public Resource Center.

Roberta Salper, Fellow — member, Central Committee of the Puerto Rican Socialist Party, a pro-Communist group.

Richard J. Barnet, formerly Co-director — author of *The Giants — Russia and America* (1978). Professor Hollander of Harvard reviewed the book and judged that it "shows a revisionist benign attitude towards everything the Soviet Union says and does and a pervading suspiciousness towards American policy makers."[24]

Susan Weber — former editor of the IPS' magazine, *The Elements,* which is now being published by Waskow's Public Resource Center. One indication of her political views is that before coming to IPS, Ms. Weber worked in the Soviet Embassy as an editor of their magazine, *Soviet Life* and was registered with the Government as an employee of a "foreign power".[25] She is now employed by New Directions, the lobbying organization which emerged from Common Cause.

IPS Projects and Subsidiaries:

The **National Priorities Project (NPP)** is led by Marcus Raskin, a former co-director of IPS. Its goal is to transfer funds from U.S. defense to "more productive social goals." In the process, the project publicizes the theme that the United States has more than enough military power and that U.S. military power is the major threat to the world's peace.

Government Accountability Project (GAP). Ralph Stavins is the Leader. He is assisted by Saul Landau, a fellow. The project is designed to encourage present or former members of U.S. intelligence organizations or other government employees to "blow the whistle" on projects they oppose. The purpose is to discredit American intelligence and other government projects. A notable example of GAP's work was the encouragement and support they lent to John Stockwell to write *In Search of Enemies,* a book on the CIA in Angola.

Bay Area Institute (BAI)

The BAI is the IPS affiliate in San Francisco. It sponsors the Pacific News Service and other leftist causes on the Coast. Among advisers and staff are T. D. Allman, widely published free-lancer known for consistently reporting against U.S. policies in Asia and against American intelligence in general; Professor H. Franz Schurmann of the University of California at Berkeley, author of several articles favorable to North Vietnamese and Cambodian Communists; Richard Boyle, leftist writer, a former member of Fair Play for Cuba Committee; Danny Siegel, activist journalist who in 1976 under the auspices of the NLG traveled to the Philippines to organize opposition to U.S. Pacific policies among American servicemen;[26] and Frances FitzGerald, author of *Fire in the Lake*, who was one of the more successful advocates of the position that the North Vietnamese were right and the U.S. wrong. BAI is also a principle backer of the radical magazine, *Mother Jones*.

Transnational Institute (TNI)

The TNI is the major IPS vehicle for affecting international politics. It brings together foreigners championing IPS' favorite causes with Americans in a position to give those causes favorable publicity. One can gain some insight into TNI by considering its former director, Orlando Letelier, who had been foreign minister of Chile under Salvador Allende's pro-Communist government.

When Letelier was killed in his auto by a bomb in November 1976, his briefcase was recovered intact from the wreckage. It contained a set of correspondence and records which have provided a clear inside look for the first time at how the IPS and its related organizations fit into the pro-Communist propaganda network. These will be quoted frequently in succeeding chapters, but among other things the letters showed that Letelier had received a lump sum of $5,000 and was receiving $1,000 monthly from Beatrice Allende in Havana, daughter of Salvadore Allende, and wife of the number two man in the Cuban intelligence service. This and other evidence in the correspondence proved that Letelier was in the pay of an international propaganda network based in East Berlin and administered by Cuban and Chilean Communists, but ultimately controlled and mainly financed by the Soviet KGB.

Among other revelations in the documents were the following:

— Letelier's "case officer" was Julian Rizo, number one in Cuban intelligence in the U.S. Rizo, first secretary of the Cuban UN mission, was also liaison with terrorist organizations in the U.S. including the Weathermen and the Puerto Rican FALN and such foreign groups as the PLO and the Chilean Communist terrorist MIR organization. Rizo used the Cuban diplomatic pouch to transmit materials between Letelier in the U.S. and his contacts in Cuba.

— Letelier was active in organizing support for a Communist-dominated "International Commission of Enquiry Into the Crimes of the Military Junta in Chile," which met in Mexico City in February 1975. This conference was run by the World Peace Council, an international Communist front. Letelier's function was to recruit "respectables" to add a facade of neutrality to the proceedings. He succeeded in lining up several prominent Americans, including Congressman Michael Harrington, of Massachusetts. The Letelier documents showed that some of Harrington's expenses for the trip to Mexico had been paid by Letelier.

— Letelier's wife was active in organizing a "National Legislative Conference on Chile," which was designed to attract liberal members of Congress and other Americans, with the aim of cutting off all economic and military aid to Chile. Throughout his papers the word "liberal" is always in quotes. In one letter to Beatrice Allende he says, "I think that given the nature of its sponsors and of the front that this Committee is taking care of in the United States, it is preferable that information about it not be spread from Havana, because you know how these 'liberals' are. It is possible that Congressmen serving as patrons could be afraid that they would be linked with Cuba, etc., and eventually drop their support of the Committee . . . ." Here and elsewhere in his papers, Letelier shows this contempt for the "liberals" being recruited for these fronts, and he illustrates his awareness of the need for the cooperation of "innocents" and semi-innocent, and of the means by which to secure it.

— There is another clear indication that Letelier and the IPS were not working for true democracy in Chile or elsewhere, but rather for their own brand of Socialism. In another letter to Beatrice Allende he says that he is doing everything possible to oppose the movement to back Eduardo Frei in Chile as a possible alternative to the Junta. Frei, president of Chile just before Allende, was a popular leader and a true democrat who had defeated Allende in the previous election and was only prevented from running for another term by the Chilean constitution. He would be a good democratic alternative to the Junta, but Letelier says, "I think this would be one of the worst things for the popular movement in Chile. But it is an alternative that could eventually emerge, in view of which it is indispensible that the Left have clear ideas. Needless to say, I am working at different levels to counter acceptance of this little game on the part of various North American elements, especially those with relations with the various presidential candidates of the U.S. Democratic Party."

— In another paragraph he says to Beatrice Allende, "Perhaps some day, not far away, we will be able to do what has been done in Cuba." In other words, he and the IPS were working for a Cuban-style Communist dictatorship in Chile, not for democracy.[27]

Other fellows of TNI include:

Eqbal Ahmad — Also active in the Campaign to Stop Government Spying. See above.

Saul Landau.

Tariq Ali — also Editor of Communist newspaper "Red Mole" in London. Active in 4th International Trotskyite Party in Europe.

Basker Vashee, an Indian from Zimbabwe-Rhodesia — A Marxist affiliated with Joshua Nkomo's terroist ZAPU party.

The Fund for Peace Constellation

Next to the IPS, the most important far left think tanks are the three "Centers" grouped around the Fund for Peace. These are located in Stewart Mott's two small white row houses at 120 and 122 Maryland Avenue. They share the buildings with several other far left organizations, including the Women's International League for Peace and Freedom and, until recently, Women's Strike for Peace. Both of these have close ties with the Women's International Democratic Federation and the World Peace Council, well known to be international Communist fronts.[28] Another occupant of these two small buildings is the Coalition for a New Foreign and Military Policy, which consistently advocates unilateral disarmament and appeasement of the Communists. The small amount of office space used by these many organizations crowded into these two small buildings raises some doubts about the amount of true academic research conducted there and suggests that a large part of their work is publishing, lobbying, and media contacts. Located conveniently three blocks behind the Capitol building, many of the personnel of there groups are highly active in conducting seminars for congressional and executive office staffers and testifying before congressional committees.

The Center for International Policy (CIP)

The Center for International Policy in fact says in its statement of purpose that it "works towards its goals through a *network* of journalists, former diplomats, and international officials here and abroad." Most CIP publications deal with U.S. assistance to foreign countries and consistently attack U.S. aid to the "repressive" regimes of countries cooperating with the U.S. in opposing the Communists, such as South Korea, the Philippines, Indonesia, Argentina, Brazil, and Chile. None of their publications have touched on repression in such Communist countries as Cambodia, Viet Nam, North Korea, or Eastern Europe.

The activities of its officers are an indication of CIP idealogy. The director is Donald L. Ranard, who was formerly head of the Korean Desk at the State Department. Ranard is responsible for having stimulated Congress and the media to start the "Koreagate" investigation. He was also the star witness before Congressman Don Fraser's sub-committee on International Organizations, which conducted the investigation. This affair, which dragged on for more than a year, did succeed in embittering U.S.-South Korean relations and smearing the South Korean government in the media. Thus both IPS and Congressman Fraser accomplished their purposes. But, as sometimes happens, the affair caused some difficulties for both Ranard and Congressman Fraser when it came out that Fraser had given Ranard a $2,000 "consulting contract." The accusations of conflict of interest levelled against Fraser for these payments to Ranard and several other witnesses were a factor in Fraser's upset loss in the subsequent Congressional election.[29]

William Goodfellow, CIP deputy director, will appear in the subsequent chapter on Cambodia as an apologist for the brutal Pol Pot regime. In Phnom Penh shortly before the Communist victory, Goodfellow authored an article on the Op Ed page of the *New York Times* in July 1975 saying that the reports of massacres in that country were false and the results of "self-serving propaganda." This article was still being distributed by the CIP and the American Friends Service Committee more than a year later when the evidence of Cambodian Communist genocide were overwhelming. And CIP has never issued a correction or any further study of Cambodia.

Goodfellow has also been doing research on Chile for purposes of recommending against private or public economic cooperation with that country. A letter in the Letelier Papers from Elizabeth Farnsworth of the North American Congress on Latin America, a pro-Communist lobbying group (see below p. 52), speaks admiringly of the good work that "Bill Goodfellow" is doing on this subject.[30]

Other present and former staff or advisors include:

The late *Orlando Letelier*

Susan Weber Former editor of "Soviet Life" in the embassy of the U.S.S.R. (See above.)

Donald M. Fraser, Chairman of the Board of Advisors (Former Congressman, now Mayor of Minneapolis.)

Richard R. Falk, Professor of International Law, Princeton. Active in anti-defense and anti-CIA movement.

Edward Snyder, Friends Committee on National Legislation.

David Aaron, With the National Security Council in the Carter Administration, where he was in charge of the Task Force on reorganization of the Intelligence Community and was also influential in the decisions on the neutron bomb. (See neutron bomb chapter.) He was formerly an assistant to Walter Mondale, when Mondale was a Senator, and served on the staff of the Senate Intelligence Committee.

Anthony Lake, Head of the Policy Planning Office of the State Department in the Carter Administration. Formerly a Director of International Voluntary Services, a pacifist organization. Served on the National Security Council under Kissinger and resigned because of disagreement over the Cambodian incursion. Close association with the Institute for Policy Studies. Brought into the State Department by Cyrus Vance in 1976 to direct the Transition Team.[31]

In May 1980, D. Gareth Porter joined the staff. Porter appears in the following chapters as one of the most active defenders of the bloody Pol Pot regime in Cambodia as well as the Vietnamese Communists. (See also the Appendix for more details on Porter's published works.)

The Center for Defense Information (CDI)

Out of more than 2,000 retired American admirals and generals, the Fund for Peace group has been able to find only two that will consistently recommend unilateral American disarmament and appeasement of the Communists. Rear Admiral Gene R. LaRoque (Ret.), CDI director, is a kindly man who resembles George McGovern in both appearance and ideas. Brigadier General B. K. Gorwitz (Ret.) is the deputy director. The CDI publishes a monthly, *The Defense Monitor*. Here and through other books, articles, speeches, and conferences the CDI constantly promotes unilateral American disarmament and minimizes the Communist military build-up. For example, CDI produced a movie, *War Without Win-*

50

ners, featuring Paul Warnke, Admiral LaRoque, General Gorwitz, and others, which claims that the U.S. has nuclear superiority over the Soviets and consequently recommends American disarmament. Also, CDI produced a study, *Soviet Geopolitical Momentum: Myth or Menace?* which denies that the Soviets have been having any increase in influence around the world in recent years.

The CDI is often quoted by the *New York Times, Scientific American,* and other periodicals without comments as to its far left tendencies. It is also frequently quoted on Radio Moscow.

Other members of the staff and advisory board includes:

James J. Treiers, Economist

William J. Flannery

Dr. Earl C. Ravenal (also on Board of IPS)

Dr. Herbert Scoville (also active in anti-CIA studies)

Harold Willens (co-founder of Interfaith Center to Reverse the Arms Race.)

The Center for National Security Studies (CNSS)

This third member of the Fund for Peace trio was founded in September 1974 at a conference on the CIA "hosted" by Senators Edward Brooke (who in fact did not attend) and Philip Hart, held in a hearing room of the Senator Office Building. The conference report claimed that "the dignity of the setting and the bipartisanship of the hosts lent weight to the proceedings and the papers". All of the speakers were notable opponents of the CIA and of a strong American Foreign policy. They included Richard Barnet of IPS; Fred Branfman, then Director of the Indo-China Resource Center; Richard Falk of Princeton and the CIP; Victor Marchetti and John Marks, authors of *The CIA and the Cult of Intelligence;* Herbert Scoville, Jr. of CIP; and David Wise, author of a number of anti-intelligence books, most recently *The Politics of Lying.*

The first Director of CNSS was Robert L. Borosage, head of the Washington office of the NLG who had formerly worked at the IPS. Borosage later left CNSS to become Director of IPS and Morton H. Halperin took over as head of CNSS. Halperin had also been a long-time critic of the CIA. In 1977 he acquired a second job as head of the Campaign to Stop Government Spying, launched by the NLG at a large conference in Detroit. (See below.)

The only defender of the CIA at the 1974 Washington conference was William Colby, then Director of the Agency. He agreed to appear to explain agency policy and was rewarded by being

harangued for more than an hour by participants like Fred Branfman, Daniel Ellsberg, Senator James Abourezk, Borosage, Halperin,
Congressman Michael Harrington, and others. Colby comments
ruefully in his autobiography on the bias of this conference.[33]

The proceedings were later published in a book edited by Borosage and Marks, *The CIA File*. Since then the CNSS has been a leading critic of the CIA, the FBI, and other American intelligence and
law enforcement activities. It publishes a monthly newsleter, *First
Principles*, and has sponsored a large number of books and research
papers. By 1976 the atmosphere allowed it to be more violent in its
attacks, and it published a book with a harsher title, *The Lawless
State: The Crimes of the U.S. Intelligence Agencies*, by Halperin,
Borosage, Jerry Berman, and Christina Marwick.[34] It is notable that
among all the CNSS output, including articles in *First Principles*
and books and pamphlets, there is no study of the KGB or any other
Communist intelligence organization. It is as though the CIA and
FBI were working in a vacuum, carrying out endless nefarious
deeds for their own sakes.[35]

Other present or former members of the staff and advisory
council include:

Jerry J. Berman

Mark Lynch (also with the American Civil Liberties Union.)

Nicole Szulc—collaborated with Phillip Agee in his *Inside the
Company, CIA Diary;* daughter of journalist Tad Szulc.

North American Congress on Latin America (NACLA)

The Congress was founded in 1966 by some members of the
Students for a Democratic Society (SDS). Its stated purposes are
research, publication, and action on the subjects of U.S. methods of
"exploitation and domination" of Latin America through "corporations, unions, church, and intelligence agencies." It sought to attract
people "who not only favor revolutionary change in Latin America,
but also a revolutionary position towards their own society." In this
it has succeeded. Prominent members of the Congress include:

Michael Locker — associate of Orlando Letelier.

Brady Tyson — former advisor to Andrew Young on Latin
America at UN.

Michael Klare — left wing writer on Latin America subjects,
frequently lecture for World Peace Council in Cuba and
Europe.

Nicole Szulc

Carl Oglesby — former President, SDS.

Gabriel Kolko — revisionist historian who blames the U.S. for the Cold War.

Saul Landau

NACLA's Berkeley office is headed by Jon Frappier, a former member of the Weathermen and of the Venceremos Brigade (young Americans who travelled to Cuba to be trained in revolutionary techniques). An affiliate of the Berkeley office is *Research Associates International (RAI)*, an organization active in research against CIA activities around the world. The London correspondent of RAI is Steve Weissman, as associate of Philip Agee. NACLA and RAI are cooperating on a computer data bank on American intelligence activities.[36]

The Pacific Studies Center (PSC)

The Pacific Studies Center is an affiliate of NACLA, concentrating on studies of American activities in the Pacific area. In 1972 PSC published *The Trojan Horse: The Strange Politics of Foreign Aid* edited by Steve Weissman, attacking U.S. foreign aid as disguised imperialism.[37]

A close associate of NACLA is Richard Feinberg, former Peace Corps volunteer, who was working as an economist at the U.S. Treasury's Office of Development Policy. Among the Letelier Papers was a letter from Elizabeth Farnsworth of NACLA to Letelier about a report being prepared on Chile: "Richard Feinberg, who is co-authoring our report with me, will contact you for an interview. Do not tell anyone else he is working on the project please. It wouldn't help his work at Treasury (obviously)." Soon after this correspondence became public, Feinberg resigned from Treasury and was hired by Anthony Lake, former associate of CIP, and later head of the Carter Administration's State Department Policy Planning Staff.[38]

The activities of these centers have had considerable influence on media treatment of the CIA and American policy in Latin America. Their studies add an aura of disinterested scholarship to points of view that in fact are direct reflections of the Communist line. Leading media frequently print articles by members of these groups, without describing their radical backgrounds. (For example, "On Mexico", *N.Y. Times* Op Ed page, 20 July 1978, by Philip Russell of NACLA.)

Citizens Committees

Citizens committees are the fourth category in the Far Left Lobby, comprising "peoples" committees, councils, coalitions, and centers. They are distinguished by their consistent backing of positions coinciding with the Communist line and never advocating opposing positions. Their stock in trade is the frequent use of names and slogans likely to appeal to liberals: "justice," "peace," "democratic," "women," civil rights," "human needs," etc. But behind this facade it is possible to see the hard consistent line favoring Communist tyranny and dictatorship, and the contempt for true liberals so clearly expressed by Letelier's remark, "You know how liberals are."

Committee for Public Justice (CPJ)

The Committee for Public Justice was formed in November 1970 by Lillian Hellman. The CPJ's other principal organizer was Ramsey Clark, a former Attorney General, who has made a reputation for speaking on America's "crimes" against Vietnam and Iran.[39] The CPJ has concentrated on "monitoring the FBI, CIA, and other law enforcement organizations, including the Justice Department. Its criticisms have been sprinkled in with enough elements of truth to attract genuine liberals. But it has consistently advocated policies weakening these organizations.[40]

Among the members of its Executive Council and advisory committee are:

Eleanor Jackson Piel, Co-Chairman (also member of NECLC)

Morton H. Halperin

Aryeh Neier, ACLU

James A. Goodman, Washington representative

Barry Commoner

J. K. Galbraith

Jessica Mitford. She and her husband, Robert Truehaft, are admitted Communist Party members.

Philip Stern

Roger Wilkins, former Chairman—now on editorial board of *Washington Post.*

Discounting somewhat for exaggeration, CPJ's influence on the media can be summarized from their own 1979 Report, which says "Articles from our *Justice Department Watch* have been reprinted as is or adapted, for such newspapers and periodicals as *The N. Y. Times;* the *Los Angeles Herald-Examiner; The Nation; Inquiry, Juris Doctor* (a magazine for lawyers), Newhouse News Service (with 22 newspapers); and the *Milwaukee Journal.* Additionally, reporters regularly telephoned our staff for comments and leads, and relied on *Justice Department Watch's* findings to develop articles of their own."

The Indochina Resource Center

The Indochina Rescource Center (now the Southeast Asia Resource Center) has consistently backed the North Vietnamese and Cambodian Communists and has continued to defend them in recent years in spite of the growing evidence of their brutality. The Center conspicuously marked itself by refusing to join in a letter to the North Vietnamese co-signed by several other activists including Daniel Ellsburg and Joan Baez. These activists had opposed the United States during the Vietnam War. But now they were appealing to the North Vietnamese to stop killing their own people. The Center refused to associate itself with any such criticism of a Socialist country. Leading members include:

> *Fred Branfman* — former Director of International Voluntary Services
>
> *Gareth Porter*
> *David Marr*
> *John Spragens*

Campaign for Economic Democracy

This is Jane Fonda's and Tom Hayden's organization, a successor to their Campaign for a Democratic Foreign Policy, which in turn replaced their Indochina Peace Campaign.

Fonda and Hayden also refused to sign the appeal to the North Vietnamese. Jane Fonda is a classic case of a prominent entertainment figure being recruited as a far left propagandist. Her final conversion evidently occurred in 1969 in Hollywood where she was working on the movie, *They Shoot Horses, Don't They.* Through her neighbors, Donald Sutherland and his wife, Shirley, daughter of a Canadian radical, she got to know many others in New Left circles in Los Angeles, including Fred Gardner and Mark Lane, the radical attorney who was then promoting his ideas about the Kennedy assassination and would later be an attorney for the Rev. Jim Jones of Jonestown, Guyana.[41] She went on from there to become an activist in such causes as Viet Nam, disarmament, and nuclear power.

Marjorie Tabankin, head of VISTA in the Carter Administration and former director of the Youth Project (see above), also worked with Jane Fonda and Tom Hayden in the Campaign for a Democratic Foreign Policy.

Clergy and Laity Concerned

Formed in the 1960's to back North Vietnamese and Viet Cong, Clergy and Laity Concerned since the Communist victory has backed other far left causes. Its members also refused to sign the letters appealing to the North Vietnamese to moderate their oppressive policies. Members include

William Sloan Coffin, Riverside Church

Don Luce

Fred Branfman

The Rev. Thomas Lee Hayes — former sponsor of the Tri-Continental Information Center in New York, a Communist front.

Organizing Committee for a Fifth Estate

An offshoot of Norman Mailer's "Fifth Estate," the Organizing Committee for a Fifth Estate receives some financial backing from the Youth Project. Its leading members are

Margaret Van Houten

Frank Donner

Philip Agee

Victor Marchetti

Marcus Raskin (IPS)

Anthony Russo — Ellsberg's co-defendant in the Pentagon Papers case.

Perhaps the most significant activity of this organization was to act as the original publishers of *Counter-Spy* magazine, which then spawned *Covert Action Information Bulletin*. These publications have identified — and mis-identified — hundreds of undercover American intelligence personnel. The murder of the CIA's station chief in Athens and the shots fired at the home of the CIA's station chief in Kingston, Jamaica, followed publication of their identities by these organizations.

In 1977 the Organizing Committee for a Fifth Estate merged into the *Public Education Project on the Intelligence Community*

(PEPIC), which in turn later merged into the *Campaign to Stop Government Spying,* described above and in the CIA chapter.

Riverside Church Disarmament Program

The Riverside Church is one of the landmarks of New York City, with its tall tower overlooking the Hudson. In 1976 the Rev. William Sloan Coffin became senior minister after resigning as chaplain at Yale, where he had been notable for his attacks on American support of South Viet Nam and on other elements of a strong foreign policy. He was one of the founders of Clergy and Laity Concerned, a group which opposed the U.S. policy in Viet Nam and continues to back causes paralleling the Communist line.

Coffin organized the Disarmament Program as a major activity of the church and brought in Cora Weiss as director. Ms. Weiss had also been prominent in groups opposing U.S. support for South Viet Nam, and continues to be influential in the Rubin Foundation (founded by her late Father, Samuel Rubin) and in the anti-Israel Jewish organization, Breira.

Under Coffin and Ms. Weiss, the Riverside Church Disarmament Program has become highly active in promoting a policy of unilateral American disarmament. For example, in the Fall of 1980, it sponsored a "Study/Action Series" of lectures on the arms race with the following topics:

October   1 — "The Tilt Towards War", Professor Alan Wolfe,
             author of *The Rise and Fall of the Soviet Threat.*

October   8 — "Military Adventures Abroad Mean Repression At
             Home".

October 15 — "Arming South Africa — The worsening situation
             in South Africa and how violation of the arms embargo by the U.S. has contributed."

October 22 — "Poverty and the Pentagon".

October 29 — "The Arms Race Begins on the Backs of Native
             Americans".

Coffin, Ms. Weiss, and another member of the Riverside Church program staff, the Rev. Michael Clark, make frequent appearances at other conferences promoting unilateral American disarmament and minimizing the danger of a Communist military build-up. A recent example was a "Statewide Conference of Military Disarmament" in Hartford, Connecticut, on April 26, 1979, where keynote speakers included Coffin and Richard Barnet of IPS. Michael Clark,

who was billed as having visited Russia and learned their commitments to peace at first hand, chaired a workshop, "The Arms Race
and the Soviet Threat". In September 1979, Clark and Ms. Weiss
were featured speakers at an "Interdisciplinary Conference on the
Arms Race" at Amherst College, East Woodstock, Connecticut,
sponsored by the Committee on Arms Limitation.

Women Strike for Peace

Founded in 1961 after the Soviets violated the atomic test-ban
treaty by detonating an atomic bomb, Women Strike for Peace for
several months was in the forefront of agitation against a resumption of testing *by the United States* and was conspicuously silent in
protesting the Soviet violation. Since that time it has continued
to work for unilateral American disarmament and to downplay the
threat of Communist arms build ups. It has had close relations with
two international Communist fronts, the Women's International
Democratic Federation and the World-Peace Council. Its activities
are described more fully in the chapter on the neutron bomb.

Until 1980 it shared office space in the two row houses at 120
and 122 Maryland Avenue with the three Fund for Peace Centers
described above. Another tenant is the Women's International
League for Peace and Freedom, described below.

Among the leading officers and members are:

Edith Villastrigo
Paula Echeverria
Bella Abzug

Women's International League for Peace and Freedom (WILPF)

The Women's International League for Peace and Freedom
also has close ties with Women Strike for Peace and the Communist
front Women's International Democratic Federation. It has offices
in Philadelphia and Geneva in addition to its Washington office in
one of the Fund for Peace buildings. WILPF publishes a monthly
newsletter, *Peace and Freedom,* and, like Women Strike for Peace,
it advocates American disarmament, opposes nuclear power, and
publishes frequent criticism of repression in foreign regimes allied
to the U.S. in opposition to the Communists, but it ignores repression in Communist countries.

Innocents

Several older organizations that formerly were truly liberal and had considerable prestige as such have come increasingly under the influence of the far left. They include:

The American Civil Liberties Union (ACLU)

The ACLU was founded by Roger Baldwin, a sincere liberal. But with Baldwin long since retired, the ACLU has lurched far to the left, even removing an internal regulation which prohibited Communists from becoming members. Among the ACLU's executives and advisory board are

Ramsey Clark
Arthur Kinoy, NLG member
Frank Donner, Director of the ACLU Political Surveillance Project
William Kunstler
Carey McWilliams

The American Friends Service Committee

The American Friends Service Committee began as a Quaker organization. But in recent years it has become so identified with far left causes that many Quakers now disown it. Its top board members are still Quakers, but many of its executives are not.

Carnegie Endowment for International Peace

The prestigious Carnegie Endowment has also shown signs of strong far-left influence. Alger Hiss, of course, was director for a time in the late 1940s. Staff includes

Alessandro Casella — a far left propagandist. (See Viet Nam Chapter.
Fred Kaplan — author of pamphlet published by IPS and article in *Scientific American* backing unilateral U.S. arms reduction and opposing neutron bomb. (See Neutron Bomb chapter.)
Michael Klare — Far left writer, also a member of NACLA.
Roger Morris — former director of Humanitarian Policy Studies Program. Associated with David Wise in his anti-CIA book.

The Carnegie Endowment sponsors *Foreign Policy* magazine, which has generally published radical and pro-appeasement articles.

The True Liberals

Of course, liberalism and the far left are anything but identical. Indeed much of the far left's efforts are aimed at fostering the false impression that liberals support most of their goals. They do not.

Historically, genuine liberals have been opposed to tyranny in all its forms. *SANE* and the *Fellowship of Reconciliation* are good examples. Though they both opposed the United States role in the Viet Nam War, they signed the above-mentioned open letter to the North Vietnamese that appealed to them to open up their society. *Social Democrats U.S.A.*, the Socialist party that advocates the democratic road to Socialism, has been notable for its anti-communist stands. Then, of course, there is the AFL/CIO — the foremost bastion of political liberalism at home and perhaps the strongest bulwark against Communism in the world.

The actions and stands of these organizations show that truly humanitarian liberals can be anti-Communist, making the groups of the Far Left Lobby even more conspicuous in their unwillingness to ever criticize Communist crimes.

EFFORTS TO CONTROL
THE WORLD'S MEDIA:
"DEVELOPMENTAL JOURNALISM"

In 1972 UNESCO embarked on a new study program, origi-
nated by the Soviet bloc and supported by many third world countries, that illustrates the relentlessness of Communist propaganda
efforts and the long-range thinking behind them.

Masquerading under plausible rhetoric about "the need for
economic growth in the less developed countries" and the importance of "mobilizing" the media to contribue to this effort, the
UNESCO program was actually a scheme to bring about Government ownership of the press, censorship of privately-owned international news services, and government-controlled world-wide news
agencies. It was soon given the name of "Developmental
Journalism."

The original UNESCO declaration tied the use or control of the
media with familiar Communist code words like "the need to combat war propaganda, racism, and apartheid." At a preparatory conference in Paris in December 1975, the Yugoslavs introduced an
amendment to the draft which equated Zionism with Racism. When
the U.S. delegate attempted to protest, he was refused the right to
speak and walked out, followed by twelve delegations from democratic countries. The remaining seventy-two delegations, who completed the terms of the draft, were mainly from third world and
Communist nations. One third world speaker went so far as to declare that freedom of the press is nothing but an excuse for "exploitation by the rich nations".[1]

First head of the UNESCO Commission studying this problem
was Sean MacBride, an Irishman who has been active in left wing
causes most of his life. At one time chief of staff of the outlawed

Irish Republican Army, he also served as UN overseer of Namibia. He received the Nobel Peace Prize and also (a more doubtful honor) the Lenin Peace Prize.[2] He later became the director of UNESCO.

MacBride's staff on the UNESCO Press Commission was heavily weighted with leftists. One of the senior officers was Kaarle Nordenstreng, a Finnish Marxist professor of journalism at Helsinki, who was also president of the International Organization of Journalists (IOJ), a Communist front based in Prague.

The IOJ has also been deeply involved in the campaign for a UNESCO code of developmental journalism. Founded in 1946, it has been one of the most active Communist international front groups, specializing in efforts to influence media in the third world. Though it claims to be a "non-governmental body" and as such was given consultative status with UNESCO, its statement of premises says that "mass media must not be in private hands ... as a social instrument they belong in the hands of society as a whole and its organizations".

The IOJ, which organizes seminars for journalists and assists journalism schools in Communist and third world countries, also produces textbooks and guides to specialized areas of journalism. In 1976 it produced a hard-cover book containing a variety of attacks on American media, calling them "the finest brainwashing system in the world." (Continuing the Communist practice of playing back local sources, many of these attacks were quotations from American writers.)[3]

The drive for a UNESCO code, like so many Communist campaigns, contained just enough elements of truth to make it believable in many circles. Third world countries do have a plausible complaint that the major international news agencies fail to give them the coverage they feel they deserve and are inclined to report only the sensational or exotic or the bad news. But this is the perennial complaint of all smaller areas, and is heard continually even within the United States from smaller towns or cities.[4]

But the answer is not a world-wide restrictive code of behavior for the media, but rather one or more news agencies managed by third world countries. There has been an effort by free world representatives in UNESCO and private organizations in the U.S. to furnish advice and assistance to third world countries for creating such an independent news service to be run by developing nations.[5]

The UNESCO campaign ran into unanimous opposition from

the democracies. In spite of the efforts of MacBride and the IOJ, it also lost the support of several third world countries, and at the UNESCO Commision meeting in November 1978, the earlier drafts were revised to eliminate all references to government control of the media.[6]

So press freedom has survived for the present. But the IOJ and MacBride and his associates have not given up. MacBride has been recommending new measures, including efforts to "license" foreign correspondents (for their "own protection" in hazardous areas) and to establish a "journalistic code of ethics". So far these have not been approved by free world journalists associations or the UNESCO votes, but the efforts continue.[7]

PROVEN COMMUNIST AGENTS
IN THE MEDIA —
SINGAPORE, MALAYSIA,
AND FRANCE

Of all the countries in the free world, Singapore and Malaysia in recent years have uncovered the largest number of Communist agents in the media. These two governments have been especially vigilant against such subversion because their recent history has been marked by a bloody struggle against Communist insurgency. The Communist networks they have exposed during the past decade provide several valuable analogies to similar activities that may be going on in the United States.

Singapore and Malaysia are small, but they have an importance in the world's strategic and raw materials picture far out of proportion to their size. Malaysia is a leading exporter of two strategic materials, tin and rubber, while Singapore is a vital port, fourth largest in the world, commanding the Malacca Straits, a key waterway on the shipping lanes for oil and other basic materials from the Middle East and Africa to Japan and the rest of East Asia. Both countries are among the best governed of the former British colonies, with a large degree of free enterprise, a prosperous population, and two of the fastest economic growth rates in the world.

The Malayan Peninsula with Singapore at its tip hangs down from Thailand like a ripe fruit. It would be a choice plum for Communist conquest. All during the 1950s, a fierce Communist guerilla movement tortured Malaysia, a movement only put down, after great loss of life, by a skilled application of counter-insurgency waged jointly by the British administration and local non-Communist citizens. The Malaysian Communist Party (MCP), organized in the 1920s by agents of the Comintern, carried out this uprising. Although backed by the Soviet Union, this work was done mainly by Chinese undercover Communists working out of the Comintern's Far Eastern Bureau in Shanghai. These agents recruited followers mostly from the Overseas Chinese, people who had migrated to Malaysia from China.[1]

The British gave Malaysia its independence in 1957 after the back of this rebellion had been broken, but mopping up operations to subdue the hold-outs continued for three more bloody years until 1960, when the remnants, numbering less than 500, retreated into the jungles along the Thai-Malaysian border. Singapore split off from Malaysia to form an independent city-state in 1965.

Thus both countries have a history of waging a life and death struggle against Communist subversion. And after the fall of South Viet Nam in 1975, the survivors of the guerillas in the Thai-Malaysian jungles heated up their activities. Viet Nam, maintaining its army at almost full strength, soon took over all of Laos, installing a puppet regime without a word of protest from the U.S. or the rest of the world. This brought it face to face with Thailand along the long Laotian border.

Thailand, Malaysia, and Singapore felt increasingly threatened by further Communist expansion. The domino theory seemed to be operating. This has been discounted by many commentators in the U.S., but as one American politician visiting the area said, "You should go out there and talk to the dominoes." By 1976 Malaysian feelings were summed up by the local correspondent for the *Far Eastern Economic Review*, Mr. K. Das, who concluded a dispatch on the Viet Nam threat and growing guerilla activity by writing, "That the barbarians are at the gates is not in doubt."[2]

Under such pressures, the governments of Singapore and Malaysia became more alert than most in watching for Communist subversion. Persons guilty of pro-Communist activities were put under detention. In 1976, a year after the fall of Saigon, the government turned up evidence on a shocking scale. In May, the Singapore government reported finding a network of MCP cells, including units in the armed services, universities, and labor unions. There was a control post in Kuala Lampur, the capital of Malaysia, training camps elsewhere in Malaysia, a guerilla camp in Thailand, and elaborate plans for infiltration and terrorism.[3]

In June 1976, Singapore took into custody two leading journalists — the editor of the largest Malay-language newspaper, *Berita*

Harian Singapore, and his chief assistant — accusing them of being Communist agents and using their paper to promote Communist propaganda. A few days later, Malaysia caused a sensation by arresting the top journalist in the country, Abdul Samad Ismail, editor of Malaysia's most important newspaper, the *New Straits Times.* Samad had also been a popular novelist and columnist for years and was well known for helping to promote Malaysian identity.

Arrested at the same time was Samad's "accomplice," Samai Mohamad Amin, news editor of *Berita Harian* (the Malaysian counterpart of the similarly named Singapore paper). The government accused both men of being in effect "Judas goats" in leading Malays into accepting Communism.

On September 1 Samad confessed on television that he had in fact been a Communist for "three quarters of his life" and had been using his position to further the cause of Communism. He said that he had been successful in making many younger members of the leading Malay political party, the UMNO, "see things my way." He also indicated that he had been receiving directions from outside the country. (He is believed to have been controlled by a senior Communist underground agent in Indonesia ever since 1957, the year of Malaysian independence.)

Two days later Singapore announced that the two journalists they had arrested had been working in league with Samad. This ring of agents, the government statement said, had been using their newspapers and their influence among political leaders to execute a six point strategy: soften the Malay environment for Communism; diminish the Malays' faith in their religion, Islam; knock out those Malay leaders who are obstacles to the spread of Communism and build up those who are helpful; create disunity among Malay leaders and organizations opposing Communism; create despair and hostility toward the Government among Malays; and project Communism in such a manner that the Malays will turn to it to solve their problems.[4]

Two weeks later the investigation reached even high echelons of the government. The Malaysian Security Service arrested two Deputy Ministers, Abdullah Majid and Abdullah Ahmad, close advisors of the former Prime Minister, Tun Abdul Razak, on similar charges. Both confessed on television to Communist activities and Soviet connections.

Then in February 1977 came another shock. The Malaysian government announced the arrest of Chan Kien Sin, former editor-in-chief of a leading Chinese daily and Chief Executive Secretary of the Malaysian Chinese Association, a crucial group in the ruling National Front Government. Chan also confessed on television, saying he had been a Communist for 30 years and had used his position on the paper to promote Communist propaganda.[5]

Thus in the space of a few months the Malaysian and Singapore governments uncovered Communist agents as editors of the most important newspapers in English, Malaysian, and Chinese, the three leading languages in both countries. In other words, a large part of the press in these two small but vital countries had been under Communist domination for several years.

Later in February 1977, Singapore announced the arrest of another group of pro-Communists under the leadership of a lawyer, Gopalkrishnan Raman. During the succeeding weeks the public confessions of these people and correspondence found in their possession revealed the existence of a wide network of influence in the media at home and abroad, in the universities, in labor unions, and in religious bodies. Their methods for infiltrating such opinion groups and influencing the media bear many resemblances to the work of the American Far Left organizations described in the previous chapter.

Raman, the group's leader, started his Communist activities in London where he studied law from 1966 through 1968. There he met a number of Communist students from Singapore and Malaysia and also made contact with London-based radicals including A. Balakrishnan, the head of the Maoist Workers Institute, and Malcolm Caldwell, an instructor at the London University School of Oriental Studies and editor of the *Journal of Contemporary Asia*.[6]

Caldwell was a specialist in Southeast Asia. Although he was a member of the British Labor Party, it is now evident that he was a Communist, generally following the Maoist Chinese line as opposed to the Soviet. This pro-Chinese slant is apparent from his writing and later activities. For example, he was one of the most active apologists for the Pol Pot regime in Cambodia, even after the evidence of its brutality was overwhelming. In 1978, he and two American reporters were the first Western newspapermen to be allowed into that country. For two weeks these three sent back favorable reports that played down the horrors. But the day before they were to leave Cambodia, Caldwell was killed by an assassin, who penetrated their government guest house in Phnom Pehn. This gunman was apparently with the underground Cambodian group opposing the Pol Pot government and supporting the Vietnamese. Caldwell was targeted in retaliation for his support of Pol Pot and to embarrass the Pol Pot regime before the world.[7] (For further details on this significant incident, see the following chapter on Cambodia.)

Starting in the 1960s, Caldwell was a leading member of a group of European pro-Communists working on propaganda and subversion in Southeast Asia. When Raman returned to Singapore in 1968, Caldwell and Balakrishnan advised him to get in touch with local Communists and to recruit others into Communist cells.

One of the principal activities of Raman's group was to provide information for the campaign started by Caldwell in England and by agitators in other European countries in 1972 to put pressure on the governing party in Singapore, the Popular Action Party (PAP), to release the Communist leaders who had been detained under the Internal Security Act. This campaign was mounted through the Socialist International, whose members include the leading Socialist parties around the world, including the PAP. Caldwell was a prime mover in influencing the British Labor Party to raise this issue in the S.I., with the objective of forcing the Singapore Government to release the Communists before the general elections in 1976. The Communists hoped that such detainees, all key party members, would be able to revitalize the party before the election.

Raman and his group fed unfavorable information on Singapore's civil rights policies to Caldwell and others in this apparatus and to the media in Europe, Japan, and Malaysia over a period of several years.[8]

In May 1976 the Dutch Labor Party at an S.I. meeting moved to have the PAP expelled for "violations of human rights and detention of political prisoners without trial." Singapore, however, refused to bow to this pressure. Before action could be taken on the resolution, Lee Kwan Yew, the brilliant but outspoken leader of the PAP and Prime Minister of Singapore, announced that PAP was resigning from the S.I. Thus Raman's campaign had succeeded in driving Singapore out of the Socialist International, but it failed in its main objective of freeing the Communist politicians in Singapore before the election.

Raman and his group were also making other energetic efforts during this period to influence the media and infiltrate labor unions and student associations. Raman was legal advisor to the University of Singapore Students Union (USSU) and the Singapore Polytechnic Students Union (SPSU), which gave him an opportunity to recruit agitators and to influence student activities. For example, at one meeting of the USSU a slide show was presented on the student riots in Thailand which had brought down the Thai government in 1973, and the Singapore students were encouraged to carry on similar activities to destroy the Singapore Government. In July 1976 Raman was quoted as saying at a student meeting that the Communist Party of Malaysia would eventually overthrow the governments of Singapore and Malaysia, and these countries would turn Communist after Thailand had already done so.[9]

It is interesting that these Southeast Asian activists were thus spreading their own pro-Communist version of the Domino Theory during the same period that prominent commentators in the U.S. like Hans Morgenthau of the University of Chicago and Gareth Porter of the Indo-China Resource Center were saying the theory was "outdated" or "discredited".

Raman and his associates were especially active in influencing the media at home and overseas. Among journalists who cooperated with them was Arun Senkuttuvan, a correspondent for the *Far Eastern Economic Review*, the *Economist*, and the *Financial Times*. Senkuttuvan, arrested in February 1977, confessed at a press conference that, although not a Communist himself, he had been spreading anti-government, pro-Communist propaganda in cooperation with Raman's group. He admitted to several specific activities which provide striking examples of how Communist agents and their sympathizers spread the line:

— A number of his articles for the *Far Eastern Economic Review* and other journals deliberately exaggerated the repressive nature of the Singapore government. In one article in particular, using information he knew to be false, Senkuttuvan attempted to prove that Singapore "framed" Samad, the editor arrested by the Malaysian Government as a Communist agent.

— He was frequently given the opportunity to *brief visiting correspondents from other countries* and always gave them the same line on the fascistic nature of the Singapore Government. (This is an important point. We shall see in later chapters how leading Amercan journalists can wield great influence on visiting correspondents, molding their treatment of local issues.)

— He was a key link in one serious incident in 1976 that might have caused serious damage to relations between Singapore and Malaysia. Ever since 1965 a major aim of Communist policy in

Malaysia had been to encourage controversy between that country and Singapore, in hopes of a break in relations that would weaken both countries' ability to resist subversion. In March of 1976, Derek Davies, managing editor of the *Far Eastern Economic Review,* had an off-the-record interview with Lee Kwan Yew. Afterwards he went to his hotel room with Senkuttuvan and made a tape recording of his recollections of Lee's remarks, including derogatory comments about Malaysian officials, which the Singapore government later said was "a mixture of truths, half-truths, and serious omissions . . . that was bound to create ill-will between Lee and the Malaysian leaders." Davies told Senkuttuvan to send the tape back to the Hong Kong main office of *F.E.E.R.* Senkuttuvan made a copy of the tape for his own use before sending it to Hong Kong. Subsequently he played the tape for Raman and a member of journalists, including Tiziano Terzani, an Italian pro-Communist correspondent for several European publications, and K.S.C. Pillai, a reporter for Agence France Presse.[10]

Through Raman a transcript of the tape was also given to two Malaysian communists, Dominic and James Puthucheary. Dominic is a lawyer who has studied in the United Kingdom, where Raman had first met him. Practicing in Malaysia, he was the legal adviser to the Rubber Workers Union and was also active in University of Malaya circles, using both sets of contacts to spread Communist doctrine. His brother, James, was prominent in the Malaysian government and on the staff of the Prime Minister, Datuk Hussein Onn. He was associated with Abdullah Majid, the Deputy Minister who was subsequently arrested as a Communist agent.

Raman and Senkuttuvan in their confessions both said that James Puthucheary had described the tape contents to the Prime Minister in an effort to damage relations with Singapore.[11]

Raman's group was also active in forming a "Human Rights Committee," which provides a revealing example of Communist methods of organizing front groups. Ng Hiok Ngee, a Singaporean Communist who has since gone into hiding, suggested the idea in 1976 to Raman. The plan was to form a committee secretly controlled by Communists but including prominent non-Communist liberals. The committee could be used to put further pressure on the government, publicizing the plight of the detainees and eventually forcing their release. The committee would also maintain contacts with international organizations like Amnesty International and the U.N. Commission on Human Rights and could furnish

71

materials to media at home and abroad on the repressive practices of the Singapore government. Members of Raman's group succeeded in recruiting a prominent doctor, a well-known Catholic priest, and a leading non-Communist politician, but the project was abandoned later in 1976 when Singapore resigned from the SI and the government began a more vigorous crack-down on Communist activities.[12]

Why did these Communists and their sympathisers make such complete confessions of their activities? There have been no accusations of torture. One reason may be that the government had enough evidence to exert sufficient mental pressure to persuade them to make full confessions in the hopes of lenient treatment and short jail sentences.

But there may be another, more ominous explanation: that many of these people simply feel that Communism is the wave of the future, advancing inexorably in Southeast Asia. They themselves on several occassions have enunciated their version of the Domino Theory—that after the fall of Viet Nam, Laos, and Cambodia to the Communists, Thailand, Malaysia, and Singapore would soon follow. They may have felt that the worst they could suffer under the relatively benign governments of Singapore and Malaysia would be a few years in jail, after which time the Communists would take over, they would be released, and they would emerge as heroes of the revolution, with the prospect of prominent positions in the new regime.

These confessions bring to mind the American story about an old Southern preacher at a revival meeting. One of his parishoners was on his feet confessing to a long list of "sins" with lady members of the congregation, when the preacher cut him short. "Brother," he shouted, "You ain't confessin'. You's braggin'."

A good example is the confession of Abdul Samad Ismail, a Malaysian author who is the most important member of all these groups and managing editor of the *New Straits Times*. In describing Ismail's confession on television, K. Das writes in the *Far Eastern Economic Review* that it "was only occasionally marred by a baleful smile that spoke more for cunning than intelligence . . . without any sign of contrition or of any doubt as to the righteousness of his cause. . . . Never in the history of television confessions—so plentiful in Singapore and Malaysia—had an audience been treated to the spectacle of a man, patently a public enemy, cocking a snook at the Government with such elan and sophistication."[13]

After the North Vietnamese victory in 1975 and the subsequent move of Viet Nam into the Soviet camp opposed to the Chinese, it became more difficult for other Asian Communists to remain neutral between China and Soviet Russia. Most of the leading agents uncovered in Singapore and Malaysia admitted allegiance to the Malaysian Communist Party, organized by Chinese agents of the Cominform, with the Soviets further in the background. After the Sino-Soviet split the MCP became mainly pro-Chinese except for one small pro-Soviet splinter group.

So most of the agents described in this chapter were pro-Chinese Communists, including Caldwell, Raman, and the members of their networks. It was also true of all the agents of Chinese extraction, who apparently retained an element of nationalistic allegiance to the Chinese Communists as opposed to the Soviets. But among the Malay agents uncovered, it is apparent that many were either playing both sides of the street or were active Soviet agents. There have been racial tensions between the Malays and Chinese in Malaysia and Singapore, and it would not be unusual for Communists of Malay extraction to ally themselves with the Soviets in opposition to the Chinese.

Abdullah Majid and Abdullah Ahmad, the Malaysian Deputy Ministers arrested in 1976, had been members of the MCP in the 1950s, but confessed to Soviet ties in 1976.

Samad, the leading Malaysian journalist, and his accomplice S. M. Amin, admitted to membership in the MCP but are believed to have been working for the Soviets.

Soon after the sensational arrests of Samad, Amin, and the two Deputy Ministers, there was a wholesale departure of Soviet officials from their embassy in Malaysia.

The Soviet ambassador returned to Moscow "on holiday" right after Samad's arrest. Then soon after Samad confessed on television, two more officials from the Soviet embassy who have been identified as KGB agents also left the country on "holidays." One was Beksultan Basayev, an expert in Malay politics and long active in Asia, and the other was Yuri Myakotnykh, a KGB veteran who had been expelled from the Congo in 1963 for subversive activities.

A fourth was Igor Dmitryeyev, a KGB officer who taught Russia at the Mara Institute in Kuala Lumpur. Known to be a regular drinking partner of Samad's associate, Amin, he also left the country abruptly in 1976 to the surprise of his Mara Institute colleagues.

These revelations of widespread Communist subversion in Singapore and Malaysia have been virtually ignored by the American media or simply treated as evidence of a repressive Government, thus following the line that Caldwell, Raman, and the others were attempting to promote.

For example, the *New York Times* ran two long articles by a correspondent in Singapore, David A. Andelman. The first on June 23, 1976, reported the arrests of Samad and Amin and treated those patronizingly as simply the result of the "frenzy" of anti-Communist fear in the Malaysian government and the fact that Prime Minister Lee of Singapore was "known to fear Mr. Samad as an extraordinarily able and *honest* journalist" (emphasis added). The second, a front page, two-column piece on April 4, 1977, reported on the arrests of Raman and his network. It presented these mainly as "a new campaign to repress dissent that has crippled the political opposition and a fledgling human rights movement" and a further effort to prop up Lee's "dictatorship with a democratic facade."

There has been little recognition in U.S. media of the problems these two small strategic countries faced in over-coming the bloody Communist guerilla campaigns in the 1950s and in resisting the continuing subversion since then by Communist encroachments from all sides. In fact the Malaysian government has been notable for being one of the most democratic of the former British colonies. And in Singapore, reports of repression have been greatly exaggerated. The PAP has been running a one-party system for several years, but political opponents have not been detained unless known to be Communists.[14] Both countries inherited the Anglo-Saxon jury system, but they have found it necessary to pass laws eliminating trial by jury for cases of Communist subversion after several incidents during the 1950s emergency when witnesses refused to testify in open court after receiving threats of reprisals from the Communist underground.[15]

The cases of Singapore and Malaysia indicate that Communists will go to great lengths to successfully infiltrate and manipulate the media, even in relatively small countries like these. But in contrast to these countries, Western countries have paid little attention to subversion of the media. As noted in Chapter I, our FBI is not even empowered to investigate such activities, and only one Western journalist has ever been arrested as an agent of influence for the Soviets: Pierre Charles Pathé, news of whose arrest came in July 1980.

Pathé is an elderly Frenchman whose father was prominent in

the French movie industry and founded Pathé News, which used to distribute newsreels in the U.S. He was arrested by the French security services in July 1979, but the case was not announced until a year later after it had come to trial and Pathé had been sentenced to jail for five years.

After he had published an article favorable to the Soviet Union, Pathé was approached in 1959 by a KGB agent working in UNESCO. As a sympathiser, Pathé did not have to be bought, but the Soviets did give him periodic financial assistance and the money to start his own newsletter, *Synthesis,* which developed a small but influential circulation among journalists and members of the French Senate and Chamber of Deputies. In 1967 his control was turned over from the UNESCO official to a KGB agent working in the cultural section of the Soviet Embassy in Paris.

Arrested in 1979 while meeting with his KGB control, to whom he had just given a batch of papers, he was accused of planting stories in the French press or in his own newsletter designed to sow discord among the NATO allies and discredit the western secret services, especially the CIA. Many of these were written for him by the KGB. Over the twenty year period he or his KGB ghostwriters wrote more than 100 such articles. Because of his many connections, he was also in a position to give the Soviet gossip about prominent journalists or officials for use in recruitment or blackmail.

Robert Moss, reporting on this case in the London *Daily Telegraph,* commented that "by putting Pathé behind bars, the French Court of State Security publicly recognized that this form of Soviet covert action . . . may represent a danger equal to traditional espionage." *Paris Match* said, "In sending Pathé to jail for five years without considering his age or state of health, the judges firmly condemned him as a spy without him actually being one. For them, Pathé is tangible proof that in France there are innumerable 'ants' of the KGB, 'ants' that are both insignificant and dangerous. These ants tirelessly and in little doses are the vehicles of false ideas."[16]

This case has been ignored by American media. But it provides an ominous lesson for the U.S., as do the events in Singapore and Malaysia. If the Communists have spent enough time and effort over the past twenty years to subvert prominent journalist and government officials in France and these two small Southeast Asian countries, what efforts have they been making to influence the people controlling the media in a much more important target, the United

States, "glavny vrag," their principle enemy? Have they been as successful as they were in France, Singapore, and Malaysia? How many "ants" exist in the United States?

THE SELLING OF SIHANOUK AND THE CAMBODIAN COMMUNISTS

Among all the propaganda campaigns to be described in this volume, the efforts on behalf of the Cambodian Communists and Prince Sihanouk had some of the most direct and disastrous effects on U.S. policy. And none of these campaigns has been so clearly revealed by later events to have based on falsehoods. For five years (1970-75) American media were influenced by this propaganda to build up Prince Sihanouk in his Peking exile as an important factor in Cambodian politics, with whom the U. S. should negotiate to end the bloodshed. At the same time many American commentators and media were portraying the Cambodian Communists as honest idealists, "gentle people," whose country was being ravaged by American bombs, and who, but for our violent opposition, would be willing to form a coalition government with other parties in their country.

In fact, after the fall of Cambodia in April 1975, that nation's Communists were found to be among the most brutal tyrants in history. Their forced evacuation of Phnom Penh and other cities at gunpoint, during which the old and young, even those in hospital beds, were forced to walk on foot into the countryside, was one of the worst cases of genocide in modern times. More than two million are estimated to have died in this holocaust within two years, either from exposure, starvation, or execution by the Communists.

As for Sihanouk, the events of 1975 showed him to be precisely what the U.S. Government had claimed he was—a powerless figurehead for the Communists. For several weeks after the Communist takeover he was not invited back to his capital and feared to go uninvited. When he finally returned, most of his staff decided not to

77

accompany him. He was horrified at what he found. He made one quick tour abroad, mechanically reading a few set speeches, but breaking down and crying frequently in private when describing conditions to friends. For the next two years he was held incommunicado in Phnom Penh, stripped even of his phony title, living a Spartan life in part of his former palace.

Cambodia's Recent History

Before describing the propaganda on Cambodia, it is necessary to outline briefly the developments of recent years in this country, which, although small, has had a complex history. The Cambodian Communist Party was formed as part of the Indochinese Communist Party during World War II. The top leadership of the Cambodian Party (or Khmer Rouge) worked continuously underground from 1942 onwards. Only in 1976 did the world learn the identity of the true heads of the Khmer Rouge: Pol Pot and Noun Chea.

Although all Communist Parties like to work secretly, no other Red leaders in history have managed to remain so deeply undercover as these leaders of the brutal Khmer Rouge. Pol Pot, who had never been heard of outside the inner circles of Indochinese Communism until 1976, has in a few years taken his place alongside Hitler and Stalin as one of the three most blood-stained tyrants in modern history.

In 1946 the Indochinese Communist Party had been split into its three national branches: the Cambodian Party known as the Pracheachon, the Lao Dong (Workers') Party in Viet Nam, and the Lao Peoples' Party in Laos. But it is now apparent that the Vietnamese only considered this to be a move of expediency and that they nursed an objective of reuniting the parties eventually and creating a combined Indochina Federation of Communist countries under their domination after they took power in Viet Nam.[1]

During the 1950s, the Cambodian Communists were a small party operating underground in Phnom Penh and other cities and in guerilla bands in the countryside. After the French gave Cambodia its independence in 1955, Prince Sihanouk served as Premier under his Father's monarchy until 1960 when the king died. Sihanouk was then declared head of state and did away with the kingship.

During the 1960s, Sihanouk attempted to steer a neutral course among several dangerous political rocks: on the one hand, Communist subversion in his own country, backed by the Viet Nam

Communists as well as less directly by the Russians and the Chinese, and on the other hand, anti-Communist forces, including the South Vietnamese, the United States, and anti-Communists in his own government. This two-way struggle was further complicated by the fact that Cambodians of all beliefs tended towards a fear and dislike of the Vietnamese, who have been their enemies for centuries ever since in the period from 1500 to 1757 A.D. when the Vietnamese moved gradually down the eastern portions of the Indo-Chinese peninsula, driving the Khmers and other less aggressive peoples before them. Many elements of opinion in Cambodia feared that the more numerous and aggressive Vietnamese would literally swallow them up and obliterate them as a nation after they lost the protection of the French.[2]

Some of the Cambodian Communists, however, had been trained in North Viet Nam and had close political ties there since the days of the unified Indochinese Communist Party. They continued to get support from Hanoi.

Sihanouk was making strenuous and complicated efforts to maintain the neutrality of his country in the turmoil going on all around it. Until 1963, he accepted millions of dollars in U.S. development aid.

In 1963, with the political struggles heating up and with Communist pressures growing, he broke off diplomatic relations with the U.S. and South Viet Nam and refused further U.S. aid. Communist subversion in his country continued, however. In 1965 he declared the Communist Party illegal. Many Communists, most of whom had been concealing their sympathies, fled from Phnom Phen and went underground or into the guerilla movement.

Under increasing pressure from the Communists, Sihanouk began to cooperate with their efforts against the South Vietnamese and to extend them great concessions in the way of transit rights and permission to use Cambodian territory against the Saigon Government and the United States. In the late 1960s the border areas of Cambodia became a de facto staging area for the North Vietnamese army. Most Cambodians were pushed out of the region, and by 1969 there were an estimated 40,000 North Vietnamese and Viet Cong soldiers along the borders. The southern ends of the routes making up the Ho Chi Minh Trail from North Viet Nam were in Cambodia. And Communists were also allowed to land supplies at the port of Sihanoukville and transport them in great volume to their army over Cambodian roads in Chinese trucks. Thus the whole area along the border also became a rest and reassembly sanctuary for Communist troops, large supply dumps, camps, and hospitals. If they were under pressure in South Viet Nam they could retreat across the border without fear of hot pursuit by the South Vietnamese or Americans. Though the presence of the hated Vietnamese was causing growing bitterness among the Cambodian people and many government officials in Phnom Penh and Sihanouk was becoming increasingly unhappy with the situation, he was unable to extricate himself from his agreements.

The Bombing Campaign

In 1968, when Chester Bowles was visiting Phnom Penh, Sihanouk proposed to him that the U.S. bomb the sanctuaries along the border, saying that he would not object as long as his acquiescence was kept secret. President Johnson did not take up this offer, but early in 1969 when the matter was raised again by the U.S. commander in Viet Nam, General Abrams, President Nixon gave his approval.[3]

A major bombing campaign of the 10 mile border region followed, with elaborate precautions set up to prevent publicity and avoid embarrassing Sihanouk. Since he was continuing to engage in his complicated maneuverings between the North Vietnamese, China, and the Soviets, it would have put him in an impossible position to have to admit he approved of the raids.

How did Communist propaganda and the American media react to these raids? The secrecy of the bombing, for a time, was in the interest of all parties involved:

—Sihanouk did not protest the bombings because he wanted them. A few months after they had started Sihanouk restored diplomatic relations with the U.S. and then invited President Nixon to visit his country.

—The Communists did not protest or even mention the bombings because they did not want to admit that they had 40,000 North Vietnamese troups and countless Viet Cong inside Cambodia.

—The U.S. government did not announce the bombings, not to deceive the American people, but to avoid embarrasing Sihanouk.

The cabinet officials concerned with defense were informed, as were key Congressional leaders, including Senator Richard Russell, Chairman of the Senate Armed Services Committee; Representative Mandel Rivers, Chairman of the House Armed Services Committee;

and Representative Thomas Morgan, Chairman of the House Foreign Relations Committee. Members of the Senate Foreign Relations Committee "informally agreed to bombing enemy sanctuaries in Cambodia after being assured by Secretary of State William Rogers that the supplies there were being used against Americans on the South Vietnamese side."[4]

The bombings in effect did help to save American lives. General Earl Wheeler, Joint Chief of Staff at the time, told the Senate Armed Services Committee that U.S. casualties in South Viet Nam, running at about 1,250 per week before the raids, dropped to less than half that afterwards. Wheeler said that the raids "harassed the enemy, destroyed his supplies, kept him off balance, and relieved pressure on Allied forces. Extensive loss of personnel and material inflicted on the enemy saved American lives. Sihanouk's restoration of diplomatic relations with the U.S. and his invitation to President Nixon to visit his country should leave no doubt that Sihanouk approved the bombings.

But while the Communists did not complain publicly about the raids, they soon incorporated them into their propaganda within Cambodia. One of the leading American experts on Communist propaganda, Douglas Pike, formerly with U.S.I.A. in Indochina and later at MIT and the State Department, published in 1971 a thorough analysis of Communist propaganda inside Cambodia. Among the four major themes (which will be described more fully below) was the point that American air strikes were bringing death and destruction to the Cambodian people.[5] Although almost all Cambodians had been expelled from the sanctuary areas by the Communists and virtually none were killed by the sanctuary bombings, the American media later bought this Communist propaganda line completely in criticizing the bombing. They also thoroughly misinterpreted the reasons all parties involved were reluctant to talk about the bombings publicly.

The first leak about the raids occured almost immediately in 1969. This was a report by William Beecher in the *New York Times* on May 9. Though this did not cause much of a stir at the time, it did concern Nixon and Kissinger, who were alarmed that such a closely guarded defense secret had been given to a reporter by someone high in the defense organization. This was one of the first and most serious leaks causing Nixon to start wiretapping the National Security Council staff and some reporters and to launch the

Plumbers operation. The leak also forced the U.S. to stop the bombing, and thus, the administration later said, cause additional loss of American lives.

In 1973 more details of the bombing emerged. A former Major, Hal M. Knight, who had resigned from the Air Force, testified before the Senate Armed Services Committee on July 14 on the raids and the double entry bookeeping system. His testimony started a storm of indignation among some senators and congressmen and many of the media. The *Times* ran an indignant editorial, and on July 20 *Times* columist Tom Wicker viewed the situation with alarm. On July 25 the *Times* published a front page article by Seymour Hersh reporting that Secretary Rogers had testified that Sihanouk had been informed of the bombing and hence that it was not a violation of neutral territory. But then the *Times* sent a cable to Sihanouk inquiring whether he had been aware of the bombing. Sihanouk, deposed in 1970, had taken refuge in Peking and in July 1973 was visiting the ruler of North Korea, Kim Il Sung, in Pyongyang. Sihanouk cabled the *Times* from the North Korean capital saying that he had not been aware of the bombing, adding that the raids "simply proved that the U.S. was preparing for the overthrow of his government." The *Times* ran the story without comment.

The *New York Times* has a record of decades of knowledgeable reporting on American diplomacy. But it must have reached some low point of naiveté to cable such a question to this Cambodian prince, sojourning in a Communist capital, and then to take his reply at face value and print it without comment on the first page. We can only ask what sort of reply Seymour Hersh expected the Prince to make. Would he cable from his host's headquarters in North Korea that he had in fact known all about the bombing?

Yet this allegation that the U.S. had bombed a neutral country without its government's knowledge or consent grew to be one of the favorite examples of the American government's villainy among the anti-anti-Communists during succeeding weeks and until the present.

On August 8, 1973, the *New Yorker* in its "Talk of the Town" section, which is often used to lecture the American administration, rose to new heights of indignation:

> In March of 1969, Secretary of State Rogers, testifying before the Senate Foreign Relations Committee, said "Cambodia is one country where we can say that our hands are clean and

our hearts are pure." At that moment with Secretary Rogers knowledge and assent, we were bombing the neutral country of Camodia; the administration was keeping our illegal bombing secret and the Pentagon was falsifying the record of our raids. In a military parallel of Watergate, the White House presided over a crime—the illegal bombing of a neutral country and the taking of uncountable lives, and then over an historically unprecedented cover-up . . . it acted lawlessly, it acted in secrecy, and it lied.

Even today the legend persists that the U.S. acted without Sihanouk's knowledge, that it killed large numbers of innocent Cambodians (although in fact few Cambodians were left in the sanctuaries), and that it kept the raids secret simply to fool the American people.

As late as March of 1977, no less an expert on U.S. foreign relations than Ben Bradlee, executive editor of the Washington *Post,* was quoted as saying that the news suppression that angered him the most during his career in Washington was the bombing of Cambodia. "The people who were being bombed knew it." he said. "The Godless Commies knew it. Only the American people didn't.[6]

It is difficult to believe that sophisticated journalists like Ben Bradlee and Seymour Hersh would not know that the reason for secrecy was not to fool the American people, but to protect Sihanouk, and that they would be taken in by such an obvious propaganda line.

The Cambodian Incursion

The sanctuary bombings in 1970 slowed down the North Vietnamese operations in Cambodia considerably but had to be halted after the leak and were not enough to drive the North Vietnamese out of Cambodia. The anger among the Cambodians against this presence grew, and along with it, hidden opposition to Sihanouk, whose intricate policy of playing all sides was now beginning to be considered ineffective. In early 1970 Sihanouk left on a trip to France, planning to continue on to Russia and China in order to persuade all three countries to use their influence to get the North Vietnamese out of Cambodia. But he had not yet left Paris when he was deposed by a unanimous vote of the Cambodian National Assembly. Lon Nol, his Prime Minister, was named Head of State.

There have never been any accusations by even the most dovish commentators that the U.S. was behind this coup (although Communist propaganda soon took up this line). It was evidently a true popular movement, at least among the Cambodian elite, although large numbers in the countryside still had great affection and loyality to the Prince.

The Communists were evidently as surprised by the coup as the Americans, and for three days they muted their propaganda output while they developed a party line. The Soviets maintained an embassy in Phnom Penh, and although they soon began to back the Khmer Rouge, they managed to keep this embassy until the 1975 Communist victory in a complicated effort to play both sides.

Meanwhile Sihanouk continued on from Paris to Moscow and then to Peking, where he settled down in exile under the protection of the Chinese Communists.

Anti-anti-Communists in the U.S. have since blamed Nixon and Kissinger for not attempting to negotiate with Sihanouk to bring about his return to power in a "neutral" government. This was precisely the line being peddled by pro-Chinese sympathisers at that time. But the facts now show that this would have been impossible.

The U.S. in fact *did* prefer to approach Sihanouk and would have preferred to see him still in power in Cambodia in a "neutral" government, but the possibilities for that had evaporated. Within two days of his arrival in Peking, and without waiting for any U.S. approach, Sihanouk took sides with the North Vietnamese and turned violently against the U.S. and the Lon Nol government. He issued a statement blaming his overthrow on the CIA and defending the Vietnamese Communists in Cambodia as resisting "American imperialism".[7]

Kissinger was meeting secretly with the North Vietnamese in Paris during this time in an attempt to resurrect the peace negotiations on the Viet Nam War. When he offered to discuss the neutralization of Cambodia, he was rudely rebuffed by Le Duc Tho, the chief Vietnamese negotiator, who blamed the U.S. for Sihanouk's overthrow and said that the three Indochinese people—the Laotians, Cambodians, and Vietnamese—were now united in the fight against colonialism.[8]

The North Vietnamese called the new Cambodian leaders "pro-American rightists." The Khmer Rouge, with North Vietnamese backing, announced the formation of the National United Front of Kampuchea (or FUNK, after its French initials). On April 6 Sihanouk announced from Peking the formation of a coalition between his followers and FUNK, to be named the Royal Government of National Union (or GRUNK).

Then the North Vietnamese made it starkly clear that there was no hope for compromise by launching a series of attacks on the Cambodian Republic's forces all across southern and eastern Cambodia in cooperation with the Viet Cong and Khmer Rouge. There were major attacks in 24 locations between April 3 and 24, and growing harassment of shipping on the Mekong River.[9]

The U.S. now faced an entirely new situation in Indo-China. Cambodia under Sihanouk had provided the Communists with transit rights down the Ho Chi Minh trail and by sea from Sihanoukville, as well as with sanctuaries all along the border. But now the U.S. saw the possibility of a Communist take-over of the entire country. This would have represented an even more serious threat to a satisfactory settlement of the Viet Nam war and an orderly withdrawal of American troups with the preservation of an acceptable free government in South Viet Nam.

After two more weeks of agonizing debate within the U.S. administration, Nixon decided on April 28 to order the "incursion" into the Cambodian border areas by South Vietnamese and American forces.

The later propaganda line was that our actions had somehow "driven the North Vietnamese deeper into Cambodia" and hence widened the war for that poor country. In fact, the incursion was ordered *three weeks after* the North Vietnamese had themselves burst out of the border areas and started major operations further into Cambodia.

Kissinger later commented sadly that the opposition in the U.S. had led again the "perennial error of our military policy in Viet Nam: acting sufficiently strongly to evoke storms of protest but then by hesitation depriving our actions of decisive impact."[10]

The incursion did lead to the largest storm of protest of the entire Indo-China war, with accusations that we were invading a "neutral' country and expanding the war to include this small "gentle" people. The hysteria culminated in the riots at Kent State and the death of four students.

The Fall of Cambodia

But contrary to the accusations of the opponents of the incursion, the U.S. and Vietnamese troups were withdrawn within the initial time limit. After the withdrawal, no further U.S. troops were sent to Cambodia, but there were advisors, and a major bombing campaign was launched against the Cambodian Communists.

So the situation in mid-1970 can be summarized as follows:

—Most of the elite of Cambodia—the best educated, the military, the business classes, and the small aristocracy—were disillusioned with Sihanouk and strongly against Communism and the Vietnamese.

—Most of the peasantry and all the clergy were also anti-Comcommunist and anti-Vietnamese although many still maintained a loyalty to Prince Sihanouk.

—The Communists were a small but well-organized minority in the beginning. There were the original cadres from the Pancheachon like Pol Pot and Noun Chean and radical intellectuals like Khieu Samphan. There was also an element of Khmer Krom; i.e., Cambodians who had lived in Viet Nam and been recruited by the Communists there.

Thus a large part of the population with any political loyalties at all was strongly united behind the new Republican government and against the Communists. This contrasted with the situation in the early days of the war in Viet Nam when there were many political and religious factions competing with each other. The Buddhists were a case in point. In Cambodia there is only one Buddhist sect, the Hinayana or "Small Wheel" Buddhists who received their religion directly from India. This sect has generally been more otherworldly and pacifistic than the Mahayana or "Big Wheel" sect, which received its benefits from India by way of China and has traditionally been more activist. In Viet Nam, both sects are active and are split into many sub-sects, which held many shades of political loyalties during the Vietnamese war. But in Cambodia the single Hinayana sect became strongly anti-Communist early in the struggle and was surprisingly militant about it. These Buddhists were alienated very early by the brutality of the Khmer Rouge, a development ignored by American media but hinted at frequently in more knowledgeable dispatches from Cambodia. As early as the middle 1960s, the Khmer Rouge were executing Buddhist monks who would not cooperate with them, and this continued up through the 1970s, driving the Buddhists into an active role in supporting the new Republican government. Dispatches described the Buddhists actively aiding the troops and allowing monastery and pagoda grounds to be used as training areas.

It is part of the tragedy of Cambodia that this small nation, which initially was united behind a single Government in opposition to the Communists, was not able to make effective its will to survive as a free people. It was plagued by the inefficiency of its own Government and by the gradual loss of will of the United States in Indo-China, and above all by a clever and relentless Communist campaign of propaganda that confused its own people and misled the outside world, including the U.S. public.

Sihanouk's "coalition government," GRUNK, was given much publicity by the Communists and by American media, but after the fall of Phnom Penh it was found to be a fiction, like most coalitions in which the Communists take part. In practice it was used by the Communists for two purposes: 1) to throw dust into the eyes of Americans and other foreigners, leading them to believe that Sihanouk had some power and that there was a reasonable government as an alternative to the Cambodian Republican government in Phnom Penh, and 2) to fool the large numbers of people inside Cambodia who were still loyal to Sihanouk and to hold them on the same side as the Communists against the Lon Nol government. Soon after the fall of the Republican government in 1975, GRUNK was seen to be completely without power. By April 1976 it was dissolved and Sihanouk "resigned" his position as Head of State and retired from public life.

The war dragged on during the early 1970s. There was increasing corruption and inefficiency on the Phnom Penh government side, but there is no doubt that the great majority of the people retained a preference for the Lon Nol government and opposed the Communists.

By 1972 in the United States, the antiwar movement had become so powerful that the government was having increasing difficulty providing adequate aid to the Cambodians. The Communists continued to gain territory. Then Kissinger's diplomacy in 1972 resulted in the Paris Peace Treaty of 1973 which called for a "Cease fire" in South Viet Nam, Laos, and Cambodia.

Article 20 of the agreement called for *the end of all foreign military activity in Cambodia, the withdrawal of all foreign military personnel, and the end of the use of Cambodian territory to encroach on neighboring countries.*

Lon Nol called an immediate cease fire by his Army and offered to negotiate for a settlement, but the Communists refused and continued the fighting. Sihanouk declared from Peking that he would only negotiate if the "traitors" in Phnom Penh were put out of office.

It is notable that amidst all the controversy as to whether the North or South Vietnamese committed the most violations of the Paris peace terms, there is little doubt that the North Vietnamese from the beginning committed gross violations of the *Cambodian* provisions. They continued to maintain at least 40,000 troups in Cambodia both to support the Cambodian Communists and to pursue the war against South Viet Nam from the sanctuaries. The Ho Chi Minh Trail, which terminated in Cambodia, was built up during the 1973-1975 period into a multi-lane concrete highway until one American observer said it looked from the air like the New Jersey Turnpike, yet this was immune from American or South Vietnamese bombing by the provisions of the treaty.

When the Communists refused to negotiate, Lon Nol was obliged to continue the war and asked for further American aid. The only aid the U.S. administration could legally give him was to maintain the bombing, but the administration declared that this would stop as soon as the Communists agreed to a cease-fire and the North Vietnamese left Cambodia according to the treaty terms. But anti-war sentiment continued to escalate in the U.S. In June 1973 Congress attached a rider to a funding bill the U.S. Government calling for the cessation of all U.S. military operations in, over, or off the shores of Indo-China. Nixon took the risk of vetoing the bill, but with all workings of the government threatened with a halt without funding, he was obliged to compromise and agree to a bill that would cut off all military operations by August 15. He was forced into this compromise partly by the fact that on June 25, 1973, John Dean began to testify before a Congressional Committee about Nixon's involvement in Watergate.

The compromise meant that the Cambodian Communists had only to hold out until August 15 for the U.S. bombing to stop. This they did. And with this final cut-off of U.S. military support and subsequent further reduced financial backing by Congress, the Cambodian government's ability to fight the Communists with their continued backing from Hanoi, China, and Russia declined steadily. The Republic fell at last in April 1975 shortly after the fall of Saigon.

It is an open question whether with continued U.S. financial assistance and some military aid and advice, and perhaps a more vigorous U.S. insistence on a reform of the Cambodian government, the Cambodian Republic might have been able to survive. It would have been much more possible if we had also continued sufficient aid to the South Vietnamese to allow them to fight on. But in any event free Cambodia and South Viet Nam collapsed within a few weeks of each other.

Then began the bloodbath in Cambodia. Lon Nol fled to safety, but the other top members of his Government showing great heroism, remained with their people. Sirik Matak, In Tam, and Lon Nol's brother, Lon Non, who had been accused in the American press of being corrupt and inefficient, all elected to stay, and in the event were among the first to die. Sirik Matak and In Tam were shot almost imediately. Lon Non was reported by the Communists to have been "beaten to death by an angry populace, and his body thrown into a hole that had been dug to transplant a banana tree." The victorious Communists began to drive the population out of Phmon Penh and other Cambodian cities and villages at gun point—the young, old, sick, and wounded—in an exodus that some commentators said was the most brutal since Genghis Khan. Phnom Penh was soon reduced to virtually a dead city. Thousands attempted to flee across the borders to Thailand and even into Communist occupied Viet Nam.

The Communist government remained mysterious for several months. Khieu Sampan and Ieng Sary, the previous overt leaders, were superceded at the top by men who had been unknown in the West, notably the new Premier, Pol Pot. The government in fact was a classic Communist totalitarian oligarchy, and Sihanouk had no power whatever. His patriot followers failed to return with him to Cambodia and took refuge elsewhere abroad, and those who had supported him within the country disappeared, presumed to have been eventual victims of the holocaust.

The Chinese provided Sihanouk with asylum and ostensible support. But they were also enthusiastically supporting the Cambodian Communists. They must have known these fanatical men had no intentions of giving Sihanouk any power. There is no reason to think the Chinese ever took Sihanouk seriously as anything more than window dressing.

Communist Propaganda Treatment

How did Communist propaganda handle these events, and how did this propaganda in turn affect the U.S. media?

By the end of 1970, after a brief pause to analyse the unexpected overthrow of Sihanouk, the Communists developed a propaganda line which they proceeded to push in the Cambodian villages where they had access and to purvey to the outside world. This consisted mainly of four points:

—Lon Nol and the other leaders of the new government are lackeys of American imperialism.

—They overthrew the legal government of Prince Sihanouk, who is a fine man.

—In doing so they brought death to Cambodian civilians in the form of air strikes and artillery fire.

—Our goal is to overthrow Lon Nol and bring Prince Sihanouk back to Phnom Penh.[11]

Launched within a few weeks of Sihanouk's arrival in Peking, these were the major themes developed by Communist propaganda from that time up until the fall of the Republican Government in 1975. Messages of support to the new National Government of Union (FUNK) and the Royal Government (GRUNK) were broadcast frequently over Radio Peking and Radio Hanoi, and there were several sympathetic reports of Sihanouk's visits to North Korea and the visits of Cambodian Communists to Peking. In July 1970, the North Vietnamese radio broadcast friendly greetings from Premier Pham Van Dong to Sihanouk.[12]

Chinese, North Vietnamese, and North Korean broadcasts and print media through these five years continued to disseminate support for Sihanouk as well as the Cambodian Communists; attacks on the Republican government, the gang of seven "traitors" (Lon Nol, Sirik Matak, and the others at the top), and denunciations of the U.S. for supporting the Republic and for the U.S. bombing. Typical was a broadcast from China in April 1974 which lyrically described a "fraternal banquet" in Bucharest attended by Khieu Samphan and Ieng Sary, and at which Manescu, chairman of the Rumanian Council of Ministers, gave a speech supporting the Cambodian people. Samphan also spoke, condemning the U.S. and supporting "Samdech Norodom Sihanouk, Head of State and Chairman of the National United Front of Cambodia.[13]

Soviet output was rather guarded from 1970 through 1972, while the Russians apparently made some effort to play both sides. But after the Paris accord in 1973, they must have decided that the fate of the Republican government was sealed, for they came out fully in support of the Cambodian Communists and Sihanouk, even though the latter was still ensconced in Peking. An *Izvestia* article, November 23, 1973, appears to be an effort to sound as though the Soviets were on the bandwagon all along:

> On March 18, 1970, reactionary forces with Washington's support carried out a coup and removed Sihanouk. The Khmer people, united around the United National Front of Cambodia, rose in resolute struggle against the reactionary regime. In early May 1970, the Royal Government of National Union was formed. A telegram of greeting was sent to Sihanouk on May 10, 1970 by A.N. Kosygin, Chairman of the U.S.S.R. Council of Ministers, emphasizing that the Soviet Union welcomes the formation of GRUNK and the strengthening of the united anti-imperialist front of the Indochinese peoples . . . The struggle that you are waging together with the country's partriotic forces against the aggressors will continue to find sympathy and support from the Soviet Union." [There had been no mention of this telegram in Soviet broadcasts in 1970.][14]

From 1973 onward the Soviet press and radio continued to echo these lines.

Effects on U.S. Media

For a few months in 1970 after Sihanouk was ousted, the *New York Times* took a neutral position. It published factual reports from Phnom Penh on the new Republican government, dispatches by Henry Kamm mentioning the large number of North Vietnamese troops still inside the country, and a sympathetic interview of Sirik Matak by Gloria Emerson. But the tone gradually changed to one more critical of the Government and downplaying the threat posed by the Communists. Anthony Lewis's column on April 30 argued against any American intervention and urged a "neutralization of Cambodia on the old basis" (as though the old basis had ever been neutral). And on April 30 *The Times* also wrote an editorial against any form of U.S. intervention, then joined in the general hysteria in the country when the incursion came. From then on, even after all U.S. troops had been withdrawn on schedule by July, the *Times* reflected a growing negative attitude towards the Republic's government and a tolerant attitude towards the Communists. There were few reports of Communist brutality, although such evidence was beginning to appear in other sources; no mention of the significant fact that the Buddhists were becoming united behind the government and against the Communists; and continuing belief in the line that we should negotiate with Sihanouk.

A few typical examples:

On January 11, 1972, the *Times* ran an interview with Sihanouk by Stanley Moore, an Australian, in which the Prince was quoted as saying that he "disliked the phrase, 'Communist forces,' applied to those fighting the Lon Nol Government, since many non-Communists were fighting too." On August 12, 1973, there appeared an interview edited by the Italian journalist, Oriana Fallaci, entitled, "Sihanouk, the Man We May Have to Settle for in Cambodia."

There were frequent (and justified) accounts of corruption in the Cambodian government but no recognition of the extent to which corruption is a way of life in Asia or of the problems of controlling it in a new small nation in wartime. And there was continuing petty criticism of the Cambodians on other subjects. For example, *Times* correspondent Sidney Schanberg sent a dispatch on March 7, 1973, criticizing a Cambodian major for taking an afternoon nap when the enemy was within three miles of his position. This criticism shows a surprising ignorance of local customs. Throughout the lowlands of Indochina where the noon temperature is always in the 90s it is the general custom to sleep after lunch. Most offices, restaurants, and shops close for one to two hours. A Cambodian would no more think of missing this local equivalent of a siesta than an American would miss a night's sleep. Thus it was natural for the major to do this unless an attack was imminent.

The American bombing, the only means the U.S. had after 1970 of supporting the small Cambodian army militarily against the combined force of the Khmer Rouge and the North Vietnamese, came in for continual attacks. Generally the damage to civilian property and the loss of civilian life caused by this bombing were greatly exaggerated. Commentators towards the end of the war and since have spoken of 1 million civilian deaths and implied this was mainly the result of U.S. bombing. Actually even Sidney Schanberg has said that only a small portion of these deaths were the result of our bombing.[15]

The original incursion and our bombing were continually cited as the only reasons Cambodia was then at war. Commentators generally ignored the fact that the Cambodians themselves had overthrown Sihanouk and that the North Vietnamese attacked three weeks *before* the American incursion. A good example of this tendency to blame U.S. policies for all Cambodia's troubles was Gloria Emerson's statement on WNET Channel 13, New York as late as January 31, 1975, in which she attacked "the American pretense for going into Cambodia to find the North Vietnamese Headquarters . . . and they pushed and shoved their way into Cambodia, a quiet and gentle country, looking for a building they expected to find like the Pentagon."[16] (One wonders whether she still considers Cambodia a gentle country.) Most of the rest of the "northeastern liberal press," which depends so much on the *New York Times* as a source, echoed these replays of the main Communist propaganda lines. *Harpers,* the *Atlantic,* the *New York Review of Books,* and the *New Yorker* all followed the same pattern.

The major broadcasting networks generally reflected similar lines. But they went further, dramatizing the American involvement and ignoring the reasons for it. CBS was proceeding according to this pattern as early as the U.S. incursion in 1970. On May 6, a CBS correspondent in South Viet Nam interviewed the troops of Alpha Company who were about to embark on the fighting. He asked them four questions:

Do you realize what can happen to you?
Are you scared?
Do you say the morale is pretty low in Alpha Company?
What are you going to do?

These questions prompted Senator Robert Dole to ask, "Does Freedom of the Press include the right to incite to mutiny? . . . I believe a CBS reporter has come perilously close to attempting to incite mutiny by playing on the emotions of soldiers just before they were to go into battle . . . . I can think of no other war in our history where this sort of thing would have been permitted."[17]

By the beginning of 1975 with the fortunes of the Republican government declining, the clamor in the media increased, echoing the main Communist lines. On February 11, the *Times* ran an article by O. Edward Clubb, a former U.S. Foreign Services officer who has usually taken positions somewhat sympathetic to Communist regimes in Asia, which said that the "U.S. has always displayed an irrational opposition to revolutionary regimes" (like the Khmer Rouge). On February 13 there was a column by Anthony Lewis urging a coalition government with the Communists. Lon Nol offered to step aside on March 1 if that would bring peace, and on March 3, the *Times* ran an interview with Senator Mike Mansfield recommending a coalition government following Lon Nol's offer. In the same issue was a signed article by Prince Sihanouk written at the *Times'* request.

On February 13, a *Times* editorial said "One striking thing about the Kissinger position [of supporting Saigon and Phnom Penh] is how little it has to do with the wishes of the Vietnamese or the Cambodians. They must go on with the war, however destructive, because the end result of the political alternative might weaken Henry Kissinger's diplomatic position vis à vis the Soviet Union."

On February 25, Tom Wicker's column echoed the position that the war was all the fault of U.S. intervention. "It was the U.S. invasion of 1970 that brought full-scale war to a country that had been at peace, however uneasy. The real disaster is that of the gentle and unwarlike Cambodian people."

On February 27, the *Times* ran an interview with Senator Mansfield in which he said letting Cambodia fall would "force the Cambodians to face up to their own future with no help or hindrance from the U.S., and that's the way it should be, and that's the way it's going to be!"

On March 13, the *Times* published an article reporting, a proposal of Senators Jackson and Mansfield to send Mansfield to Peking to negotiate a peace with Sihanouk.

In the same issue was a long report from Phnom Penh by Sidney Schanberg examining the possibilities of a bloodbath if the Communists won and reporting that although there had been some stories of brutality from Communist occupied areas, these were probably exaggerated, and most observers did not expect any such developments. "Most Cambodians on the non-Communist side seem to want to believe that a future insurgent government will be more nationalist than Communist . . . . There are those who believe that Khieu Samphan and others like him will move somewhat to the right . . . to remain independent of Hanoi . . . . Unlike Administration officials in Washington and some American Embassy officials, most Cambodians do not talk about a possible massacre and do not expect one."

A month later Phnom Penh had fallen and the massacre had started.

Saigon surrendered to the North Vietnamese in the same month of April 1975. For many months after Phnom Penh's surrender, Communist propaganda played the line that this Communist victory was the victory of the people against American imperialism and its lackeys. Many in the U.S. media echoed this line.

But the horrendous bloodbath that began immediately after the fall of Phnom Penh presented a major embarrassment for Communist propagandists. They had several alternatives. One was to deny it, which they tried to do for several months. (See Chapter VIII.) But when denials were overwhelmed by the facts, this became difficult The next alternative was to disassociate themselves from it. This the North Vietnamese and Soviets eventually did. (See also Chapter VIII.) Chinese Communists and their sympathizers, however, were left in the unpleasant position of having to defend the Khmer Rouge because they turned out to be one of the few buffers against the aggressive Soviets and North Vietnamese. But all Communists could and did agree to try to blame the horrors in Cambodia on American policy.

There is no direct evidence that Peking stimulated this effort. But there are indications that the stimulus did come from media and research people in the U.S. with sympathies for the Chinese Communists. And there is also the fact that the effort fit in directly with the pro-Khmer Rouge and pro-Chinese party line.

A key figure in this campaign was William Shawcross, a British journalist who reported on the Indo-China war for several years from Washington. Many of Shawcross's articles for the *Far Eastern Economic Review* in 1976 and 1977 began to expound the thesis that Nixon and Kissinger were responsible for the horrors in Cambodia. They had authorized the bombing of a "neutral country," they had "refused to negotiate with Sihanouk in Peking to bring about a neutral coalition in Phnom Penh," and finally they had authorized the invasion of this "neutral country," which "forced the North Vietnamese deeper into Cambodia and expanded the war."[18] In 1979 Shawcross published *Sideshow*, a book on which he had been working for four years. Based on extensive interviewing of participants and documents obtained under the Freedom of Information Act, from the State Department, the CIA, and the Pentagon, *Sideshow* expounded the same theories of Nixon's and Kissenger's responsibility for Cambodias horrors.

Shawcross's conclusions do not fit the facts summarized briefly earlier in this chapter. His book was severely criticized by the liberal British weekly, *The Economist*, which said "This is not history . . . . Mr. Shawcross's book is free of (the right) questions, and free of answers too. It is too busy doing something else to be considered even remotely fair."[19]

Nevertheless, Shawcross became a star for those who were anxious to divert attention from Communist crimes in Cambodia and soften the horrors of this ally of Communist China in the axis against the Soviet-Viet Nam grouping in Asia. Frances FitzGerald contributed an endorsement, saying "*Sideshow* is a brilliant book. It is an extraordinary piece of investigative reporting, a careful history, and a fine piece of political analysis . . . ." Miss FitzGerald will appear in Chapter VII supporting the theory that Communism is the logical heir to the Buddhist tradition. She is on the Board of the Pacific News Service, located in San Francisco, which is affiliated with the Institute for Policy Studies, and has been noted for its pro-Mao stance. Richard Dudman of the *St. Louis Post Dispatch* wrote a favorable review for the *N.Y. Times*. Dudman was one of the few American reporters allowed into Cambodia by the Pol Pot regime at the height of the horrors and came out with reports that contained some reservations but were generally favorable to Khmer Rouge efforts to "rebuild."[20]

Among many others, Shawcross acknowledges the help of Elizabeth Becker of the *Washington Post* (the other American reporter whom Pol Pot allowed into Cambodia with Richard Dudman); Laurence Stern, managing editor of the *Washington Post;* and Tiziano Terzani, one of the few Western reporters who was able to stay on in Saigon after the Communist victory. He also expresses his debt to some key members of the Far Left Lobby including the Center for National Security Studies; its directors at that time, Robert Borosage (now Director of IPS), and the Field Foundation.[21]

A hint as to Shawcross's own political beliefs occurs in a striking paragraph in his earlier book, *Dubcek*. It seems likely that his beliefs resemble those of many leading figures in the Far Left Lobby. His book is a biography of the Czech premier who attempted to bring about "Communism with a Human Face" or "The Prague Spring" in his country. Dubcek was ousted as a deviationist as a result, and his country was invaded by an overwhelming force of the Soviets and other Warsaw Pack nations, using more tanks than they had employed in the final invasion of Germany.

In his summary chapter, Shawcross makes the following statement:

[It is interesting] to ask whether the failure of Dubcekism

was simply a function of the Czech environment or whether the system itself was inherently unstable and impracticable . . . . If Dubcek's Socialism with a Human Face can be shown to be more than a tantalizing but illusory vision . . . . then the experiment of 1968 holds great promise. For Dubcek was trying to create a Marxist democracy genuinely responsive to the wishes and aspirations of its people. If he was succeeding, he has then provided the world with a real alternative to *the blind arrogance of American capitalism, to the satisfaction of the bourgeois–democratic mixed economy, and to the mindless inhumanity of the Soviet dictatorship.* (Emphasis added.)[22]

This surprising paragraph indicates that Shawcross not only rejects American free enterprise but that he also scornfully rejects "the bourgeois-democratic mixed society", which can only refer to his own Great Britain and other Western European countries that are experimenting with democratic socialism.

That leaves only some of "Communism with a Human Face", since Shawcross also dislikes the extreme form that developed in the Soviet Union. So it appears that Shawcross is one of those well-meaning idealists who are searching for the "right kind of Communism", not democratic socialism but a dictatorship of the proletariat that will somehow be the answer to the world's problems. Such people have come and gone through several cycles since 1917. First they rested their hopes on the Soviet Union. Then many became disillusioned and either rejected Communism or turned to splinter Communist parties. After 1946 many belived that Mao might be the savior, the "right kind" of Communist dictator. Now many have again become disillusioned, or split into factions by the attacks on Mao by the latest Chinese rulers.

Shawcross, publishing in England where people are apt to write pro-Communist views more frankly, has revealed his opinions more clearly than most American writers. But it is probable that many of the Americans who have been following the Communist line so closely in their writings share the same point of view.

Shawcross's theories on Cambodia were taken up eagerly by many others in the media, who were anxious to blunt the impact of the horrors. Tom Wicker and Anthony Lewis echoed his lines in their columns in the N.Y. Times.[23] The Educational Broadcasting Corporation interviewed Shawcross for TV.[24] His book was recommended by Peter Osnos, Foreign Editor of the *Washington Post*,

Walter Berkov in the Cleveland *Plain Dealer,* and Harrison Salisbury in the *Chicago Tribune. The New Yorker's* "Talk of the Town" joined in.[25]

Whether or not deliberately, Shawcross provided another salvo in the Communist propaganda offensive to convince the American public that we should not interfere in *any* attempts by Communists to take over other countries.

In summary, most of the major media accepted the four main lines of the Communist propanda campaign on Cambodia outlined above:

—They were overly critical of the Cambodian government and army without any appreciation of their difficulties as a new undeveloped country emerging from colonialism in the midst of a civil war.

—They exaggerated the importance of Sihanouk, causing many of our opinion leaders to follow the dead-end street of recommending negotiations with him.

—They minimize the faults of the Cambodian Communists, even though there was increasing evidence of their brutality.

—They ignored the importance of the North Vietnamese occupation of eastern Cambodia, treated the bombings and incursion into these sanctuaries as attacks on a gentle, neutral country, and exaggerated the effects of these actions in prolonging the war.

The total results were to frustrate American policy in Cambodia. Of all the case histories to be described in this volume, none will so clearly show the effects of Communist propaganda in emasculating our foreign policy.

Communist propaganda affected our media. The media in turn had profound impact on the opinions of students, intellectuals, and groups of opinion leaders, who in turn influenced Congress. At the same time the Far Left Lobby organizations probably exerted direct influence on Congress.

Communist propaganda, however apparently had greater effect on the media and on Congress than it did on the general public. The American people seemed to have a reserve of common sense, patriotism, and loyalty to simple principles that provided an inertia against the sophisticated arguments being voiced to justify our abandonent of small countries fighting for their existence in Indo-China.

At the height of the hysteria in the media, in Congress, and in student bodies over the Cambodian incursion in 1970, the Gallup Poll found that 50% of the people approved of the Government's policy in Cambodia, 35% disapproved, and 15% had no opinion.[26]

This phenomenon will be apparent in other case histories in this book, where the public appears to favor a stronger policy than do the major media or Congress.

In retrospect, our abandonment of Cambodia was a disgraceful retreat from American honor and commitments to defend the freedom of countries facing aggression. This small country was unified in its fear and dislike of the Vietnamese and abhorrence of Communism. The Cambodians appealed for aid and fought hard by themselves, tying down large Communist forces for five years. Yet we spurned them. The actions of Congress in cutting off our aid marked a tragic abandonment of the principles declared by President John F. Kennedy in his inaugural address in 1961: "we shall pay any price, bear any burden, meet any hardship" to defend freedom around the world.

WHITEWASHING
THE NORTH VIETNAMESE

The worldwide propaganda campaign in support of the struggle by the North Vietnamese against the United States was one of the largest campaigns in history. After the North Vietnamese victory, it continued with slightly less intensity, but in a new direction. Once the U.S. had withdrawn from Indochina, the propaganda had two new objectives: 1) to persuade the U.S. and other democracies to grant political recognition and economic aid, and 2) to convince the American public that our involvement in Viet Nam had been a gigantic mistake, that we had been opposing a sincere movement for national liberation, and therefore that, in the future, we should not interfere in other countries' internal affairs. Or to use a phrase that became popular in the media, we should not try to be "the policeman for the world."[1]

The first objective was of primary interest to the Vietnamese, who were facing tremendous economic problems. The second objective, however, was a particular aim of the Soviets. By taking advantage of this "first defeat ever suffered by the U.S.", Soviet propaganda could do much to convince the American public that we should never again become involved in such foreign adventures.

This chapter will describe this propaganda campaign and the reactions of U.S. media against the background of events in Viet Nam since the Communist victory in 1975. Finally, it will also describe the reactions of several leaders of Western public opinion to the growing evidence of repression and brutality by Vietnam's Communist government. The contrasts between the reactions of these prominent individuals to such cruel events are a ready-made "controlled experiment" which allows one to determine who in fact are true believers in human rights and who are so dedicated to Communism as to be unshaken even by the worst barbarism, so long as it is committed in the name of socialist progress and with the blessings of the Soviet Union.

The Communists' First Year (1975-76)— Propaganda vs. Reality

Soon after Saigon fell in April 1975, Communist propaganda began to promote two new themes:

—The defeat of the South Vietnamese government represented the victory of the revolutionary South Vietnamese people over Thieu's puppet regime and above all over American imperialism. It was also a trimph for the forces of a democratic socialist Viet Nam and for the aims of the Father of a unified Viet Nam, Ho Chi Minh.

—According to the terms of the Paris Peace Treaty, and because of the United States' responsibility for the heavy damage of the war, the U.S. should provide Viet Nam with massive help in reconstruction.

Hanoi radio and print media continually repeated these themes all during the rest of 1975 and 1976. Soviet radio and print media concentrated mainly on the first.[2] Far left groups in the U.S. and those ultra-liberals who followed their line also echoed these themes. They also pounded away at the "lesson" that our support for South Viet Nam had been a hideous mistake and that we should not again become involved in such foreign intervention. This theme was used as an argument against *any* American support for those fighting Communism anywhere, for example, in Angola, Ethiopia, or Afghanistan.

In fact the scenario of this non-interventionist propaganda line had been promoted in the U.S. for many years before 1975 by those who wanted the U.S. to quit the war. Incidentally, it is a mistake to refer to such people as anti-war or as pacifists. The movement's leaders decidedly favored the military objectives of the North Vietnamese. They opposed America's role in the war—not North Viet Nam or the Soviet Union. Back in 1972 Senator Ted Kennedy had said that the U.S. should get out of Viet Nam and "let the Vietnamese settle their own problems," causing Singapore's brilliant but sharp-tongued prime minister, Lee Kwan Yew, to say that in view of the massive Communist interference in Viet Nam on the other side, Senator Kennedy must be "out of his mind." In the same year, Frances FitzGerald, the young free-lance writer who became one of the leading intellectual spokesmen of the anti-war movement, published her *Fire in the Lake.* This was serialized in the *New Yorker* and then became a prize-winning best seller. In her concluding paragraphs, Miss FitzGerald predicted that "behind the dam of American troops and American money the pressure is building toward one of those sudden historical shifts when individualism and its attendant corruption give way to the discipline of the revolutionary community. When this shift takes place . . . the moment has arrived for the narrow flame of revolution to cleanse the lake of Vietnamese society from the corruption and disorder of the American war. . . . It is the only way the Vietnamese can restore their country and their history to themselves."[3]

The Reality

Statements such as Kennedy's and FitzGerald's began to be proved false almost immediately after the Communist take-over. The North Vietnamese set up a typically authoritarian Communist regime in Saigon. Though given token titles, southern leaders of the Viet Cong gradually dropped out of sight. Madame Nguyen Thi Binh, the frozen-faced Viet Cong Foreign Minister so visible at the Paris peace negotiations with Kissinger, was named Education Minister, but soon "resigned" and disappeared from view. In August, according to some reports that filtered out a year later, there was actually a show of force by the North Vietnamese against the South Vietnamese Communist officials of the former Provisional Revolutionary Government (PRG). On one tense Saturday, army tanks and soldiers surrounded the homes of all the leading PRG officials. By nightfall the crisis was over, and the PRG men disappeared from view.[4] Few of those former Southern officials have appeared on subsequent lists of the top rulers in Hanoi.

Some Viet Cong went so far as to begin fighting again in underground opposition *against* the Communist government.

All members of the former South Vietnamese Army, former government officials, and those who had done any business with the government or the Americans were required to report for "re-education." At first those sympathetic to the regime reported that such people were able to return to their families after a few months. But evidence began to filter out from refugees that in fact large numbers were being held indefinitely and that the prison population was growing.

Persecution of religious groups began immediately. Detailed word later reached the West that in November 1975 twelve Buddhist monks had burned themselves to death in protest against government repression. This news was virtually ignored by American media, in contrast to the wide coverage given to the self-immolation of *one* Buddhist priest in protest against the South Vietnamese Government in 1963.[5]

The An Quang Buddhists in the years before the Communist take-over had been one of the most active groups agitating for peace and reconciliation and opposing the Thieu government and the American presence. But they soon found themselves persecuted by the new Communist masters. On April 6, 1977, the police carried out a nighttime raid on the An Quang pagoda and arrested their top leadership.

The Catholic Church also came under severe pressure. All orphanages, schools, hospitals, and leprosauriums were seized. Some churches in the largest cities were allowed to remain open, but large numbers in the countryside were taken over. Services were allowed, but priests were under continual pressure to include political messages in their sermons, especially criticism of American imperialism and support for government policies. Catholic education was forbidden. And priests who violated these rules or appeared too independent-minded were apt to be arrested and to disappear into the gulag.

On February 15, 1976, the Vinh Son Church in Saigon was surrounded by police. Only sketchy details have filtered out through the censorship, but apparently those meeting inside decided to resist out of desperation. A 15-hour gun battle ensued, killing one policeman and two of the church group. Fifteen of the resisters were arrested. Redemptorist Father Tran Huu Thahn was also arrested for complicity in this resistance and has been in prison ever since. He had been a notable figure before the Communist take-over as an agitator for political freedoms and negotiations with the Communists.

By the summer of 1977 there were three hundred Catholic priests and six bishops in prison.[6]

Many other South Vietnamese who had earlier opposed the South Vietnamese Government and called for peace negotiations were being rounded up and imprisoned on a wide variety of accusations. Many now began to face imprisonment, starvation, and death at the hands of the government they had helped to bring to power in hopes it would create national reconciliation.

Mr. Tran Van Tuyen, for example, 64 years old and former chairman of the South Vietnamese National Assembly bloc opposed to the Thieu government, had a long record of agitation for human rights, democracy, and negotiations with the Communists. A democrat and a socialist, he continually advocated liberal policies during the many governments that followed the independence of the South in 1954. During the Diem administration, he was imprisoned on Con Son Island, and in the closing years of the war, government newspapers regularly attacked him as a "pacifist" for his advocacy of negotiations with the Communists. Active in demonstrations for the release of political prisoners and for more freedom of the press, he was chairman of the South Vietnamese chapter of the International League for Human Rights, a world-wide organization whose American leaders include Roger Baldwin, a founder of the American Civil Liberties Union and former Congressman Donald Fraser.

Two months after the fall of Saigon, Tuyen was taken into custody by the Communists. The Vietnam office of the International League for Human Rights was forced to close. Shortly thereafter, Tuyen was classified as "obstinate" by re-education authorities. Ordered to write a "confession," he turned in just two sentences: "I have committed no crime against the Vietnamese fatherland or the Vietnamese people. If I have done anything wrong, it is only in the eyes of the Communist Party of Viet Nam." Not until later did Tuyen's family learn that he had died in jail.[7]

Pro-communist propaganda was quick to try to off-set the reports of such repression. In October, 1976, the Indochina Resource Center and Gareth Porter released a statement on "Human Rights in Vietnam: a Reply to Theodore Jacquenay," with biographical sketches of Tuyen and three other prominent Third Force men imprisoned by the Communists, attempting to show that they had all been collaborators of a repressive South Vietnamese regime. Regardless of the accuracy of this statement, it was soon overwhelmed by the evidence of mass imprisonments that continued to pour out of Viet Nam.

Here are brief profiles of other prominent Third Force and even pro-Communist early victims of this growing terror:

Bui Tung Huan. Prominent anti-Thieu senator before Communist victory. Formerly Rector of Hue University, secular leader of An Quang Buddhists, a sect militantly against the war and the American presence. Elected to Senate in 1970 on a "Lotus" slate, whose platform was peace and national reconciliation. Repeatedly jailed by South Vietnamese government. Four months after Communist take-over, arrested after protests by An Quang Buddhists against persecution of their faith by Communists. At last word was gravely ill in Vietnamese gulag.

Nguyen Cong Hoan. School teacher, elected to South Vietnamese National Assembly, member of Third Force bloc in National Assembly opposing war, but never prominent in politics. After Communist conquest, elected to a new "unified" National Assembly in Hanoi. Attended sessions for two years and was able to travel widely in North and South. Witnessed so much tyranny and oppression that decided to flee country in small boat. "I saw the country from both the ruling class and the people's point of view," Hoan told a U.S. Congressional Committee, "and I decided I had to go."[8]

Nguyen Van Hieu. High ranking Communist cadre, 30 year party member. Led the 1968 Tet Offensive on Saigon. At last report, in Tran Hung Dao prison.

Nguyen Van Tang. 30 year Communist party member, deputy mayor of Binh Chanh. Now in Le Van Duyet prison.

Hai Chien Thang. Formerly National Liberation Front (Communist) Commander in Chief of Saigon district. Now in Le Van Duyet prison.

Nguyen Huu Giao. Former president of Hue Student Union. Organized burning down of American Information Center, Hue. Now in Le Van Duyet prison.[9]

These are only a few names from the hundreds of former Third Force and Viet Cong leaders imprisoned, and thousands of other less prominent citizens whose loyalty to the present regime was suspect.

A massive system of prisons and "reeducation camps" was set up all over South Viet Nam, and extending into the North. Hundreds of buildings were pressed into service, former schools, churches, barracks, dormitories, and warehouses. The system became like the Soviet Gulag Archipelago on a smaller scale.[10] Conditions in these prisons and camps varied from the boring down to the hideous, depending partly on the presumed political status of the prisoner or on the random carelessness which always seems to occur in such prison systems (the irrational inefficiency that has been described in the Nazi prison camps and the Soviet Gulag).[11] Theodore Jacquenay quotes one refugee, a doctor who had escaped from the Gulag. "We were put into a jail cell, about 4 by 8 meters, with 50 other people. All doors and windows were closed, opened only twice a day to give us food. Two bowls of rice per day only and a little salt ... The lavatory was one small pan per cell, which prisoners were permitted to empty twice each day, and which slopped over onto cell floors ... People were forced to write confessions ... sometimes new confessions many times each day ... Sometimes people went crazy with these confessions, living under such conditions. I saw many such cases, screaming, yelling people. I could not treat them with any form of psychotherapy ... Many people hanged themselves."[12]

Father Gelinas, a Jesuit priest who lived in Viet Nam for 20 years and remained in Saigon for 15 months after the Communist conquest, testified before the same Fraser Congressional Committee in July 1977. He documented a minimum estimate of 300,000 prisoners in 1977 with the statement that he believed that more than 60% of all people with high school or college educations in the South Vietnamese cities had been rounded up, and that former American military barracks and officers' quarters in Saigon were filled with prisoners, as many as twenty to a room.[13]

Other estimates of the total number of prisoners ranged as high as 800,000.[14] Reports from refugees indicate that large numbers of "reeducation center" prisoners are being slowly starved.

Did the Vietnamese Communists plan this massive tyranny from the beginning—like the Cambodians—or did they find themselves pushed into it by continuing opposition, "poor harvests," and other excuses made by some of their sympathizers?

Though the Far Left Lobby sought to disseminate a benign impression of the Communist regime's intentions, one of its own releases provides ironic and chilling evidence that the Vietnamese Communists planned their gulag from the beginning. In the *Indochina Chronicle*, published by the Indochina Resource Center in July 1974, months before the Communist victory, there is a review by Professor Franz Schurmann of *Tradition and Revolution in Viet Nam* by Nguyen Khac Vien. Vien is one of the leading intellectuals in North Viet Nam, described by Schurmann as a Marxist writer of "serenity, toughness, and principaledness." As an example of Vien's toughness, Schurmann admiringly quotes him as saying, "The Saigon army, bureaucrats, police, and their families comprise five or six million people out of a total population of seventeen million. We cannot take care of them."

Without demur Schurmann interprets this as meaning that Vien says the Vietnamese Communists, after the victory, will leave these people, comprising one third of the population, to starve. (This would be an even harsher policy than that of the Cambodian Communists, who have starved or executed "only" about one fourth of their population.)

This issue of *Indochina Chronicle* was part of the Indochina kit distributed by the American Friends Service Committee. One wonders if the Friends were aware of all its contents.

Franz Schurmann, a professor of History and Sociology at the University of California, Berkeley, is director of a project known as "America's Third Century." He is also affiliated with the Pacific News Service in San Francisco, which shares offices with the Bay Area Institute, an affiliate of the Institute for Policy Studies.[15]

The Communists, incidentally, were also facing increasing economic problems in Viet Nam. These were blamed on war damage, population shifts, and floods and droughts. But it is probable that the greatest difficulty was the inevitable impact of Communist doctrines on good agricultural and industrial practice. (As one commentator has said, "In the Soviet Union, the Communist revolution was followed by 40 years of 'poor harvest weather'.") Many of the North Vietnamese new edicts had serious impacts on economic progress in the South. More than 800,000 families of former tenant farmers who had been given their land under the South Vietnamese land reform program had this taken back and turned into collectives by the Communists. The lively free markets in Saigon and other cities were crippled. Price controls and rationing strait-jacketed trade. Instead of a gradual recovery from the war, there was a steady decline in production.

The Propaganda Campaign

The Soviet and Vietnamese Communist propaganda machine, of course, presented a much more attractive picture of Viet Nam after the fall of Saigon in 1975. After their victory in April 1975, the Communists took immediate steps to control news internally, closing down all newspapers, magazines, and radio and TV stations to ensure that the official government version of any event was the only one disseminated.

Today in Viet Nam there are just a few official newspapers and magazines and a single TV channel broadcasting only from 7:30 to 9:30 P.M. with government propaganda. Throughout Saigon, says Father Gelinas, books, magazines, newspapers, and tape recordings and other vestiges of the free world were taken from peoples' houses and burned in large bonfires in the streets.[16]

The Hanoi regime also took immediate steps to control news reported to the outside world. All foreign correspondents were forced to leave except for a few who had been highly sympathetic to the Communists. *Time, Newsweek,* and *New York Times* reporters left immediately after the fall of Saigon. AP and UPI correspondents remained for a few weeks but were evicted after they began to send overly frank accounts of executions and evidences of opposition. Only a few sympathetic reporters remained, including Tiziano Terzani, Italian correspondent for the German magazine *Der Spiegel,* who later wrote an admiring book on the "victory," and Nayan Chanda of the *Far Eastern Economic Review.* But even the latter was obliged to leave after several months.

But these blatant attempts to control who did the reporting and what got reported were only the most obvious means of shaping our false perception of life in Viet Nam after the Hanoi victory. As we noted earlier, the Soviet and Hanoi propaganda objectives were to make us believe that the defeat of the South Vietnamese government was a triumph of the revolutionary South Vietnamese people over Thieu's puppet regime and American imperialism and to make the U.S. assume responsibility for the heavy damage of the war and thus help Viet Nam with massive reconstruction aid. These versions of reality began appearing with sinister regularity in Western media.

As the first year after the conquest wore on, the propaganda for aid to Viet Nam heated up with a flurry of TV and press commentary on progress in Viet Nam. One of the most obvious exampes of propaganda was an article appearing in the *New York Times Magazine* on April 25, 1976, the anniversary of the fall of Saigon, entitled "Vietnamizing South Viet Nam," praising the new regime and expressing optimism about progress. The author's name was given as "Max Austerlitz," identified only as "a long-time observer of Asian affairs who recently spent several months in Viet Nam." I had never heard of a "Max Austerlitz," and, having some interest in Viet Nam, I telephoned the *New York Times* for more information. But the editor in charge of the article was evasive, refusing to identify him further. I then turned the matter over to Accuracy in Media Inc., the private Washington organization that monitors media performances. Together we were able to determine that "Max Austerlitz" was a pseudonym and that the author in fact was Alessandro Casella, a Swiss citizen of Croatian descent, with a long record of radical writing and research on Asian affairs. Casella had been in Indonesia in 1965 during the Communist attempt to take power that culminated in Suharto's overthrow of Sukarno, and was writing pro-Communist reports at that time. In the early 1970s he wrote several articles with a pro-Communist slant for the *New York Times Magazine* under his own name, one favorable to Mao Tse Tung, one praising Sihanouk, and another that went so far as to declare that American treatment of North Vietnamese prisoners was as "reprehensible" as the North Vietnamese treatment of Americans.

In April 1976 Casella was head of the U.N. Office of Refugees in Viet Nam, hardly a post that qualified him to write objectively about conditions there. And a government that had been expelling all Western correspondents would hardly have tolerated a U.N. official who was likely to write critical articles.

In the same month as the Austerlitz article, a special U.N. mission completed a study of the Viet Nam economy. Chief of Mission was Dr. Victor Umbricht, also a Swiss, a top executive of the CIBA-Geigy Co. in Basel. The report recommended an international aid program of no less than $432 million for Viet Nam. After the results were leaked to a few sympathetic media, a favorable article by Kathleen Teltsch appeared in the *Times* June 3, 1976. The report, however, was not made available to the public. When I called Dr. Umbricht's office at the U.N. for a copy, I was told it had been "prepared for the Secretary General's use and would not be released." I later obtained a copy (in French) from a friend at another medium (not the *Times*).

The report had several notable parallels to the Casella "Austerlitz" article in the *Times*, providing an optimistic picture of conditions in Viet Nam and glossing over the suppression of human rights. It appeared to be as another stage in the apparently organized effort channeled through the U.N. and sympathetic journalists to promote foreign aid for Viet Nam.

A major new theme in Vietnamese propaganda during 1975-76 was the campaign against the refugees. The large number of refugees—the first wave and those who continued to escape—was a major embarrassment for Communist commentators. It was hard for the propagandists to argue convincingly that it had massive popular support when such large numbers of people were fleeing desperately. The refugees were living proof of the opposite. The propaganda followed two somewhat contradictory lines:

Most of the refugees were misguided and would want to return.

Most of them were the scum of Vietnamese society: brutal generals, corrupt businessmen and politicians, torturers, police, prostitutes, pimps, and other lackeys of the Americans.

These lines appeared first in publications of the Far Left Lobby and its sympathetic allies. For years apologists for the Vietnamese Communists had been attempting to explain why every Communist victory was accompanied by hordes of South Vietnamese refugees fleeing to the areas controlled by the South. For example, in April 1975 the American Friends Service Committee distributed a flyer by Edward Block entitled "Vietnam: Why the Refugees?" In 1972 and 1973 Block had been in Viet Nam as an employee of the U.S. Agency for International Development on refugee problems. After his resignation he became affiliated with a number of the Far Left Lobby organizations in attacking the U.S. effort in Viet Nam. The flyer's point is that the refugees were not fleeing from Communism but from fear of additional American bombing.

But this assertion did not explain why the population continued to flee to the smaller areas still controlled by the South Vietnamese government during the final collapse. During those weeks the Vietnamese Air Force was doing next to nothing, while the remaining Government-held areas were being shelled. The refugees were leaving the "safe" Communist areas for the dangerous areas held by a crumbling government! Communist propaganda—and its American echoes—could only portray the refugees as irrational, panic-stricken people. But after the fall of Saigon and the complete cessation of fighting, it was unmistakable that the refugees actually preferred the risk of death at sea to life in the new socialist paradise. Communist propagandists faced a tough task. But the purpose of propaganda is to convey opinion, regardless of truth. Thus the Indochina Resource Center in the *Indochina Chronicle* article, September 1975, "Where is Home? Indochina's Evacuees in the United States," passed along the line that large numbers of the "evacuees" (not refugees) were misguided, were swept up in irrational panic, or were seeking a "good life" in America. (By implication the latter is prima facie evidence of corruption.) The propaganda also stressed the disorganization of the American evacuation effort, claimed there were attempts at coercion in persuading Vietnamese to leave, and enlarged on the themes of corrupt generals, torturers, heroin pushers, embezzlers, and murderers.

One of the most notable libels, one which persists to this day, concerns the AP's famous photograph of General Nguyen Ngoc Loan shooting a Viet Cong "suspect" before the TV cameras during the Tet Offensive. In fact, this "suspect" was a Viet Cong officer caught red-handed in civilian clothes with two guns during a battle outside the central An Quang pagoda. General Loan, like other Vietnamese, knew well that soldiers' wives and children were being murdered by the Viet Cong (facts also reported by AP but soon forgotten by the American media). And under the rules of war, a combatant found armed and fighting in civilian clothes can lawfully be executed.[17] Thus General Loan shot an enemy he was entitled to shoot. Yet this picture has become one of the classic propaganda items used to besmirch the reputation of the South Vietnamese. It appeared again as late as February 1979 in an editorial in the *New York Times* saying Loan should be expelled from the U.S. for having shot this "suspect."

The depth of the campaign in 1975 was reached with Herblock's cartoon in the *Washington Post* showing the Statue of Liberty with a worried expression on her face, looking at a procession of seedy-looking Vietnamese entering the country. The cartoon was captioned, "Give me your drug pushers, pimps, prostitutes, your torturers and embezzlers."

Direct Communist propaganda—*i.e.* printed materials and broadcasts from Moscow, Hanoi, and Peking—sought to depict Vietnam as a place full of brave efforts to restore a war-damaged country and bring about national reconciliation. In the United States, the Far Left Lobby and its well-meaning collaborators echoed this line. A typical example was Don Luce, of Clergy and Laity Concerned, who testified before the House Subcommittee on International Organizations in June 1977 that he had visited Viet Nam in April and came back "with a very optimistic feeling about a society that is working very hard to rebuild. I found a very equal distribution of food. I found a very deep concern about the human rights of everyone."[18]

Two "churchpersons" from Church World Service of the National Council of Churches gave similar testimony. The Rev. Paul McCleary, Executive Director, and Ms. Midge Meinertz, "Director for Southern Asia," had been given a tour of one "reeducation camp." They found the food "delicious: chicken, pork, rice, fruit." They visited a neat clinic, and several small houses for the camp "members," four men to a house. The Rev. McCleary went so far as to say that the Vietnamese Communists have done a better job of reconciliation with their domestic opponents and "healing the wounds of war" than has the U.S. in welcoming back its deserters and draft dodgers.[19]

This optimistic line was reflected almost exactly in the American

TV networks and the "liberal" northeastern media from the time of the Communist victory up through 1977.

The major networks, the *New York Times,* the *Washington Post, Time, Newsweek, Harpers,* and the *New Yorker* generally pictured the Communist take-over as an inevitable victory of a popular movement against outside interference.

All of these media virtually ignored the testimonies of the many refugees coming out of Viet Nam who could give authoritative evidence on the horrors. *The New York Times* ran a few such reports over the two year period, but these were generally offset by more optimistic stories under large headlines. ("ELECTION OF PANEL TO RULE CITY WARD REPORTED BY SAIGON," 8 July 1975; "VIETNAMESE SALUTE INDEPENDENCE DAY," 14 July 1975; "LIFE IS PEACEFUL IN DELTA," 16 September 1975; etc.) Although the AP and UPI frequently reported the testimony of refugees and experts such as Jacquenay and Father Gelinas in their dispatches, the other media carried almost nothing.[20]

Response to Tyranny: The Test of True Humanitarians

By late 1976 when the evidence of brutal oppression in Viet Nam was becoming overwhelming, it began to have some influence on humanitarians in the United States, including many who had been prominent in the anti-war agitation. Activity starting among these former movement people was to prove highly revealing as to their true sentiments and motivations. Reactions to Communist Viet Nam's tyranny became one of those historic tests of peoples' true sentiments about Communism, indicating on the one hand who was truly humanitarian and willing to speak out against tyranny in any guise, and who was so dedicated to Socialism (or Communism) that he or she was willing to forgive it anything, no matter how tyrannical.

The first to take action was S.A.N.E., the Committee for a Sane Nuclear Policy, a liberal organization in Washington, D.C., which had a history of opposition to the war dating back to 1964. In October 1976, the Board of Directors addressed a letter to Dinh Ba Thi, the Vietnamese observer at the United Nations, expressing concern about reports of more than 200,000 political prisoners and of the imprisonment of many former opponents of the war, including members of religious groups. S.A.N.E. appealed for an accounting of all prisoners and for permission for a neutral group to inspect the re-education camps. The Executive Director of SANE, Sanford Gottlieb, reported sadly that no reply was ever received.[21]

Next a group was formed around the Fellowship of Reconciliation, a pacifist organization with offices in New York and Amsterdam, which had also been active in opposing the war and had frequently been received cordially by North Vietnamese officials. FOR Executive Director James Forest, who had been jailed for 18 months during the war for burning his draft card, began circulating an appeal within the peace movement. The letter expressed continuing friendship for the Vietnamese people and denunciation of American "crimes" against that country, but it also voiced concern over reports of large numbers of prisoners, maltreatment, and violations of human rights. It asked for permission for neutral organizations like Amnesty International or the U.N. to make on-site inspections.

The 112 signers included many former anti-war activists such as Joan Baez, Daniel Ellsberg, Sanford Gottlieb, Tom Cornell of FOR, Homer Jack, Staughton Lynd, and the Rev. Richard John Neuhaus. Neuhaus had been a founder of Clergy and Laity Concerned, one of the most active anti-war groups, but had later resigned and become editor of *Worldview*, a human rights magazine. A number of other liberals also signed, including Kay Boyle, Jerome Frank, Congressman Donald Fraser, Erich Fromm, Allen Ginsberg, Ken Kesey, Roger Baldwin (founder of the ACLU), Aryeh Neier (President of the ACLU), Edward Koch (then a Congressman and later Mayor of New York), and Paul O'Dwyer. Another signer was Robert Ellsberg, son of Daniel and editor of the liberal magazine, *Catholic Worker*.

For several weeks attempts were made to present the letter privately and without publicity to the Vietnamese U.N. observer. The signers hoped that this would be more effective in getting action. But Mr. Thi ignored all letters and phone calls. On December 22, James Forest, Robert Ellsberg, and Daniel Berrigan went to the observer's home, found no one there, and slipped a note under the door extending season's greetings and suggesting a phone conversation. That also raised no response. So as a last resort the group called a press conference for December 29, 1976, and released the letter publicly. The conference was held at the office of the International League for Human Rights on 46th Street near the U.N.[22]

Between the first discussion of this letter and the public announcement there was tremendous pressure on the signers to withdraw their names. Here the separation between true humanitarians and dedicated pro-Communists was most evident. Anti-war activists most closely connected with the Far Left Lobby not only refused to sign but *actively attempted to prevent the publication of the letter*. Most vehement in opposition were Fred Branfman of Clergy and Laity Concerned and William Kunstler, one of the top men in the National Lawyers Guild. Kunstler said, "I refuse to criticize *any* Socialist government in such a fashion." John McAuliffe, director of the Indochina Program of the American Friends Service Committee, said that "all reliable sources indicate that the Vietnamese are carrying out the awesome task of reconstruction with extraordinary humaneness." Claudia Krich, former co-director of the AFSC for South Viet Nam, said that in Viet Nam the reeducation camps are really called "Study-practice sessions." But the leader of the campaign to quash the letter was Gareth Porter of the Indochina Resource Center, which had been the most active coordinating center of anti-war planning up until the Communist victory. Porter spent days campaigning against the letter. He spent literally hours on the phone haranguing Daniel Ellsberg, trying to persuade him to withdraw his name. Ellsberg says, "morning after morning, I'd wake up with arguments going on inside my head, and then for the rest of the day, I'd be hammered both ways by people I have a lot of respect for." But Ellsberg did not withdraw. And Joan Baez also withstood similar pressure.[23]

Despite incidents like this letter, the Far Left tried to maintain that all was well in Viet Nam and that the U.S. should grant massive aid. In September 1977 Viet Nam was admitted to the United Nations. To celebrate this event, Friendshipment, a group backed by the National Council of Churches and linked to the Indochina Resource Center, organized a two-day seminar at the Union Theological Seminary in New York and a "reception" at the Beacon Theatre.

The events have been described by Mrs. Le Thi Anh, a Vietnamese pacifist and a Hoa Hao Buddhist who lived in the U.S. from 1964 to 1971 under a UNESCO grant for writers and was a leading activist in the anti-war movement here. She spoke at anti-war rallies, lectured on campuses, and spent a five-day vigil in front of the White House. After returning home in 1972, she witnessed the Communist takeover in 1975, returned to the U.S. with her husband, and after several months became convinced that the

Communists had simply installed a tyranny far worse than any existing before. "I finally understood what the U.S. had been trying to do in Viet Nam," she said.

Mrs. Anh was invited to the reception because of her former "anti-war" credentials. She gave the following description:

Of the 350-400 Vietnamese gathered at the Beacon Theatre, only a dozen or so were there to celebrate. The remainder were there to protest. Among the protestors who stood outside in the rain was Nguyen Cong Hoan. [the Hanoi Assemblyman who fled Viet Nam in 1976. See above.]

While inside, Mrs. Cora Weiss, the Friendshipment coordinator, in a pink evening dress, welcomed the VN delegations to the applause of her American audience. Outside, Hoan stood in the rain and denounced the new regime to the cheers of his rain-soaked compatriots. They carried posters denouncing the well-concealed Viet Nam gulag and the Nazi atrocities being perpetrated against their own people in Viet Nam....

When I presented my invitation, an American woman searched me from head to toe for at least two minutes ... put her hands under my armpits. Then I was allowed to come in and shake hands with the smiling delegation.

Except for one speech by the VN Deputy Foreign Minister, all other speeches were by Americans.... There were so few Vietnamese supporters that the seminar and the Beacon Theatre show were put on entirely by the Americans. They did all the singing; not one single Vietnamese song was heard during the "Vietnamese celebration." A group of Americans performed a costumed show in what seemed to be an American version of the traditional Vietnamese dragon dance.

If the Ngo Dien speech is one indication, the Vietnamese will use the UN forum to press for U.S. aid for reconstruction. "U.S. Imperialists" and their lack of responsibility in refusing to repair the damage they have caused in Viet Nam were mentioned many times, in the speech and in the seminar."[24]

In 1977 and 1978 conditions in Viet Nam worsened. Even apologists of the new regime in the U.S. admitted that the Vietnamese were suffering from administrative problems. They had two more poor harvests, which were blamed on the after-effects of Amercan defoliation, on "flooding", or on "droughts". Low rice rations, hunger, and even starvation were reported from many parts of the country.

The worsening conditions meant an increase in the flood of refugees. While the early wave had been mainly those with connections to the previous regime or those who had advanced educations or occupations, the new waves included many more simple farmers and laborers with no economic or political allegiance. Vietnamese are distressed if obliged to leave their land and the tombs of their ancestors. Never before in history, even during the previous occupations by foreign conquerors—the Chinese over several hundred years, the French, or the Japanese—had so many Vietnamese felt compelled to pull up their roots and risk death by drowning or starvation.

When one of the farmers among the refugees was asked by a Congressional Committee how he succeeded in organizing his escape without being betrayed to the police, he said, "No one is informing to the police any more. Every one is against the government and would like to leave.[25]

The government began a crack-down on all small businesses which up until then had been tolerated. By one decree in March 1979 all the inventories and capital of private businesses were seized. These measures fell particularly hard on the ethnic Chinese communities in the south, particularly in Cholon, the Chinese area of Saigon. Private businessmen and their families were faced with the choice of starvation or moving to the New Economic Zones, which reports said was almost equivalent to starvation. There was some resistance. One report that later emerged told of bodies strewn throughout the streets of Cholon.[26]

In 1978 occurred the Vietnamese invasion of Cambodia and in 1979 the Chinese invasion of Viet Nam. Both events were accompanied by further dislocations and repression within Viet Nam, directed particularly against the Chinese.

1977 and After—U.S. Media Reactions

In the 1975-76 period, the evidence of such tyranny in Viet Nam had drawn little mention in the print media and was virtually ignored on TV. The many prominent refugees testifying before Donald Fraser's Congressional Committee and making statements at several press conferences were ignored by the major networks.[27] Now in 1978 there was some pick-up in media interest, and a few mentions on TV. But it is striking that most such mentions referred to the ethnic Chinese refugees from Viet Nam. This raises the questions as to whether some of this attention was stimulated by persons having sympathy for the Chinese Communists, who were engaged in a major confrontation with Viet Nam. It was just at

117

this time that the Vietnamese politburo suffered their first major defection in history. Hoang Van Hoan, a leading member and former close friend of Ho Chi Minh, defected and fled to Peking in a disagreement over Vietnamese policy toward China. He began to issue statements critical of the Vietnamese tilt towards the Soviets and persecution of their Chinese minority.[28]

The sudden increase in coverage of the refugees by American media, and especially the Chinese refugees, occurred during this same period.[29]

Still the hard core ultra-liberals and the Far Left Lobbyists continued doggedly to paint a favorable picture of Viet Nam. The Public Broadcasting Service as late as January and April 1978 was showing documentaries filmed in Hanoi and airing radio programs taped in Paris, with rosy-hued accounts of the reconstruction and national reconciliation in Viet Nam and the crimes of the American imperialists.[30]

On August 3, 1979 the *N.Y. Times* published an article on the Op Ed page by Robert Richter, identified only as having "recently completed a documentary film in Viet Nam, 'Viet Nam, an American Journey' ". The article makes the startling claim that the thousands of people fleeing Viet Nam are comparable to the Tories who fled to Canada after our Revolution and the slaveholders who fled to South America after our Civil War. Richter then proceeds to blame the problems in Viet Nam on American bombing, napalming, defoliation, and mining and burning of rice paddies. The article continues, by mentioning that Viet Nam is burdened by 500,000 prostitutes, 800,000 orphans, and a Chinese middle class of profiteers who "no longer fit into Hanoi's socialism." The conclusion of the piece is that the American "Federal law banning aid and trade to Viet Nam should end so that normal relations can resume and we can help rebuild the country we helped destroy."

In the same issue of the *New York Times* appeared the first of a series of six articles on Viet Nam by Seymour Hersh. Hersh had spent 10 days in Viet Nam, one of the few American correspondents to be admitted since the early months of Communist rule. His articles seemed to reflect his gratitude for this favor, painting a universally rosy picture of conditions there. The opening article passed along almost without comment the remarks of the Vietnamese Secretary of State for Foreign Affairs that the U.S. was primarily responsible for the failure of the two countries to achieve normalization of relations, that his country would stop the "unauthorized" flow of refugees, that Viet Nam opposed any conference on the neutrality of Cambodia and rejected Sihanouk as a possible head of a neutral Cambodia, that the Chinese in Viet Nam are being treated no worse than the Japanese in America after Pearl Harbor, that those unemployed or undernourished in South Viet Nam were suffering only because "they don't want to work hard," and so forth. Another article is a long interview with a "non-Communist editor" whose newspaper was supposedly "flourishing" in Ho Chi Minh city, and who described the freedom he enjoys. The editor "expressed anger at the people in the United States who have been criticizing Viet Nam for its policies on refugees." Nowhere in his series did Hersh show his noted investigative talents to determine the truth or falsehood of conflicting claims about the "reeducation centers," about of the real story on Americans missing in action, of the state of religious freedom, of the Soviet Navy's use of Cam Ranh Bay, or of any of the other crucial issues in American-Vietnamese relations.

True liberals, however, were becoming increasingly disillusioned. In May 1979, a number who had signed the 1977 appeal to the Vietnamese government composed another letter. This time the leading spirit was Joan Baez, but this letter was more outspoken. Among the most prominent of the 85 signers were Daniel Berrigan, Pat Brown, Cesar Chavez, Douglas Fraser, Kay Boyle, Norman Cousins, Sanford Gottlieb, Staughton Lynd, James Michener, I.F. Stone, and Charles W. Yost. Again the hard-core members of the Far Left Lobby refused to be associated. Jane Fonda and Tom Hayden ignored Joan Baez's appeal. And Daniel Ellsberg did not sign this time around. "The only thing he wanted to talk to me about when I called him," says Miss Baez, "was my future in the anti-nuclear movement."[31] (See Chapter XII.)

Attacks on Joan Baez and the other singers were not long in coming. On June 24, 1979, another ad appeared in the *New York Times* head lined "The Truth About Viet Nam," with several paragraphs of the usual descriptions of the villainies of U.S. policies in Viet Nam.

A striking feature of this ad in comparison to similar pro-Vietnamese appeals of earlier years is the complete absence of any of the well-known idealists. Few names of signers are recognizable to any one except a student of Far Left politics, and a large number of the singers are known Communists. The list included Carl Bloice, editor of the Communist *Peoples World*, and Charlene Mitchell and Pauline Rosen, senior CP members.

The list is also heavily sprinkled with lesser known names from other organizations in the Far Left Lobby, including the U.S. Peace Council, the Mobilization for Survival, the National Lawyers Guild, the Women's International League for Peace and Freedom, the National Alliance Against Facist and Political Repression, the Center for Constitutional Rights, Clergy and Laity Concerned, and—one more jaw-breaking name—The National Center to Slash Military Spending.

Two days later, a similar ad appeared in the *Washington Post*, sponsored by the U.S. Peace Council, an offshoot of the World Peace Council, a known Communist front. Here the principal signer was Wilfred Burchett, the Australian journalist who has been identified as a Communist. Again the ad was conspicuous for the lack of the usual well-known liberal names.

It appears that backers of Vietnam have finally exhausted the support of the large number of humanitarian liberals who were seduced for so many years in to backing the policies of this tyrannical regime, undermining American policy, and encouraging the final collapse of the South Vietnamese government.

One of these liberals in France has made a public confession of his tragic error. Jean Lacouture, a journalist who reported on the Viet Nam war for *Le Monde* and other papers and generally sided with the North against the South Vietnamese and the U.S., has recently written a book in which he admits his "shame for having contributed to the installation of one of the most repressive regimes history has ever known." In an interview in Milan's *Il Giornale Nuovo* he says, "my behaviour was sometimes more that of a militant than of a journalist. I dissimulated certain defects of North Viet Nam because I believed that their cause was just enough so that I should not expose their errors . . . . I believed it was not opportune to expose the Stalinist nature of the North Vietnamese regime right at the time that Nixon was bombing Hanoi." He adds that he and other journalists were "intermediaries for a lying and criminal propaganda—ingenuous spokesmen for tyranny in the name of liberty."[33]

So we have gone through another cycle where many liberal humanitarians became so enamored of Communism that they were manipulated into assisting another Communist victory and the conquest of another important segment of the free world. Each particular generation of humanitarians wakes up to its error, recoils, and mends its ways. But meanwhile the unfortunate people of Viet Nam are left to suffer under Communist tyranny while the humanitarians in this country who aided in their downfall continue to enjoy the fruits of American democracy. And meanwhile also the Communists do not suffer from the liberals' recoil. They have their victory in Viet Nam. They have achieved another conquest of another important segment of the free world and can be prepared for the next one, in which another group of well-meaning innocents can be persuaded to help them bring about yet another Communist conquest.

How many Jean Lacoutures still exist in American media today? How many American reporters or TV commentators do not realize that they are being used as "intermediaries for a lying and criminal propaganda"? What is the next target for Communist conquest, or the next campaign to undermine American security or economic progress at home that they are being manipulated into helping?

Though the veil of illusion which obscured the nature of the Vietnamese Communists was being swept away, the propaganda campaign still showed striking success in undermining America's will to resist Soviet agression. The second objective of the campaign, to convince us that the U.S. had made a great mistake to attempt to interfere in another country's internal affairs and be "the policeman of the world", was still having its disastrous influence.

A few months after the Communist victory in Viet Nam, two factions in faraway Angola were fighting a third faction backed by the Communists. When they appealed to the U.S. for help, Henry Kissinger recommended we support them, but Congress refused. Congressional opponents said we should "not get involved in another Viet Nam". The Communists, with massive Cuban and Russian support, soon won. A disgruntled CIA employee, John Stockwell, with the assistance of the Institute for Policy Studies, later published a book, *In Search of Enemies*, which declared that the entire effort in Angola had been an attempt by the CIA to find "another war to fight after its defeat in Viet Nam."

Similarly, after President Carter took office, an anti-Communist faction in Ethiopia appealed to the U.S. for help against the Communists. Our National Security Advisor, Zbigniew Brzezinski, like his predecessor, Henry Kissinger, urged that the U.S. respond. But again Congress (and others in the Executive Branch) overruled him. Ethiopia fell to the Communists after extremely bloody fighting that went almost unnoticed in the U.S., and thus the entire Horn of Africa was dominated by the Communists. American isolationism was succinctly expressed by a scholar who should have known better, Arthur Schlesinger Jr.: "Six months ago, most America's had never heard of the Horn of Africa, and now the government is creating panic that this might affect our interests." (Shades of 1938 in England when Chamberlain's followers asked who had ever heard of the Sudetenland.)

SEQUEL: THE FLIP-FLOP ON CAMBODIA

One of the most convincing signs that an organization is being influenced by foreign propaganda is when it displays a sudden shift in opinion coinciding exactly with a shift in policy of the foreign country. One notorious example was the 180 degree turn by the U.S. Communist Party in 1941 when Nazi Germany invaded Russia. For two years before then, following the signing of the Hitler-Stalin pact, Communists in the U.S. had opposed American aid to Britain and France. Suddenly overnight when Hitler invaded, the Party came out strongly in favor of the war. Several other organizations in the U.S., including labor unions, also made the same astonishing reversal, thus unmasking themselves as Communist-dominated.[1] This type of switch in response to the Communist party line has since been appropriately called "Zig-zag Parallelism." This zig-zag also disillusioned many liberal American pacifists who who had allowed themselves to be drawn into cooperation with the Communists.[2]

Since early 1978 a number of Asian experts, media, and political figures in the U.S. have radically changed their public pronouncements on the Khmer Rouge. Others have not. The reasons for both change and constancy are significant.

In a previous chapter, we summarized the voluminous reports after the Communist victory on the barbarity of the Khmer Rouge regime, which was driving the population out of the cities at gunpoint and massacring all those suspected of links to the former government.

Reliable reports continued to accumulate from diplomats, journalists, and a horde of refugees. Secretary of State Henry Kissinger issued a statement on June 24, 1975, that there was good evidence of a huge death toll among Cambodian civilians. Freedom House in

New York City compared the plight of the Cambodian people to the annihilation of the Jews by the Nazis.

Communist propaganda and the reaction of American media to these Cambodian horrors went through two phases. From 1975 through 1977 the reports were ignored or discounted by many in the media who had been sympathetic to the Khmer Rouge and opposed American assistance to the Cambodian Republican government. Beginning in 1978 however a peculiar shift began to take place.

Phase I: Indifference or Disbelief (April 1975 through 1977)

As the months wore on in 1975, Communist propaganda could no longer ignore the reports of massacres and attempted to refute them. For example, on July 7 Radio Moscow carried the following commentary:

A propaganda campaign against Cambodia has been unleashed in the West. Rumors and allegations are being spread about the so-called tragic fate of its 6 million people . . . . In the U.S. the *Christian Science Monitor,* for instance, plays up all reports coming in from Cambodia in intentionally lurid forms, consciously striving to pit public opinion against the positive steps being taken by the triumphant Cambodian people. And it is not difficult to gauge why this is being done. The victories scored by the patriotic forces of Cambodia, and the total collapse of the puppet of the imperialist circles, Lon Nol, bungled everything for the Pentagon, which was striving to consolidate positions west of Indochina.

The resolute measures of the new revolutionary government were not to the liking of some parties, measures ousting all representatives of the capitalistic west who had cooperated with the puppet regime and all the local reactionaries. The international reactionaries are bitterly angry over these measures being taken by the National Unity Front of Cambodia and the Royal Government of National Unity, which are aimed at totally liquidating the whole political structure of the old administration . . . .

In rural areas the land is being redistributed . . . According to reports, the rice harvest that is being collected this year is a good one.[8]

This viewpoint was echoed by many in the U.S. who had been sympathetic to the Khmer Rouge. Within a week of the Moscow broadcast, the *New York Times* published a William Goodfellow article on the Op-Ed Page taking exactly the same line:

The evacuation of Cambodia's larger cities has been sensationalized in the Western press as a "death march." In fact it was a journey *away* from certain death by starvation, for at the time the former Phnom Penh Government surrendered, starvation was already a reality in the urban centers, and widespread famine only a matter of weeks away . . . . The available evidence suggests that recent reports in the Western media, based on United States intelligence sources, of hundreds of thousands, or even millions, perishing from starvation, are self-serving exaggerations planted to discredit the new Government.

These same sources gave birth to a flurry of sensational "bloodbath" stories, nourished with "eyewitness accounts" that made headlines in the days immediately following the surrender. . . . Now that the war has at last come to an end, there is reason to believe that after initial difficulties are surmounted, the new Government's all-out efforts to increase food production will transform Cambodia into a land self-sufficient in food and within a few years into a rice-exporting nation as it was before it was ravished by war.

Goodfellow is Vice President of the Center for International Policy (CIP), one of the Fund for Peace organizations described in the chapter on the Far Left Lobby. His name appears favorably in the correspondence discovered in the briefcase of Orlando Letelier, the Communist agent-of-influence killed when a bomb exploded under his car in Washington.[4] The CIP has consistently followed a line opposed to a strong American foreign policy and sympathetic to Communist countries. As the evidence of Khmer Rouge atrocities accumulated, it published no emendations of Goodfellow's article, and it has conspicuously failed to publish *any* further studies on Cambodia.[5]

As long as a year later, Goodfellow's piece was being included in an "Indo-China Kit" distributed by the American Friends Service Committee, another example of this organization's un-Quaker-like toleration of brutality and militarism in Communist countries.

There were several other notable efforts to refute the bloodbath reports. Anthony Lewis in his *Times* column on May 12, 1975, said that the stories were overblown and that any violence was probably the result of revenge for America's past misdeed—"our cultural arrogance, an imperial assumption that by superiority or sheer power our way of life must prevail." Sidney Schanberg, who had been the *Times* correspondent in Phnom Penh until a week after the fall, wrote in June from New York that the bloodbath reports were exaggerated and added that American authorities have a stake in such theories.[6]

But the most glaring sins of the media during this period were ones of omission rather than commission. An examination of the record of TV coverage reveals a deafening silence on the subject for months at a time, which is all the more striking when compared to the large amounts of air time devoted earlier to *American* misdeeds like My Lai. From April 1975 through December 1976, according to an analysis by Dr. Ernest Lefever of Georgetown University, the three major networks spent four hours and fifty-five minutes on Cambodia, only seven minutes of which were on the bloodbath. Moreover, some of those seven minutes were devoted to skepticism that it was in fact occurring. During the subsequent eighteen months, the three major networks carried only ten brief references to brutality.[7]

The editorial judgments during this period are surprising. The TV networks felt obliged to carry Secretary of State Kissinger's statement in June about large death tolls. And in January and July 1976, CBS reporter Peter Collins spoke from the Cambodian-Thai border on reports of the massacres. But otherwise, reporting on Cambodia consisted of trivia. For instance, in October there were accounts of Sihanouk's arrival to visit the UN as Cambodian "head of state," but no mentions of the slaughter. And on March 9, 1977, both NBC and Walter Cronkite on CBS reported the sensational news that the U.S. had lifted travel restrictions to Cambodia (plus Cuba, Vietnam, and North Korea)! President Carter was quoted as saying that Americans should be free to go anywhere. But there was no comment on the continuing horrors in Cambodia or the fact that the Pol Pot Government had shown no signs of allowing *any* Americans to travel there—or that any Americans were interested in going.[8]

The print media performed only slightly better. The *Times* editorial page denounced the massacre on July 9, 1975, comparing it to the "Soviet extermination of the kulaks or the Gulag Archipelago." And the *Times* also printed some of Henry Kamm's detailed reports from Thailand. But the rest of the news pages were not as enterprising. Ernest Lefever's study found that in the *Times* and other leading papers there were 63 stories on the bloodbath, only one of which made the front page—in the *Washington Post* of February 2, 1976. Most of these stories, according to Lefever, were hedged with doubts or apologies for the Cambodian Communists.[9]

A study by Accuracy in Media showed that throughout 1976 the *New York Times* and the *Washington Post* combined contained only 13 mentions of human rights violations in Cambodia compared to 124 for Chile and 85 for South Korea. The performance of the major networks was similar: 16 for Cambodia compared to 137 for Chile and 90 for South Korea.[10]

Groups in the Far Left Lobby and other institutions showed the same partiality for the Khmer Rouge. In September 1975, Ieng Sary, then second in command of the Cambodian Government, arrived in New York and spoke at the United Nations, announcing that the cities of Cambodia had been "cleansed." His speech received a standing ovation. Later he was given a reception at the Union Theological Seminary, sponsored by the Indo-China Resource Center, an organization which had been one of the most active groups agitating against American support for the South Vietnamese and the Cambodian Republic. Gareth Porter, then Co-Director of the Center, introduced Sary, who made a speech attacking the U.S. for our conduct during the Mayaguez crisis. Neither Porter nor any one else during the question period raised the matter of the massacres in Cambodia.[11]

Porter has been one of the most energetic members of the Far Left Lobby in opposing American policy in Indo-China and in supporting the new Communist governments there. In 1977 he left the Indo-China Resource Center (which became less active after the Communist victories) and joined the Institute for Policy Studies. On May 3, 1977, he appeared before the House Subcommittee on International Organization hearings on "Human Rights in Cambodia." He argued that the reports from Cambodia were greatly exaggerated, that the number killed was probably in the range of a few thousand rather than a million or more, and that they were understandable as the aftermath of a violent civil war. He also had complimentary things to say about the new government's "food policies," thus echoing the line taken in the Moscow broadcast quoted above and other similar statements from Radio Peking. Also testifying at this hearing was David Chandler, an associate at the Harvard East Asian Research Center who had spent some time in Cambodia in the Foreign Service. Chandler stated that perhaps thousands of people had been killed or "allowed to die" by the new regime but that "to a large extent, American actions are to blame.... we dropped more than 500,000 tons of bombs.... We may have driven thousands of people out of their minds.... We bombed Cambodia without knowing why."

Porter's and Chandler's testimony stimulated some indignant comments from committee members. William Goodling, for instance, a Republican of Pennsylvania, said to Dr. Chandler, "It is just unbelievable to me that you would say that because we bombed Cambodia—that may be the reason they are killing their own people."

And Stephen Solarz, a New York Democrat, engaged in a long and acrimonious exchange with Porter, concluding, "I know there are still people publishing books contesting whether 6 million Jews were killed by Hitler.... I don't know whether 1 million (Cambodians) were killed or 1.2 million or 800,000 ... but in light of everything that has come out already, it would be difficult for any one to sustain the proposition that hundreds of thousands of Cambodians have not been murdered by their own countrymen."

Also at this hearing was John Barron of the *Reader's Digest*. With Anthony Paul, a *Digest* correspondent in Asia, Barron had written a monumental study of the Cambodian holocaust, *Murder of a Gentle Land*, based on interview with hundreds of refugees scholars, and analysts of Southeast Asia and foreign radio broadcasts. Barron and Paul estimated that by December 1976 more than 1.2 million had been killed or died of starvation.[12]

In summary, until the end of 1977 most major media and many influential opinion leaders were reacting to the horrors in Cambodia with indifference or disbelief.

Phase II: Parallel Zig-Zags (1978 and After)

Early in 1978, however, the picture began to change. In retrospect it is now evident that the change began first in Communist propaganda.

Indo-China became the scene of violent confrontations between the Communist countries after 1975. The cooperation that existed among the Soviet, Vietnamese, Cambodian, and Chinese Communists until their victories in April 1975 had fallen apart by 1978. There is not space here to describe the complex changes, most of which are still shrouded in mystery, nor to assign the blame as to who were the aggressors and who were refusing cooperation or attempting to exert "hegemony." But by mid-1978 there was an overt split between the Cambodians backed by the Chinese on one side and the Vietnamese backed by the Soviets on the other.

This was reflected abruptly in the propaganda. As late as January 3, 1978, Radio Moscow was still following a line friendly to the Khmer Rouge, broadcasting a New Year's message of support to the Cambodian people: "In the international arena the Soviet people have constantly supported the struggle of the heroic Cambodian people and have constantly adhered to the stand of friendship between Kampuchea and the Soviet Union."

Within two days, the tone began to change. Radio Moscow started to air stories of "border tensions" between Cambodia and Viet Nam. It quoted the Vietnamese ambassador as saying that Viet Nam was resisting Cambodian aggression. On January 12, the World Peace Council, always a barometer of Soviet foreign policy, declared that it "supports the Vietnamese position." On January 19, Radio Moscow said "the Vietnamese radio asks for peace. The Cambodian radio fans hysteria." On January 26, the Vietnamese radio declared that Viet Nam "refutes the Cambodian charge that Vietnam is attempting to carry out its Federation Plan." By March, Radio Moscow reported the "Cambodian failure to respond to Vietnamese proposals for negotiations," and March 3, 1978, Radio Moscow broadcast a long commentary from *Novoye Vremya* on the "Medieval Barbarities Characterizing Cambodian Actions." From then on all gloves were off and the attacks from Radio Moscow and Hanoi on Cambodia became as fierce as they had ever been against the American "imperialists" in Viet Nam.[13]

This shift was reflected almost immediately in the American media. Although no direct evidence of cause and effect is available, the coincidence is remarkable. With the Cambodian holocaust ongoing for almost three years, there was no more reason for discovering it in 1978 than there had been a year before. After early 1977, additional evidence poured in, with one unimaginable horror piled on top of another, but the evidence differed only in degree rather than in kind from previous clear indications that horrors had taken place. Thus the only new factor as of early 1978 was the Soviet Union's new attitude. When the pro-Soviet elements in the Far Left Lobby switched instantly, this somehow made it respectable for those who look to the far left for clues to join in.

Anthony Lewis's columns in the *Times* for the first time admitted the horrors, although one column quoted William Shawcross in attempting to place much of the blame on American policy. Coverage of human rights violations in Cambodia increased considerably in the *Times,* with 48 mentions in 1978 compared to 34 in 1977. In the *Washington Post* such mentions increased from 10 in 1977 to 29 in 1978. In July 1978, more than a year after they had been published and become best-sellers, the *Post* finally reviewed two major books on the Cambodian holocaust, Barron and Paul's *Murder of a Gentle Land* and Father Francois Ponchard's *Cambodia—Year Zero.*[14]

TV mentions of the massacres also increased considerably, reaching a climax of sorts on June 8 when CBS broadcast a program anchored by Ed Bradley featuring an all-star cast of "experts" on Cambodia, including Gareth Porter, William Shawcross, and Tiziano Terzani. All of these now confirmed that horrendous massacres had in fact occurred, with Porter completely reversing the position he had taken before the House Subcommittee.

The only exception on the program was Daniel Burstein of the Communist Party (Marxist-Leninist), the Chicago-based party that supports China and opposes the Soviet Union. Burstein is editor of the party's weekly newspaper, *The Call,* and had recently returned from a visit to China and Cambodia, where he and two associates were the first Americans admitted since the Khmer Rouge victory. He testified rather lamely under sharp questioning by Ed Bradley that all reports of brutality in Cambodia were exaggerated.

The climactic and most dramatic shift in viewpoint came in August 1978 from Senator George McGovern. At a Senate Foreign Relations Committee hearing, McGovern called on the State Department to recommend an international military force to "knock the Cambodian regime out of power." McGovern had run for president in 1972 on a platform of American withdrawal from Indo-China and cessation of support for the anti-Communist governments there. In 1974, with the Communists winning in Cambodia, he declared that the Cambodians "should be left to settle their own affairs." Now he said military intervention was justified because of evidence that more than 2.5 million out of Cambodia's population of more than 6 million had died from starvation, disease, or execution since the Communist victory. His statement evoked bitter comments from the *Wall Street Journal* and others who had supported American resistance to the Communists in Indo-China. Why, they asked, had McGovern not foreseen the dangers of a Communist victory before it was too late?[15]

Thus from mid-1978 onwards, almost immediately after the USSR began opposing the Khmer Rouge, the only people defending the Cambodian regime were those with obvious ties to Peking. Burstein and the CP(ML) were the most extreme examples. Then in December 1978 occurred the strange visit of three Western journalists to Cambodia, the first and only reporters to be admitted by the Pol Pot regime after Burstein's group.

These included Elizabeth Becker of the *Washington Post*, Richard Dudman of the *St. Louis Post Dispatch*, and Malcolm Caldwell, a British instructor from London University. All had shown earlier evidence of partiality towards the Chinese and Cambodian Communists. Elizabeth Becker had been a *Post* correspondent in Phnom Penh in 1973 and 1974, when she wrote articles generally critical of the Cambodian Republic's government and sympathetic to the Khmer Rouge. Back in Washington as a *Post* writer, she showed the same sympathy for the Khmer Rouge even after the evidence of their brutality became overwhelming during 1977. In January 1978, Miss Becker attended an American Security Council press conference at which a Cambodian refugee, Pin Yathay, presented one of the most authenticated eye-witness accounts of the massacres. Pin, a civil engineer, escaped after surviving 26 months in Cambodia and witnessing the death of all his family. He told "many macabre incidents. . . . The starving people ate the flesh of dead bodies during this acute famine. Now I will tell you a story that I lived myself . . . a teacher who ate the flesh of her own dead sister. She was later caught and beaten to death, in front of the whole village, as an example, and her child was crying beside her." Halfway through this press conference, Elizabeth Becker walked out. She was helped into her coat by an employee of the American Security Council, who heard her exclaim, "I have heard enough of this junk."[16] The *Post* failed to carry a story of this press conference.

Richard Dudman had also shown strong partiality for the Cambodian and Chinese Communists. In 1970 while covering the war in Cambodia, he and some other correspondents were captured by the Khmer Rouge. Dudman was released after six weeks, and there is evidence that he was freed because of the intervention of anti-war activists in the U.S., who considered him an ally. He later wrote a book about his experiences in captivity, tending to favor the Khmer Rouge and saying nothing about their brutality, which was becoming evident even in 1974.[17]

131

Malcolm Caldwell of London University was a member of the British Labor Party but was known to be active in London's Maoist Communist circles. In 1977 he was implicated in the public TV confessions of a Communist agent-of-influence in Singapore, G. Raman. (See Chapter V.) Raman had met Caldwell while studying in London in the 1960s. Caldwell persuaded him to recruit agents in Singapore to spread propaganda and to gather information unfavorable to the Singapore government, information Caldwell used to try to discredit Singapore in European media and the Socialist International. Caldwell had also lectured and written articles defending the Pol Pot regime.

These three arrived in Phnom Penh by way of Peking in December, 1978. A Cambodia radio broadcast quoted Caldwell as saying, "I have been trying for years to create more sympathy for your country in Britain. And I know that I shall be able to carry on this work much more successfully as the result of having the opportunity to visit your country."[18] The three stayed for two weeks and were given guided tours around the country, finishing with an interview with Pol Pot himself. On the early morning before they were to leave, three gunmen broke into their guest house. Caldwell was killed. Dudman narrowly escaped when a gunman missed him from only 20 feet. Elizabeth Becker escaped by hiding in her bath tub. The assassins were believed to be members of the pro-Vietnamese underground in Cambodia. Their motives were either to discredit the Pol Pot government by showing that they could not protect their own guests, or to take revenge on pro-Pol Pot journalists.[19]

Becker and Dudman returned to the U.S. via Peking and wrote a series of articles frankly describing Cambodia's desolation: Phnom Penh was like "Pompeii without the ashes," said Dudman and there were signs of hunger, and a cowed and dispirited population. They also admitted that they had been given a Potemkin tour and were not free to interview whom they pleased. Yet they somehow managed to conclude with favorable impressions. Dudman argued that "The physical conditions may well have improved for many peasants and former urban workers. ... The new leaders are not fanatical madmen ... the crash evacuation of Phnom Pehn may well have been essential to resume food production. Cambodia is in the midst of one of the world's great housing programs." Becker concluded that the production figures given them could not be too misleading and that "the system was working."[20] The system was working indeed, if its purpose was to destroy a people and a culture.

Both these journalists reported that the Vietnamese forces in the area had been repulsed the year before and were now weaker than before. But within a week, they were proved wrong. The Vietnamese launched their long-planned final invasion and drove through to Phnom Penh by January 7. The Pol Pot government was forced to flee to the jungles.

The Vietnamese set up their puppet regime under Heng Samrin. In the first few weeks it appeared that any government, even one sponsored by the hated Vietnamese, would be preferable to the murderous Pol Pot regime. But as the months wore on and the guerilla fighting with the Pol Pot remnants continued, the Vietnamese and their puppets refused to allow imports of foods to the contested areas. So another cycle of starvation and bloodshed started for the unfortunate gentle people of Cambodia.

In summary, the reactions of American media and opinion leaders since the fall of Cambodia to the Khmer Rouge in April 1975 provided several clear cases of "Zig-Zag Parallelism." Columnist Anthony Lewis, research analysts William Goodfellow and Gareth Porter, and Senator George McGovern defended the Pol Pot regime long after the time when the evidence of their brutality was overwhelming. Then when the Soviets and Vietnamese switched from support of to opposition to Pol Pot, most such people also made the same abrupt change. A similar change took place in the coverage of most of the major media.

The *New York Times* editorial page denounced the horrors soon after they became evident, and Henry Kamm reported them in detail from Southeast Asia, but the rest of the *Times* new columns and Op Ed page showed the same swing from indifference or disbelief to strong denunciation. The *Washington Post* and the major TV networks also made a similar abrupt shift in early 1978.

Why was it only after the Soviet propaganda machine suddenly "discovered" Khmer Rough brutality in 1978 that many U.S. media and opinion leaders allowed themselves to do the same? And why was it that only the pro-Peking members of the Far Left Lobby desperately clung to their defenses of Pol Pot and his cohorts? The zigs and zags of U.S. media and "intellectuals" and their correspondence with the twists and turns of Soviet and Chinese propaganda are indeed enlightening. We like to boast of our freedom of the press, but our press may be far less free than we think.

133

THE CAMPAIGN AGAINST
THE AGENCY FOR
INTERNATIONAL DEVELOPMENT

Campaigns against the Agency for International Development (AID) and other American agencies operating abroad have been an important element in the Communists' strategy since World War II. The CIA was a natural target, as described in a later chapter. The Kremlin had more problems attacking AID because its work in fields like medicine, education, and land reform is self-evidently humanitarian, but as AID's effectiveness grew, the Communist campaign against it grew in size and bitterness.

AID grew out of the Point Four Program, organized under President Truman in 1949. This program was named from Truman's inaugural address that year, the fourth point of which called for a "bold new program for making the benefits of our scientific advances and industrial progress available for the improvement and growth of underdeveloped areas." The Agency for International Development was set up in 1961 to take over this and all other foreign assistance programs. With a budget of more than $2 billion in the peak years, AID administered a large number of projects in medicine, education, land reform, agriculture, and labor relations in underdeveloped countries. It recruited some outstanding experts in these fields, many of whom spent years overseas in hazardous or harsh conditions, assisting new nations to develop their infrastructure and accelerate their progress. In agriculture, for example, AID was a prime mover in bringing about "the Green Revolution," which made a major change in agricultural methods in the Philippines, India, Indo-China, and Latin America, with the introduction of new strains of wheat and corn, new uses of fertilizers and insecticides, and new breeds of cattle, hogs, and poultry.

AID also cooperated with private groups, missionary organizations, educational foundations, American universities, the American Medical Association, and others, in developing the educational systems and medical resources in underdeveloped countries.

The Communists began sniping at these activities almost immediately. Soviet publications and Radio Moscow broadcasts to the undeveloped countries attacked the Point Four Program as an American device for penetrating "colonial" countries and seizing control of them after the other "imperialist" powers had pulled out. When John Foster Dulles made a tour of the Far East in 1953, Soviet propaganda claimed that one of his purposes was "to lay plans to liquidate British imperial economic interests." And the Soviets portrayed an American-supported village community development program in India in 1952 as an effort to enslave the Indian people.[1]

A similar campaign continued against AID after its formation in 1961. Attacks broadcast by Radio Moscow and Soviet publications were echoed by slanders in local media. Examples include the following:

—In India in 1963 a shipment of wheat financed by AID was found to contain some rat poison, and several children in an orphanage became ill. A Communist-inspired newspaper story accused AID of trying to poison children.

—In Africa, AID's efforts to encourage birth control were portrayed by the Communists as an American attempt to limit black population growth and thus keep the white population in power.[2]

—The Communists discovered that an aviator assigned to the AID mission in India in 1965 had piloted the plane that dropped the atom bomb on Hiroshima 20 years before. They seized on this as another club to attack AID, promoting the angle that the Americans would bomb only Orientals, not whites. The pro-Communist weekly newspaper, *Blitz*, covered its front page with a headline, "Hiroshima Killer— Go Back."

The campaign became more ferocious after 1966 as the Viet Nam War heated up and AID became more active in Indo-China in humanitarian fields. In American media one of the major campaigns was directed against AID's Public Safety program. Since early in the Eisenhower Administration, American technical assistance programs had included projects to advise the underdeveloped countries in Public Safety methods. President John Kennedy expanded this program, founding the International Police Academy in Washington in 1962 and saying that the police constitute "the first line of defense against subversion in troubled Third World countries." This Academy posted public safety advisers in 40 countries in Africa, Asia, and Latin America and provided more than 10,000 foreign policemen with specialized training at the Academy over the next ten years. The police training program was a highly attractive target for Communist propaganda, which began accusing AID of training people in such techniques as making deadly booby traps and torturing civilians. As we shall see is characteristic of modern Communist propaganda campaigns, the propaganda soon began to originate in American media as well as in the Soviet organs themselves.

On October 8, 1973, Jack Anderson's column alleged that "Bomb and booby-trap experts from the CIA have been quietly training foreign police to make explosive devices at an isolated Federal School in Texas. . . . The cloak and dagger professors are on loan from the CIA to the AID. The existence of the school was first depicted in the movie *State of Siege*, in which foreign police were shown being trained to use bombs and booby traps against political opponents. . . . Most of the 165 policemen trained at the school came from the military-backed regimes such as those in Brazil, Guatemala, Thailand, Uruguay, Panama, and El Salvador. Only a thin blue line of cops is trained for the democracies."

Anderson fails to make clear that the course was designed to teach the police how to *combat* bombings and booby traps, not to create them. And he tries to give a distorted impression that only policemen from "military-backed regimes" were being trained. Actually, most requests for the course came from underdeveloped countries. The well-developed democracies of the world, such as Canada, Western Europe, and Japan, obviously have their own means of police training. Thus most trainees came from underdeveloped countries, and, unfortunately, a majority of underdeveloped countries in the world today have "military-backed regimes" (often to combat Communist subversion).

One of the most obvious themes was to accuse the Public Safety program of encouraging and training in torture techniques. Although there was no truth in such accusations, this angle of attack had considerable effect on American media.

On August 3, 1974, Anderson's column reported that "students

137

at the International Police Academy, a school run by the State Department to train foreign policemen, have developed some chilling views about torture tactics." He then proceeded to quote from essays by six students, which appeared to condone the use of torture. Accuracy in Media investigated this charge and found that Anderson's researcher had taken these quotations completely out of context and that the six essays in fact opposed the use of torture. AIM complained to the National News Council, an organization founded to monitor the media, headed by Stanley H. Fuld, a former chief judge to the State of New York, and funded by several liberal foundations. The Council upheld AIM's complaint, stating that Anderson's column was "biased and inaccurate."[3]

Jack Anderson's false charges in these columns are but one graphic example of a phenomenon which preceded his articles and has endured since, the effect being to paint AID's Public Safety Program as something ghastly. At times, charges that AID was training foreign torturers had direct repercussions.

On August 10, 1970, the body of an American was found in the back seat of a stolen car on a street in Montevideo, Uruguay. Blood was dripping through the floor boards. The man had been shot twice in the head and twice in the body. His eyes were bandaged, and his arms were pitted by 16 needle punctures. His left arm-pit had deep bruises, close to a gun-shot wound. This was the body of Dan A. Mitrione, employed by AID to teach police techniques to the Uruguayan government and kidnapped eleven days earlier by the Tupamaros, a large terrorist organization in Uruguay. Mitrione had been tortured and then tried by a Tupamaros "People's Court," accused of being a CIA or FBI agent teaching the Uruguayan police methods of torture and repression, and then executed.

Three years later, his story became the theme of an even more sophisticated Communist propaganda effort, the movie *State of Siege*. This film was co-authored by the noted director, Constantin Gavras (Costa-Gavras, the "Alfred Hitchcock of the Left"), and an Italian, Franco Solinas. The fact that Solinas is a member of the Italian Communist Party was never mentioned in the many favorable reviews the film received. Costa-Gavras and Solinas also co-authored a 214-page book containing the screen play of *State of Siege* and 80 pages of "documentation." *State of Siege* portrays the Uruguyan government as tyrannical and the Tupamaros as clean-cut humanitarian idealists. Both are gross distortions. Uruguay in

1970 was one of the most liberal democracies in the world. Politics were completely free, with several parties competing for power. The Communists had 37,000 open members, several representatives in Parliament, and their own newspaper. There was also a cradle-to-grave welfare program. The political freedom had encouraged a strong Communist effort to infiltrate the labor unions, and there was a large degree of labor unrest, but until 1970 there was no political repression and there were no political prisoners.[4]

The Tupamaros, on the other hand, had an organization of more than 1,000 members, a mix of idealists, hard-nosed terrorists, and common criminals similar to the membership of the Weathermen in the U.S. or the Baader-Meinhoff gang in West Germany. They were highly organized with secret houses and their own hidden hospital so well equipped that it was able to administer x-rays. Founded in the early 1960s, the group committed its first murder by 1966 and by 1970 had already killed nine people. Mitrione was their tenth victim. By the time they were crushed, the Tupamaros had caused thousands of deaths.

The movie implies that Uruguay was already under martial law and in a "state of siege" in 1970, but this was not the case. Not until three years later, one day after the Tupamaros had murdered five government officials, did the Parliament declare martial law. By that time the Tupamaros had killed 45 people.[5]

The principal message of *State of Siege* was that the United States had cooperated with the Uruguayan authorities in this tyrannical regime, with Mitrione assisting them as a CIA agent under AID cover, teaching the police refined methods of torture. This became a principal theme in the Communist propaganda campaign against AID: that it was training the police forces of repressive regimes in Third World countries in torture techniques.

The movie was filmed in Chile during the pro-Communist Allende regime. Offered to the Chilean government, it was turned down as being too obviously a Communist propaganda documentary. Nevertheless, it was shown in many art cinemas in the U.S. and got several favorable reviews. In the *New York Times*, Vincent Canby wrote,

> The film is an examination of an event and national policies that led to that event—including the U.S. historical role as Big Daddy in Latin America through economic programs that help others help themselves *as well as helping our industry*.... Finally it's an examination of our capacity to be shocked....

When we read about ITT in Chile or the Bay of Pigs, we are as much inclined to laughter as to grief or even surprise. . . . Self interest carried to such limits is no longer evil . . . but a kind of dumbfounding rascality, a form of scalawaggary. What makes *State of Siege* so shocking is not that it is true, but that it could be true. . . . No attempt is made in the film to define the inflation in Uruguay that first prompted the press censorship that in turn prompted the revolutionary opposition.

In short, Canby bought the Communist line completely: that the bloody Tupamaros were simply the result of inflation and "press censorship" in Uruguay. (Actually there was *no* censorship whatever until seven years after the Tupamaros' first murder and three years after Mitrione's death.[6])

Despite the willingness of Canby and others to believe accusations against AID, there is no truth in them. Dr. Ernest W. Lefever, who was at the Brookings Institution in Washington in the 1960s, conducted a survey of AID's Public Safety training program, during which he made field trips to 15 countries and found no evidence of the torture charge. Brookings is a liberal think-tank, and Dr. Lefever's doctorate is in Christian Ethics from the Yale Divinity School. Dr. Lefever, incidentally, later became Director of the Ethics and Public Policy Center at Georgetown University.

Nevertheless, *State of Siege* was selected by the American Film Institute for the Grand Opening of the Kennedy Center Movie Theatre in Washington, but at the last moment it was rejected by George Stevens, Jr., director of the Institute. He said that because it rationalized political assassinations, it was inappropriate for the dedication ceremony of a memorial to an assassinated president. This rejection was attacked by some in the press as "censorship." But in the resulting controversy the members of the Institute who had picked the film said they had done so "sight unseen."

In spite of such proofs of distortions, the Communist campaign against the Public Safety Program was successful, for Senator James Abourezk, one of the leaders in the congressional campaign against American intelligence agencies, introduced a bill to eliminate the entire program. In 1974 this passed both houses, bringing the program to an end.

In the late 1960s and 70s there were several other attacks on AID in American media. The Agency's program for assisting the development of free labor unions in emerging countries was the target of fierce Communist propaganda, since it collided directly with the Communists' efforts to develop their own puppet unions.

An example of media attacks on the AID labor union program is a Richard Dudman article in the May 3, 1969, *New Republic*. Dudman of the St. Louis *Post-Dispatch* appeared in our earlier chapter on Cambodia as an apologist for the hideous Pol Pot regime. In the *New Republic* piece, "AFL-CIO as Paid Propagandists," he criticizes the fact that since 1967 when CIA support for foreign labor unions was revealed, the support activity was transferred to AID, which is cooperating in this effort with the AFL-CIO. "To George Meany," he says sarcastically, "there are bad trade unions (Communist) and good trade unions (non-Communist) and never the twain shall meet." It is a good question why Dudman, who has had considerable experience in reporting foreign news, is not aware that Communist labor unions are in fact dummy organizations designed mainly to promote the revolution in non-Communist countries or reflect the policies of the government in Communist countries. They should certainly be considered "bad" by any sincere union official.

Other notable media attacks on AID include the following:

—An article entitled "CIAid" in *New Republic* for April 1, 1972, accuses AID of allowing funds for medical assistance to Laos to be diverted to a "secret Laotian army." A letter from AID in a later issue, however, explains that support for the Laotian army had been announced by the U.S. a year earlier, that support was not secret, and that medical funds were not diverted.

—*Far Eastern Economic Review* (April 25, 1975) interview with the general Secretary of the National Christian Council of Churches in Japan says he was told by directors of two U.S. church agencies operating in Cambodia (World Vision and Catholic Relief Services) that they were receiving large sums from AID in return for doing intelligence work. A letter from World Vision director in a later issue denies the report.

—One of the most bitter attacks, which seems to be the least justified in light of later events, is the article by Gloria Emerson on the Op-Ed Page of the *New York Times* of April 7, 1975, just two days after the tragic fall of the South Vietnamese government to the Communists. This was headed by a full page spread of Richard Avedon photographs taken in Saigon in 1971 of Ambassador Bunker; John Mossler, AID director in Viet Nam; George Jacobson, head of the Civil Operations and Rural Development program (a joint AID-military operation); and eight other top U.S. officials.

The picture has the appearance of a police line-up. Entitled "This Symbol of Immense American Power in Viet Nam," the article begins, "I have been thinking about these men in the last few weeks, remembering some of their faces and their voices, when it would be nicer to forget. I wonder if their dreams are dark and ugly things, if any of them trembled and turned away from the television films of Vietnamese refugees weeping, pleading, talking to themselves. . . ."

When we think of the results of the Communist conquest of Viet Nam, the hundreds of thousands now in the Vietnamese Gulag, including even many former Viet Cong, and the additional hundreds of thousands who have tried to flee, many drowning at sea, we could ask whether Miss Emerson's own dreams may be troubled now.

This article was quoted and the police line-up picture reproduced in the subsequent issue of *Time* magazine for April 21, 1975, adding another lash to American guilt feelings about our attempts to support anti-Communist governments abroad through AID and military assistance.[7]

But the Communist campaign's most telling effect on U.S. media was to cause them to comit errors of *omission* even more than of *commission*. It influenced them in later years to virtually ignore the good works of AID. In earlier years there had been frequent human interest stories on AID workers in medicine, education, agriculture, etc. in *Life*, the *Reader's Digest, Parade,* the *New York Times Magazine,* and others, and occasional treatment on television. After 1968 this disappeared. The Communist propaganda had its effect in painting AID as allied with the CIA or the "Military Industrial Complex" in continuing to promote agression in Viet Nam and imperialism elsewhere.

Following is a tabulation of citations on AID in the "Reader's Guide to Periodical Literature" from 1963 through 1976 classified roughly as "Favorable" and "Unfavorable".

	FAVORABLE	UNFAVORABLE
1963	4	0
1964	4	3*
1965	4	1*
1966	10	0
1967	4	0
1968	4	0

1969	1	1
1970	0	1
1971	1	0
1972	0	1*
1973	1	2
1974	1	0
1975	0	0
1976	0	0

*All in the *New Republic.*

It is apparent that after 1968 all favorable coverage dried up.

In 1973 I had personal experience with the blackout of good news on AID. An outline for an article on the work of U.S. missionaries and AID advisors in medicine and education in Viet Nam sent to the editors of almost all the general, women's, and religious magazines, elicited no interest whatever in seeing the complete article, although many of these journals were running critical articles on Viet Nam (on the orphans, or on Saigon's bar girls, corruption, etc.) One religious magazine's editor showed overt hostility to AID. "I have great respect for the work of U.S. missionaries in Viet Nam," he wrote, "but I would not allow them to be used as an excuse for praising the more doubtful activities of AID."

The *New York Times* index shows that there were *no* articles in the *Times* reporting favorably on AID activities from 1969 through 1976. And though there was no mention of AID accomplishments in Viet Nam, on January 15, 1973, the *Times* ran a full column story *with a picture* on a single AID official, who had resigned and come home because of disagreement with AID policies in that country. Instead of the hundreds of AID advisors who had given years of sacrificial service in Viet Nam, the *Times* picked one individual who had resigned and had something negative to say.

Another disgruntled AID employee receiving maximum attention in the *Times* was Edward L. Block, who had been a Refugee and Rehabilitation Officer in Viet Nam in 1972 and 1973 before resigning to return to the U.S. and write several articles in radical publications criticizing American policy. One of his major purposes seemed to be to try to explain the massive flow of refugees from Communist-conquered areas in Viet Nam, which was becoming a major propaganda embarrassment to the Communists. He wrote one article in the August-September 1974 issue of *Pacific Imperialism Notebook,* a far left magazine published by the Pacific Rim Project in San Francisco dedicated to supplying "facts and analysis on

U.S., Japanese, and European *imperialism* in the Asia-Pacific region." (Emphasis added.) He wrote another entitled "Vietnam: Why the Refugees?" in a flyer distributed by the American Friends Service Committee. Both argued that the refugees were not fleeing the Communists but instead the dangers of American bombing, lack of food, etc. This argument collapsed in the closing months of the war and after the fall of Saigon, when, without American bombings, the flow of desperate refugees became a flood.

On November 8, 1974, the *Times* ran a three-column article by Block on the Op-Ed page entitled "Dr. Dan, Successor to Thieu?" and headed by a three-column photograph of Dr. Dan so cropped and close up as to make him look highly sinister. Dr. Dan was a prominent Vietnamese physician who had given up his practice to work for the government and was considered to be one of the most honest and able of all the South Vietnamese by AID advisors and other Americans. During the closing years of the war he was in charge of the huge refugee program, working closely with AID. Block's article portrays him as a bungler, a clever politician, and a heartless manipulator of helpless refugees, who had hoodwinked AID. The purpose of this gratuitous attack on a man few *Times* readers had ever heard of and would have little interest in is obscure. But the effect was to further denigrate AID.

So, in summary, the result of the Communist propaganda campaign against AID, ably echoed by far leftists and re-echoed by American media was to discredit a thoroughly decent part of the U.S. government.

This in turn helped to reduce public support for such activities abroad and to blind the public to the good work done by AID in Cambodia, Viet Nam, and other underdeveloped countries worldwide. This then led to further doubts in the minds of the American people about the aims and activities of our government and our leaders. The campaign and its success is a classic case of the Communist technique of attempting to create shock and revulsion in the public, the Communists succeeding in creating an image of AID as an organization that was encouraging torture, bombings, and other nefarious activities. In fact, however, AID was devoted to the most humanitarian activities in medicine, education, labor relations, and land reform, and reflected some of the highest ideals of the American people both in its policies and in the character and devotion of its employees.

THE CAMPAIGN AGAINST VIETNAMESE LABOR UNIONS

The Communist campaign against Vietnamese labor unions provides one of the clearest case histories of the success of propaganda in causing bias in American media. It is also a good example in microcosm of the Communists' world-wide offensive against free labor unions, partly by infiltration and subversion of free unions, partly by promotion of dummy Communist unions, and partly by an all-encompassing propaganda effort.

The History of Free Labor in Viet Nam

Labor unions were active in Viet Nam for decades, well before U.S. involvement began. They had their origins among the large numbers of laborers and tenant farmers who grew into a class during French rule from 1862 to 1941. With oppressive conditions in mines and factories and among tenant farmers, a rebellion occurred against the French in 1940 with the slogan, "Land to the Tillers, Freedom for the Workers, and Independence for Viet Nam." One of the leaders of this revolt was Tran Quoc Buu, a schoolteacher who later became the father of the labor union movement in Viet Nam.

Imprisoned by the French on Con Son Island in 1940, Buu was later released by the Japanese and joined the anti-French underground, the Viet Minh, after the war. Disillusioned with the Viet Minh when it became Communist dominated and increasingly brutal, he left the underground and decided to devote his efforts to labor union development as the best means to help the Vietnamese people.

Under French rule union membership was forbidden for Vietnamese nationals although permitted for Frenchmen. Buu started a

Vietnamese labor confederation in 1949 with the cooperation of French labor organizers. In 1950 Vietnamese membership was legalized by the Bao Dai government. Later in 1950 the federation, called the CVT (Confederation Vietnamienne du Travail), joined the International Labor Organization, and by 1954 it had 100,000 members.

After division of the country in 1954 when the Ho Chi Minh Government took over the North, about half of all CVT members were in the North. The Communists persecuted labor leaders in the North, executing or jailing some and forcing others to flee. Two major leaders were assassinated. The free union movement was wiped out. Only dummy Communist unions remain to this day

In South Viet Nam, the Diem government followed a policy friendly to labor for a while. Union membership grew to about 500,000. The largest union within the Confederation was the Tenant Farmers Federation with 330,000 members. In his last years, Diem began to repress the unions, but conditions improved after his overthrow and during the subsequent administration of Thieu.[1]

The Thieu government carried out a major land reform program in 1970, stimulated partly by the Tenant Farmers Federation, which practically wiped out the serious farm tenancy problem in South Viet Nam.[2]

ILO data on work stoppage and man hours lost from 1967 to 1972 shows that Vietnamese unions were more active than any others in Asia, a clear indication that these were not dummy unions.[3]

Meanwhile, the Communists began waging a major propaganda campaign against the CVT after 1965, as the war heated up. By 1970 Buu was being attacked more by Radio Hanoi than any other individual in South Viet Nam except Thieu. The Communists naturally regarded free unions as a major threat to their attempts to undermine the society of the country by portraying the Thieu government as a tyranny. Buu was accused of being nothing but a CIA agent, plotting to impose restrictions on labor for the benefit of American imperialists and their lackeys.

The CVT was getting well publicized assistance from AID in training and techniques, and it would not be surprising if AID in turn fed information to the CIA, but it would be ludicrous to say that Buu was "nothing but" a CIA agent. No CIA or AID backing could produce a trade union confederation of 500,000 members. Furthermore, the CVT had hit a membership figure of at least 100,000 by 1954, well before the U.S. had much direct interest in South Viet Nam, and certainly before the CIA or AID knew much about Vietnamese unions.

The Communists also carried out an assassination campaign against the CVT. More than 100 free union organizers were assassinated from 1960 to 1974, and three attempts were made on Buu's life. This was disguised and denied by the Communists before the fall of Saigon, but it has now been reported by no less than a Communist source. Tiziano Terzani, a pro-Communist correspondent of the German magazine, *Der Spiegel,* was one of the two or three western journalists allowed to stay in Saigon for any length of time after the fall. His book on the subject, *Giai Phong (Liberation)* echoes all of the Communist propaganda lines. But he reveals that the attempts on Buu's life were the work of a Viet Cong assassination team. In fact, he interviewed the leader of the team, who spoke frankly of two unsuccessful attempts. This assassin adds that the Viet Cong tried to make it appear that the attempts on Buu's life were the work of the South Vietnamese military, and one member of the assassination team was thrown out of the Communist Party for confessing publicly on TV that it was the work of the Communists.

Some American scholars fell for this propaganda that such killings were simply infighting among South Vietnamese political and military groups.[5]

Terzani also calls Buu a "CIA agent" and says that the CVT was financed by "various organs of the 'International Right.'" One wonders if Terzani really believes the AFL-CIO is part of the International Right. Terzani's book, incidentally, received a favorable review by the *New York Times.*

Effects on U.S. Media

There were a few mentions of Buu and the CVT as CIA agents in the radical press, including the Hayden-Fonda *Focal Point* magazine and *Ramparts. The New Republic* article by Richard Dudman of the *St. Louis Post Dispatch,* cited previously in the AID chapter and entitled "AFL/CIO as Paid Propagandists," refers to "Agent Meany" and criticizes the activities of the CVT in Viet Nam. Then there was the famous Marchetti-Marks book, *The CIA and the Cult of Intelligence,* in which several paragraphs were deleted at the insistence of the CIA. One deletion immediately follows Buu's name, and would seem to imply that Marchetti is claiming that Buu was an "agent." (Among other mistakes, Marchetti gives Buu the wrong middle name.)

But the major effect on American media of the Communist campaign, as in the case with AID, was to cause errors of omission rather than commission, resulting in the labor union movement in Viet Nam being virtually ignored.

A check of *The Reader's Guide to Periodical Literature* shows that the 124 publications indexed there contained not a single article on the CVT or Buu throughout the entire history of U.S. involvement in Viet Nam, from 1955 to 1975. Even passing mentions of this subject were infrequent. For example, *The New Yorker's* sober correspondent, Robert Shaplen, once referred to "my friend, the labor leader, Tran Quoc Buu," without further elaboration. But throughout all his lengthy articles on Vietnamese politics there is no other mention of Buu or the CVT. And there was no reference whatsoever in *Time* or *Newsweek*.

A check through its index for this twenty year period indicates the same is true of the *New York Times*. Two one-inch stories appeared during the twenty years, one when Buu barely escaped assassination and the second when he attacked U.S. mistakes in Viet Nam. Then in 1974 the *Times* finally devoted one full column to Buu when he openly denounced Thieu for the first time. The *Times* apparently only found Vietnamese labor unions newsworthy when they could be used for negative coverage of the South Viet Nam government.

There was good coverage in the labor press—AFL/CIO publications, *The Machinist*, etc., and Victor Riesel's columns—but nothing in general media. Considerable treatment of Buu and the CVT does appear, however, in *The Politics of Massacre*, by Professor Charles A. Joiner of Temple University (Philadelphia, 1974), the most complete study of South Vietnamese politics.

The general media's neglect of labor unions in Viet Nam would be comparable to their covering American politics and business over the past 20 years without mentioning the AFL/CIO or George Meany. In fact, they were missing a rather dramatic and moving story, as outlined only briefly above, of the struggles of Buu and his associates to build up a free labor union movement in spite of French Imperialism, Communist subversion, and a major war within their own country.

Finally in 1975 came the fall of Saigon. Then three days later the *Times* ran a front page story on a parade of "2,000 members" of the Communist labor union organization in Saigon. Of all the evidences of the effects of Communist propaganda on the *Times*, certainly this is one of the clearest. Any journalist with an elementary knowledge of world labor union affairs knows that unions in Communist countries are simply another instrument of Government control of the population. Any union which tries to assert its independence is quickly snuffed out or emasculated—something which is currently threatened in Poland at the time this book is going to press. Communism, which claims to be the voice of the workers, simply cannot afford to allow a real and independent workers' voice. For the *Times* editors to ignore free unions in Viet Nam for twenty years and then to front-page the first demonstration by a Communist "union" is a startling example of bias.[6]

The World-Wide Campaign

The campaign against Vietnamese labor unions and its success among American media, is a clear example of the continuing worldwide Communist effort to destroy free labor unions by propaganda, or by penetration, or physical force, and to substitute their own dummy unions. Again, Poland is the most recent example, but this has been conscious Communist practice since the days of Lenin.

From the early 1900s Lenin and his associates had only scorn for the "Trade Union Mentality," which strives only for better wages, hours, and working conditions and cares nothing about overthrowing Capitalism itself.[7]

When the Comintern was founded in 1921, the 21 conditions which Communist parties had to accept in order to join included not one word about improving the lot of the working class. Instead, there are instructions to (1) infiltrate and attempt to capture existing trade unions, and (2) propagandize for a break of national trade unions from the existing International of Trade Unions in favor of a projected new International of Unions (an organization which would, of course, be Communist dominated).[8]

After World War II there was considerable hope in the West that the Soviets had given up ideas of world domination and stood for the rights of the workers. The World Federation of Trade Unions (WFTU) was founded in 1945. Disillusionment set in very soon, however, and in 1949, non-Communist trade unions withdrew and founded the International Confederation of Free Trade Unions

149

(ICFTU). The WFTU has since devoted a major effort to attacking the ICFTU. The greatest part of the WFTU consists of trade unions from the Communist countries, although some unions that are partially influenced by Communists in the democracies still belong, notably the French CGT and the Italian CGIL.[9]

In the United States the organization with the closest ties to the WFTU is Trade Unionists for Actions and Democracy, which regularly hosts visits by "trade union" officials from the Soviet Union.

Soviet efforts to promote subversion through trade unions have grown greatly since World War II. There is a special department in the KGB on labor affairs as well as a counterpart in the Propaganda Ministry. And there are KGB labor specialists in Soviet embassies in most major countries. In Washington, Ruben Grigorian holds this post, with the title of First Secretary of the Embassy, but in fact he reports to the KGB Labor Department.[10]

Red unions have been prominent in most Communist attempts to seize power, as in Chile under Allende, where the Communist unions were financed from Moscow much more liberally than the free trade unions were supported by the U.S. In the struggle for Portugal in 1975 and '76, the Communists almost succeeded in taking over the only large labor federation in the country, thanks to millions of dollars poured into the country by the KGB.

The Soviets made an energetic effort to restore the relations between the WFTU and labor unions in democratic countries by a vigorous propaganda campaign on the need for labor solidarity. The head of the Russian trade union organization spearheading this drive (the All Union Central Council of Trade Unions) was Alexander Shelepin. But he was notable for never having had labor union experience. His previous post had been director of the KGB! For a time he had some success in improving relations with Western union officials, but his past caught up with him during a visit to London in 1975. Newspapers published the facts that his KGB duties had led to involvement in a murder in Germany. Hostile demonstrations by British anti-Communist unionists forced him to enter the Trade Union Congress building for his meeting by a back door and return early to Moscow. There he was soon removed from his "trade union" post.[11]

In the 1960s and '70s the Agency for International Development in cooperation with the AFL-CIO carried out a program of education and assistance for new or weak unions in other countries. This was done through three institutes: the African-American Labor Center (AALC), based in New York City; the Asian-American Free Labor Institute (AAFLI); and the American Institute for Free Labor Development (AIFLD) in Washington. Through these institutes, AID provided much valuable support to unions in Viet Nam, Indonesia, Thailand, the Philippines; Zaire and elsewhere in Africa; and Chile, Brazil, Mexico, and Uruguay in Latin America.[12]

These American efforts stimulated vigorous counter-measures by the Soviet propaganda apparatus. Within the United States efforts began that were the first seeds of the later massive assault on the CIA, as described in Chapter XII. In 1966 Victor Reuther of the United Auto Workers, a bitter rival of George Meany and the AFL/CIO, charged that the CIA was operating through the AFL-CIO labor institutes. Senators Eugene McCarthy and J. William Fulbright picked up this charge and attempted to get a senate committee to investigate the CIA. Though their attempt failed in 1966, some of the dirt stuck, and this became a favorite theme of Communist propaganda. Any anti-Communist union in another part of the world from then on could be accused of being a "CIA tool" and an "agent of the American monopolies and multi-nationals."[13]

The massive Communist campaign was also successfully directed against the International Labor Office, a UN body based in Geneva, whose main official mission was to work for the improvement of working conditions and labor union organizations around the world. As a result of Communist efforts, the ILO became increasingly political, frequently criticizing labor conditions in the U.S. and other democracies, refusing to investigate charges of labor repression in the Soviet Union, and engaging in non-labor related issues such as the Palestine question. In 1975 when the ILO voted to admit the Palestine Liberation Organization as official observers during a heated debate in which the U.S. and Israel were viciously attacked, the American delegation walked out for the first time. A few minutes later, the PLO delegation walked in to the cheers of most of the assembly. The PLO leader, Abdel Aziz al-Wajeh, made an opening speech. He was later identified as having directed the PLO massacre of the eleven Israeli athletes at the Olympic Games as well as the terrorist attack on the Hotel Savoy in Tel Aviv, in which eleven guests were killed.

Later that year the Ford Administration gave the required two-year notice that the U.S. would withdraw from the ILO if it did not reduce its political activities. In 1977 when there was no sign of improvement, the Carter Administration formally withdrew, depriving the organization of 25% of its budget.[14]

By February 1980 the U.S. was persuaded that the majority of the ILO members were now "intent on assuring that the organization will live up to its principles and promises." The ILO Director General promised in writing to try to prevent politically motivated resolutions, and the organization showed evidence of not following a double standard when the Soviet Union and other Communist countries were challenged for practices harmful to workers. Thus on February 1980 the U.S. resumed membership.[15]

But the Communist offensive against free labor unions continued in this country and abroad. Typical of the propaganda campaign were the actions of *Counter Spy* Magazine in 1979. This journal had been started by the "Fifth Estate" organization in 1975, with the backing of the Institute for Policy Studies and the advice of opponents of American intelligence like Philip Agee (the CIA defector), Victor Marchetti, David Dellinger (one of the Chicago Seven), and Mark Lane (attorney for Jim Jones' church and James Earl Ray). During 1976 after an internal fight over policy, most of the staff resigned and the magazine stopped publication. Agee and others in 1979 started a new magazine, *Covert Action Information Bulletin*, while *Counter Spy* resumed publication under a new editor, John Kelly.[16] The first issue of the new *Counter Spy* was devoted almost entirely to an attack on the so-called involvement of the CIA in the efforts of AID and the AFL-CIO to assist labor unions in other countries. Following the practice of the old *Counter Spy* in "naming names," this issue listed more than 50 labor union officials from other countries who had simply visited the U.S. Kelly later admitted that there was no evidence that any of these persons were CIA agents, but the magazine used the mere fact that they had visited this country to besmirch their reputations and imply they were tools of American monopolies or the CIA.

Another example was the three-part Public Broadcasting Service television series on the CIA aired in May 1980 and entitled *On Company Business*. Billed as a scholarly documentary, this series produced by Allan Francovich and Howard Drach in fact was a highly prejudiced hatchet job on the CIA. In a fund-raising prospectus circulated in 1976, the producers made clear that their purpose was anything but a balanced investigation: "This film will be the story of 30 years of CIA subversion, murder, bribery and torture as told by an insider...it will show the broken lives, hatred, cruelty, cynicism, and despair which result from U.S.-CIA policy."[17] The "insider" was Philip Agee, and many of the other "experts" interviewed on the film were Agee's friends and associates, including Angela Seixas, the Brazilian woman who lived with Agee for several years in England; A. J. Langguth, who wrote the highly distorted book on the Mitrione case, *Hidden Terrors;* and John Stockwell, another CIA defector, who wrote *In Search of Enemies,* a biased account of CIA attempts to counter the Communist conquest of Angola.

The second installment of this series was almost entirely devoted to an attack on American efforts to assist free labor unions in other countries and on efforts to resist Communist subversion of the labor movement. Statements by officials of the AFL-CIO international labor institutes are taken out of context or followed by statements by Agee and his friends making these American efforts appear to be nothing but cynical attempts to use foreign labor unions as tools of U.S. imperialism. The CIA is pictured as using foreign labor unions simply as a means of subverting legally elected foreign governments.[18]

This PBS series was so biased and distorted that it aroused considerable indignation, with many persons questioning the use of the taxpayer-funded broadcasting system to sponsor so prejudiced an attack on American institutions.[19] Communist propaganda had found its way into the heart of a news medium which should belong to the American people. But as the Polish unions illustrate as this book goes to press, free labor unions and Communist tyranny cannot coexist, so the propaganda machine cranks up with all its power subtlety against these unions, as we saw in Viet Nam and as we are seeing now in Poland. We can only hope that — as the Reagan victory suggests and as media coverage of Poland may indicate — we are finally beginning to see the reality behind the propaganda.

Just how diametrically opposed are free labor unions and the Communist system is dramatically indicated by a speech buried in the *On Company Business* series itself. The producers quoted the speech out of context, intending it to be heard as support for their anti-CIA, anti-AFL-CIO, and anti-American stance, but if we remove it from the false context of the television series, it provides a vivid illustration of the graphic contrast between free labor and the Communist world.

Bill Doherty, director of the AFL-CIO's American Institute for Free Labor Development, gave the speech at a luncheon concluding a one-month training session for Latin American labor union officials:

> Concluding our luncheon today . . . I'd like to give you a thought in Spanish that comes from one of the great political and literary geniuses of this century and of the past century, the true liberator of his country, who is embarrassed from heaven by the shame that now exists in Cuba because of the dictatorship of Fidel Castro. That great Cuban, Jose Marti, once said:
>
> " 'El mundo se divide en dos ramos: los que aman y construyen, y los que odian y destruyen.' Nosotros companeros sindicalistas libres, somos que amanos y construimos. Vayanse con Dios, companeros."[20]
>
> (" 'The world is divided into two groups: those who love and build, and those who hate and destroy.' Our comrades in free labor unions are those who love and build. Go forth with God, comrades.")

Communist propaganda has been tragically effective in attacking those who love and build and in supporting those who hate and destroy.

BLOWING UP
THE NEUTRON BOMB

"Ban the Killer Bomb." "Imperialist Weapon: Kills People, Saves Property." "In the Name of Life, Stop the Neutron Bomb."

For hours during a hot Washington day in June 1977, several dozen members of the militant Women Strike for Peace marched in front of the White House carrying placards and shouting these slogans. How many of these earnest demonstrators were unsuspecting dupes and how many were actually aware of the source of their slogans is a moot point. But the catch-words they were shouting and carrying were composed in Moscow by Soviet propaganda experts more than fifteen years earlier.

The Communist campaign against the neutron bomb, a campaign which succeeded in snaring these women in its net, has been one of the most massive of all Soviet propaganda efforts, and one of the most successful. It has confused the media and public opinion, altered U.S. defense policy to our disadvantage, and blackened the reputation of the American government in the Third World and even in the eyes of our own people.

The neutron bomb story starts in the late 1950s, when American scientists at the Livermore Laboratories developed the concept of a precision atomic weapon with reduced blast and heat effects but with greater radiation of neutrons. This device could be used to kill enemy soldiers but would greatly reduce civilian casualties and destruction of homes and other property in the battle zone.[1]

Such a weapon has great advantages for certain situations. Most of all, it is particularly effective against the major threat to NATO countries: the awesome strength of Soviet tanks and armored personnel carriers massed in Eastern Europe, which by

155

1975 outnumbered NATO vehicles almost two to one. Defending against this onslaught by conventional atomic weapons would cause massive damage to West Germany and other democracies. Many doubt the West would dare to use tactical atomic bombs — and that doubt, in Soviet minds, could encourage the Communists to risk an invasion.

As soon as the possibility of developing this device was mentioned in the scientific press, the Soviets recognized its importance as a defensive weapon for Western Europe and started a propaganda campaign against it. The first big blast came from Premier Nikita Khrushchev in a speech at a Soviet-Rumanian "Friendship Meeting" on August 11, 1961. "The neutron bomb as conceived by American scientists," he said, "should kill everything living but leave material assets intact. So, comrades, this is how these people are thinking. They are acting as robbers who want to murder a man without staining his suit with blood so as to be able to use this suit."[2]

Later the same month the Russians exploded their bombshell. They resumed atomic bomb testing — a stunning violation of the agreements made three years earlier with the U.S. and other democracies. This was one of the greatest blows to the hopes of mankind ever perpetrated by the Soviet Union, and the Kremlin required a large-scale propaganda effort to contain the public relations problem. They seized on the neutron bomb development in the U.S. as one excuse for resuming the tests: "The Soviet Government considers it a duty to draw special attention of the peoples of the world to the fact that now in the United States there is much ado about projects for developing a neutron bomb, which would kill everything living but not destroy material things. Only aggressors dreaming of plunder, of capturing foreign lands, can mobilize the efforts of scientists for the development of such weapons... These plans expose the inhuman essence of modern imperialism,"[3] the Soviets said in a statement announcing resumption of their tests.

In hindsight, this two-year period, 1961-62, is one of the most tragic in modern history, with mankind's hopes for the elimination of atomic bombs dashed and the arms race resumed full scale. The sequence of events is a striking case history of the power of Communist propaganda and the lack of counter-acting propaganda by the democracies.

The first event of this case history was the Russian resumption of tests, actually a series of *forty detonations*. After the initial shock, John Kennedy and his cabinet decided to defer a decision to resume American tests and to sit back and await a ground-swell of popular protests around the world and reap to the full the propaganda value of the Soviets' moratorium violation. But *almost nothing happened*. Except for one small parade in London, there were no popular demonstrations. There were numerous editorials in the leading newspapers and statements by government leaders in the western nations and the Third World deploring Russia's action, but no further groundswell of indignation.[4]

So after several months of agonizing indecision, the Kennedy administration announced that we were obliged to resume our own testing. *Only then was there an enormous outpouring of demonstrations and denunciations around the world*. Even within the United States there were more organized attacks on Kennedy's decision than had ever been directed against the Russians' initial violation. Women Strike for Peace was formed in September 1961, specifically to put pressure on Kennedy against resuming tests, and the organization mounted vigorous protests after his decision was announced. Its first big demonstration was a one-day "Strike for Peace" on November 1, 1961. W.S.P. officers claimed to have called out 50,000 women in 60 cities, although later media estimates were smaller.

In subsequent appearances before the House Un-American Activities Committee, ten out of the twelve top officers of W.S.P. took the Fifth Amendment when asked about Communist Party membership. And throughout 1961 and in later years they agitated continually against American tests and never against Soviet actions.[5] In August 1962 their top officers attended a Communist-organized World Convention Against Atomic and Hydrogen Bombs in Tokyo. When Japanese Socialists at this parley introduced a resolution condemning the Soviet tests, the Chinese Communist delegation said the Soviet tests were "necessary to preserve peace," and the resolution was defeated. The American W.S.P. delegates voted with the Communists against the resolution, and the Japanese walked out in protest after its defeat.[6]

The following year a W.S.P. group of 65 women attended a World Women's Congress in Moscow. These American women sat placidly through continual savage denunciations of the United States, including one by a Cuban representative that caused even the *Italian* delegation to walk out in protest.[7]

Another international extravaganza occurred in July and August, 1962, a two-week Youth Festival in Helsinki. There were two delegations of young people from the United States. This was an uneasy period when men of goodwill in all countries were agitating, hoping that the great powers could be persuaded to abandon the nuclear bomb race, which now threatened to start again full scale. Several delegations to the Youth Festival carried signs reading "No Tests — East or West." Half-way through the two week conference, the Soviets again shocked the world by detonating the largest bombs they had ever used— and in considerable numbers, several kiloton high-altitude blasts in the Arctic. Immediately after this was announced, the Communists who dominated the organizing committee forbade the "No Tests" signs from being carried in any subsequent delegate marches. And when several delegates defied the organizers and raised these signs again, they were attacked by Communist goons under the leadership of Jean Garcias, the French Communist secretary of the organizing committee, who seized the signs and tore them up. This was perhaps symbolic of what happened to the world's hopes for peace during this tragic two year period.[8]

Yet after the dust settled in 1963 and 1964, world opinion generally forgot that it was the Soviets who had violated the test ban and launched mankind again on an atom bomb race. We can now see how they completely outplayed the U.S. and the other democracies in the propaganda battle. Through their propaganda organization and media manipulation, they left the impression that they had resumed tests only because of the West's aggressive intentions, and that the West was even more at fault in imperiling peace by resuming its own tests.

In denouncing the neutron bomb as a major reason for resumption of the tests, Khrushchev used propaganda slogans in 1961 that were reproduced almost exactly on the signs carried by the Women Strike for Peace protesters at the White House 16 years later in 1977. There were three principal points: (1) the neutron bomb is a "killer" weapon that destroys people; (2) it produces death by radiation, which is somehow more horrible than death from other weapons; and (3) it is an "imperialist" bomb, designed to preserve material things.

By 1977 the Soviets had developed a fourth point: that this new weapon would "lower the nuclear threshold," making atomic war likely and threatening detente.

During the succeeding months of 1977 and 1978 these points would be echoed a thousand times by the media and by signs carried by innocent demonstrators who thought their slogans were their own ideas.

In fact, none of these four statements is accurate. In relation to the amount of damage to enemy armed forces, the neutron bomb would actually *save* millions of lives. *All* bombs kill people. This is the tragic reality of war. Neutron bombs do not kill more people per pound of material used than do conventional atomic weapons. They simply have the special advantage that they can kill the same number of combatants with a lesser degree of damage to surrounding homes and property. Since the purpose of most weapons is to kill soldiers, it is illogical to criticize a weapon that can accomplish this with less destruction of civilian establishments.[9]

Such a consideration is especially important in Western Europe where the potential war theatre is the heavily populated areas of Germany, France, and the Low Countries. When we are talking about preserving material things, we are referring not only to factories and other "capitalist" property, but also to homes, churches, hospitals, museums, schools, universities, and all the other treasures of centuries of European history.

Finally, most military analysts agree that the neutron bomb would not lower the nuclear threshold, but would provide a more effective deterrent to Soviet agression and thus make nuclear war *less* likely. Later in the debate about the bomb, President Carter wrote to Senator Stennis, "I can assure you that these neutron weapons would not make the decision to use nuclear weapons in general any easier. But by enhancing deterrence, they could make it less likely that I would have to face such a decision".[10]

In the late 1960s after the new neutron weapons had been under development for a few years, the U.S. decided not to give them high priority, and they were put on the back burner. Communist criticism then fell silent, but the propaganda blueprint was filed away for possible future use.

By 1975, however, the massive Communist build-up of tanks and other mechanized weapons in Eastern Europe became a grave concern in Washington. The "umbrella" provided by conventional tactical nuclear weapons, which had been counted on as a deterrent to the Russians, was now becoming less plausible. With NATO strategists realizing that most of the casualties in a nuclear exchange would be among NATO civilians, the chances for war increased as Western defense options became more questionable. In October 1975, therefore, Secretary of Defense James Schlesinger approved a start-up of production of the neutron bomb, not as an offensive innovation but as a defensive weapon designed to reduce the likelihood of war.

Many in Congress and the Administration were later surprised by the controversy aroused when this decision was made public — especially when some of the initial opposition was on the basis of *cost*. In fact, the neutron bomb is a very minor item in the budget. The costs are estimated in the tens of millions, only a small fraction of the cost of a single B-1 bomber, for example. Senator Hubert Humphrey complained, "We have blown this neutron bomb up out of all proportions," perhaps making an unintentional pun.

In June 1977 the campaign against the bomb broke full-scale into the open with a series of Walter Pincus articles in the *Washington Post*. The series echoed all of the original Communist propaganda points: "killer warhead," "kills people but preserves buildings," etc. After the articles continued for almost three weeks, some under two-column headlines on the front page, the *Post* climaxed the series on June 26 with a lead editorial opposing the bomb.

The Pincus articles were later critized as being one-sided and unscientific as well as a replay of Communist propaganda. At an Accuracy in Media Washington Conference on coverage of defense problems in April 1978, Pincus shared the platform with Dr. Edward N. Luttwak of the Georgetown Center for Strategic Studies. Luttwak strongly condemned the Pincus articles for their irrational attacks and use of inaccurate phrases like "killer warhead," which hindered rational discussion of this complicated issue. Pincus admitted that the headline on his first story did say "Neutron Killer Warhead". "But that was written by a copy editor," he claimed. "I was away that weekend. They don't consult with reporters on how they write headlines."[11]

Examination of the Pincus series, however, shows that in fact he did use the phrase "killer warhead" in his lead paragraphs on three occasions. It was *not* the invention of some headline writer, but the result of a copy editor doing what copy editors always do: take the headline from the lead.[12]

Throughout all the articles, there is only a single mention, buried on a back page, of the main American objective in developing this weapon: to confront a Soviet tank invasion with a credible deterrent that would minimize the destruction of the lives, homes, and cultural heritage of the NATO countries. Pincus passed along all the Communist propaganda lines, but not the true aims of the U.S.[13] As Luttwak said, the *Post* series had indeed confused the issue for the public.

One expert criticized Pincus even more emphatically. Donald R. Cotter, then Assistant to the Secretary of Defense for Atomic Energy, told me in a telephone interview that Pincus had talked to him but then ignored his information and wrote mainly "a lot of baloney". Among other points, Cotter criticized Pincus' implications that the neutron bomb was secretly "buried" in the Energy Research and Development Agency budget without the knowledge even of the President or most members of Congress. Actually E.R.D.A. was legally responsible for all atomic weapons development at that time, and the President, the secretaries of the Army and of Defense, and all the responsible committees of Congress had been informed.[14]

The Pincus articles were immediately followed by a massive Communist propaganda campaign, indicating that the neutron bomb touched a new nerve. The Soviets usually carried out their campaigns by stimulating local media, with only a minimum effort in outlets in the U.S.S.R. itself. But in this case, the campaign started off full-scale in Soviet media and among front groups around the world,[15] developing into one of the largest propaganda campaigns waged by the Soviets since World War II. They must have regarded this relatively minor new weapon as a major threat to their offensive plans. The intensity, coordination, and speed with which they mounted the campaign indicate that they considered time to be vital: they had to divert the U.S. from deploying the weapon before the American military and NATO became further committed.

Within two days of the Pincus articles, they were being quoted extensively by *Tass, Pravda,* and Radio Moscow. During the July 25 through August 14 period on Radio Moscow, comments on the neutron bomb received more attention than any other topic.[16] Using this barrage as a kick-off, the Soviets carried the campaign world-wide through other organizations.

The effort outside the U.S.S.R. was spearheaded by the World Peace Council, the largest Soviet international front organization, which has affiliates or agents in 120 countries, including the United States. Founded in 1948, the W.P.C. has consistently backed the Soviet line, calling for "total and complete disarmament," but opposing any effective provisions for inspection that could detect cheating. It regularly attacks Western military maneuvers or new weapons as threats to peace, but it supports similar Communist maneuvers in Eastern Europe as efforts to preserve peace. After being expelled from France and, later, Austria for subversive activities, it settled in Helsinki where it is based today.[17]

In July 1977, only a few weeks after the Pincus articles, the W.P.C. launched a massive campaign against the neutron bomb, promoting all the major Soviet propaganda themes. It orchestrated the efforts of other organizations, including the World Federation of Trade Unions, the International Association of Democratic Lawyers, the International Federation of Resistance Fighters, the Women's International Democratic Federation, and the World Federation of Scientific Workers, which issued statements viewing the neutron bomb with horror and denouncing the U.S. for considering it. All have since been identified in a CIA report to Congress as Communist fronts.[18] (See chart on page 16.)

Communists organized meetings and demonstrations throughout the world during a "Week of Action." Peace Councils in Eastern Europe held rallies and passed resolutions. A Peace Committee demonstrated outside the U.S. embassy in Istanbul. Front groups delivered notes to the U.S. consulates in several cities of West Germany. Similar organizations in Peru, Tanzania, and Ghana sent protest notes to U.S. embassies and the United Nations.[19]

Interestingly, one country that did not join in was Communist China. Peking let it be known through several American visitors that Communist China was heartily in favor of U.S. deployment of the bomb. This presented the Soviet propaganda apparatus with an opportunity to attack the Chinese People's Republic for "kneeling before the neutron bomb idol put up by the Pentagon and trying to set the Western apostles of the bomb against the Soviet Union, thus exposing themselves as the enemies of peace and security."[20]

Soon after communist newspapers and magazines around the globe carried attacks on the bomb, non-communist media picked up a large amount of the material. NATO Secretary General

Joseph Luns, in a speech on August 26, complained that the performance of European media on this issue was based on "half-truths, untruths, and ignorance."[21]

Throughout late 1977 and 1978, major American church groups attacked the bomb, including the National Council of Churches and the American Friends Service Committee.[22] Such organizations have regularly opposed new U.S. weapons developments, and the neutron bomb was simply added to their lists of targets. In this they echoed a letter sent by the Russian Orthodox Church, recognized in the West as a KGB-controlled tool of the Soviet government, urging them to appeal to Washington to ban the bomb.[23]

In January 1978, at the same time all Western European NATO powers received a letter from Brezhnev stating that the deployment of the bomb on their territory would be a serious threat to detente, the Soviet labor union organization sent a message to American trade unions, while the Soviet organization of "Parliamentarians" (i.e., members of the Supreme Soviet), wrote appeals to the legislative bodies of the NATO powers.[24]

The campaign reached a climax in February and March 1978 with a series of three international conferences, organized openly or covertly by the World Peace Council. After the first meeting in Geneva and the second in Vienna, the conference effort culminated in the "International Forum Against the Neutron Bomb", a huge conference in Amsterdam on March 18 and 19 organized by the Dutch Communist Party and backed by the World Peace Council.[25] More than 40,000 delegates were brought from all over Europe and the U.S. There were speeches by the far-left Lord Mayor of Amsterdam, W. Polak, by several representatives from the U.S.S.R. and Eastern Europe, and by various Western European speakers, communist and non-communist. Those from the U.S. included Pauline Rosen, a long-time member of the Communist Party USA, and Daniel Ellsberg.

The conference echoed the familiar Communist propaganda line: the bomb is an "inhuman, killer weapon" that would lower the nuclear threshold and damage detente. A lavish display of Communist propaganda materials included posters in several languages which usually portrayed the bomb as a large frightening object emblazoned with the stars and stripes.[26]

Meanwhile in the United States, the campaign was led by a constellation of "citizens" groups and think tanks which habitually agitate for unilateral American disarmament and which have many close relationships with the World Peace Council and other Communist fronts. Many of these groups, in fact, are located together in two small adjacent row houses on Maryland Avenue, within walking distance of the Capitol in Washington.

These include the Center for Defense Information, the Center for National Security Studies, the Center for International Policy, and the Coalition for a New Foreign and Military Policy. Women Strike for Peace used to be housed there, but moved to 201 Massachusetts Avenue in 1979. The Center for Defense Information's monthly, *The Defense Monitor*, which consistently attacks new weapons development, carried articles against the bomb which were extensively quoted by Radio Moscow.[27]

Two other organizations frequently allied with the World Peace Council are the Mobilization for Survival and the Women's International League for Peace and Freedom, both housed at 1213 Race Street, Philadelphia. The largest of these groups, the Institute for Policy Studies, is located on Q Street in Washington.[28]

These organizations cooperate with a number of journalists who habitually pass along the same line of attack against U.S. defense policies. Walter Pincus, for example, has had close relations with this Far Left Lobby. Before joining the *Post*, he was executive editor of the *New Republic*, where he authored several articles critical of U.S. defense efforts.[29] In 1974 he was one of the speakers at the "conference" on the CIA, sponsored by the Center for National Security Studies, which was nothing more than a propaganda sounding-board for the most prominent critics of the intelligence community. When William Colby, then Director of the CIA, was the only participant to give a balanced view, he was rewarded for his openness by being subjected to an hour-long harangue by Daniel Ellsberg and other "experts."[30]

Another participant was Herbert Scoville, formerly with the Atomic Energy Commission, the Defense Department and the CIA, where he was deputy director of Science and Technology. Scoville gave a speech urging that *all* American intelligence activity by overseas agents be terminated, claiming that such intelligence can now be more effectively gathered by technical means, electronic and satellite. Scoville, too, has had close ties to the Left Lobby and became active in the campaign against the neutron bomb.[31]

All of this activity had an impact on American news media.

Leftist magazines, such as *The Nation* and *The Progressive*, published articles attacking the bomb and parroting all of the Communist slogans.[32] The TV networks in early July 1977 carried both sides of the controversy for a few weeks, then let the subject die.[33]

The New York Times also took a neutral stance in the early months and simply passed along both sides, although columnist Russell Baker ran one column entitled "Son of H Bomb," an attack on the bomb based on the threshold argument[34] — that the bomb would lower the "threshold" of nuclear warfare by making it easier to launch a united war.

Newsweek, under the same ownership as the *Washington Post*, launched its coverage with a piece repeating most of the arguments against the bomb from the Pincus articles. *Time*, however, gave a balanced presentation that did explain the value of the bomb in defending Western Europe. *The New Yorker's* Richard Rovere, in his Washington Letter, gave a long account of the controversy, coming down heavily against the bomb, again on the threshold theory. The *Bulletin of Atomic Scientists* and *Commonweal* also joined the chorus against it.

By the early spring of 1978 there seemed to be some movement in the other direction. The *New York Times*, which has usually shown uncertain support for a strong U.S. defense policy, ran an editorial in favor of the bomb as a desirable weapon to defend Western Europe. This stimulated an indignant letter to the editor from Herbert Scoville.[35]

The *New Republic*, historically a far left and anti-defense publication up through Walter Pincus' editorship, has become more anti-Soviet recently, and came out in favor of the bomb.

A weighty attack appeared in the prestigious *Scientific American*, which has always displayed a pronounced bias against a strong U.S. defense policy, but takes an optimistic view of developments in the Communist world. Publisher Gerald Piel has close connections with the anti-defense lobby and was on the original board of trustees of the Institute for Policy Studies. His wife belongs to the National Emergency Civil Liberties Committee and Lillian Hellman's Committee for Public Justice.[36] The May 1978 issue of *Scientific American* ran a lead article by Fred M. Kaplan, illustrated with maps and sketches of military maneuvers and attacking the bomb. Kaplan, then still studying for a graduate degree at MIT, also has close connections with the Far

Left Lobby. He had been a student intern at the Institute for
Policy Studies. His IPS pamphlet, *Dubious Specter, A Second
Look at the Soviet Threat,* discounts the menace of Moscow's
arms build-up, and he has also written articles in a similar vein
for the far-left *Progressive* and *The Nation.*

In April 1978 Carter announced his decision: the United
States would defer production of the weapon. This statement,
which caused consternation in Europe, was against the counsel of
many of his advisors, including Secretary of State Vance, National Security Adviser Zbigniew Brzezinski, the Defense Department, and many leading members of Congress.[37] One man who
played a key role in the decision was David Aaron, deputy director
of the National Security Council, who has also had close connections with the Lobby. During the period he was assistant to
then Senator Walter Mondale on the staff of the Senate Intelligence Committee, he was on the advisory board of the leftist think-
tank, the Center for International Policy, along with Chilean
Marxist Orlando Letelier and other radicals. (For further details
on the CIP and its relations with IPS, see above, page 48.) On
the NSC he gained the reputation for being part of "Mondale's
Mafia" and in one meeting was rebuked by no less than Attorney
General Griffin Bell for "reporting to Mondale" rather than to
President Carter or Brzezinski. Aaron is said to have steered the
neutron bomb statement through the administration machinery
in spite of Brzezinski's support for the weapon's deployment.[38]

But more important than this pressure by certain individuals,
the main force behind Carter's decision to defer the neutron bomb
was the furor in the media and the public stirred up by the propaganda campaign in the U.S. and abroad.

Ironically, the Communists received Carter's concession with
hostility, not praise, giving him no credit for restraint. Instead,
they immediately labelled the decision as a "subterfuge" or a
"diversionary maneuver" and charged the U.S. with trying to
trick the Soviets into unjustified arms reductions.[39]

Brezhnev tried a propaganda ploy with the "pledge" that the
Soviets would never produce the neutron bomb first. Carter replied that this was an inadequate response since we know that
they had no need for such a defensive weapon. Brezhnev's gesture
was compared by one commentator to the "little boy who promised to give up spinach for Lent."

The decision also caused confusion and alarm in the NATO

countries which had been counting on the defense the neutron bomb would provide. West German Chancellor Helmut Schmidt was "stunned." He had gone far out on a political limb in support of the bomb against violent political opposition from leftists, some in his own party. Other European defense officials warned that facing a Soviet attack without the neutron bomb would leave them only two options: suicide or surrender. Throughout Europe the reactions were varied, but most agreed that Carter's indecision had imperiled the alliance.[40]

Even after Carter's concession, the Communist campaign continued unabated. The bomb was attacked frequently on Radio Moscow and in Soviet publications as a "sword of Damocles" hanging over the "peace-loving peoples."[41] And the usual voices in the United States and throughout the world joined in the chorus.

By October 1978, in reaction to grave warnings from the NATO allies, Carter apparently decided that no reciprocal Soviet concessions were forthcoming. Instead, the Russian arms build-up continued. So he quietly announced that the administration would start production of neutron warhead "parts" which could be assembled in Europe if needed.

In summary, the Soviet propaganda campaign to stop the U.S. from developing, producing, and deploying the neutron bomb was strikingly and frighteningly successful, preventing us for a dangerously long time from even providing the bomb and then convincing us to limit deployment to a contingency basis. Whether or not they knew what they were doing, key opinion leaders listened to the Moscow line, and the result was a serious weakening of our ability to counter the Soviets where their threat is most serious: in Europe. The campaign also succeded in blackening America's reputation in the eyes of hundreds of millions throughout the world and in giving the Soviets an excuse for its mammoth arms build-up. United States resolve and consistency became seriously doubted, and our alliances weakened. Our own people were led to doubt the aims and humanity of our leaders.

The campaign illustrates the power of the Communist apparatus to mount a tremendous world-wide propaganda effort on command. Key Communists received awards for the brilliant success of this effort. The Soviet Ambassador to the Hague received a decoration from the Communist Party of the Soviet Union in 1979 in recognition of the success of the Dutch Communist Party in organizing the mammoth conference against the bomb in Amsterdam in 1978, a high point of the campaign. And the Chief of the International Department of the Hungarian Communist Party wrote in September 1979, "the campaign against the neutron bomb was one of the most significant and most successful since World War II .... but we have no reason to feel satisfied ... It is in our common interest to make greater efforts than so far for the implementation of this program and for strengthening the anti-imperialist unity."[42]

The success of the KGB propaganda effort against the neutron bomb should make us constantly vigilant against these "greater efforts" of the future. One goal the anti-neutron bomb campaign achieved was to help excuse the tremendous Soviet arms build-up, but the Russians have little need for military weapons when they can win their battles against the unsuspecting West so easily with words alone.

THE HIDDEN
WAR AGAINST THE CIA

The scope and ferocity of the Communist campaign against the CIA are vastly more intense than the campaigns described in previous chapters. Other campaigns have been designed to blunt or cripple American agencies such as AID or policies such as neutron bomb deployment or our assistance to the Cambodian Republic, but the propaganda campaign against the CIA has had the aim of actually *destroying* the agency. This is because the CIA's mission—countering the Communist offensive around the world—brings it into more direct confrontation with the Soviets than any other agency. If the United States is the Soviet Union's main enemy, "glavny vrag," then the CIA is the eyes and ears of this enemy, the bull's-eye at the center of the target. So the Communist war against the CIA has been the longest, fiercest, and most subtle of all.

It is tragic that many of the Western journalists, scholars, and legislators who participated in the blinding and deafening of our eyes and ears—the dismantling of the CIA—did not even realize they were acting as unwitting dupes of the KGB in this war and would never have participated if they had known what was going on. As the propaganda campaign began to succeed in the media and Congress, virtually no one in the media, in Congress, or in the executive branch mentioned that the KGB and its Soviet propaganda organs were promoting the attacks on the CIA. Perhaps the greatest irony of all is that even many top CIA officers appeared unaware that Soviet puppeteers were pulling the American strings. Men like William Colby, CIA director during the worst period, seemed blind to the fact of Soviet stimulation of the campaign and made surprising blunders in dealing with the media, blunders which substantially furthered the Soviet effort.

169

The history of this war against the CIA provides the clearest example of all of a campaign that started with direct Communist propaganda output and then gradually shifted over the years until most of it was coming from American sources. Moscow set the over-all objective: destroy the CIA. But as the years went on, tactical planning and implementation came to be carried out more and more by U.S. citizens, Communists, sympathisers, and ultra-liberals (many unaware of the Communist inspiration), along with their friends in the media, Congress, and the Federal Government. Such Americans were mainly responsible for uncovering the most damaging areas where the CIA could be investigated by journalists or Congress, devising the slogans and the exploitation of such probes, and implementing the resulting propaganda. The Soviets could then follow their usual practice of playing back such American sources in broadcasts from Radio Moscow, in print media, and in other vehicles around the world, thus further blackening the reputation of the CIA and American foreign policy.

Phase I—Propaganda from Moscow—1946-1964

The war against the CIA started on a small scale soon after peace was declared in World War II and the United States organized an intelligence agency out of the remnants of the Office of Strategic Services. The CIA provided an ideal target for Communist propaganda. Chapter I outlined the Communist technique of developing "hate targets." The Communists established an entire constellation of these hate targets revolving around the CIA, including "the military-industrial complex," multinational corporations, foreign dictators, and so forth.

The Soviets used at least three main themes in the campaign:

—The CIA is simply one more arm of American "imperialism." As such the CIA cooperates with the military-industrial complex and with multinationals to spread American influence and subvert the independence of smaller countries.

—The CIA generally sides with dictators or with "racist" regimes overseas in opposition to democratic and progressive movements.

—To carry out these policies the CIA uses the most villainous methods of bribery, corruption, assassination, blackmail, sabotage, etc.

Under Stalin, the Soviet propaganda campaign was clumsy and ragged. In *The Craft of Intelligence* (1963), Allen Dulles is slightly patronizing toward the crudity of Soviet propaganda in the 1950s. For example, Dulles describes an anti-CIA booklet printed in East Berlin which gives the wrong address for the agency and which says it is located in "Washington, N.Y.," as though the American capital were in New York State.

But in the 1960s, several factors helped make the campaign more effective. Under Stalin's successors, Soviet propaganda became more sophisticated, tailored to local opinion in each targeted country and increasingly expressed by natives, thus vastly improving credibility.

In 1959, after Khrushchev had emerged at the top in the contest for power to succeed Stalin, the KGB expanded its disinformation activities considerably. A new department to concentrate on this effort, Department D of the KGB, was organized under General Ivan Ivanovich Agayants. (See Chapter II.) And as the 1960s proceeded, disinformation activities became increasingly more numerous and sophisticated.

Notable examples of such disinformation include:

—A booklet printed and distributed in London in 1961 attacking Allen Dulles, entitled *A Study of a Master Spy* and ostensibly written by Bob Edwards, a prominent Labor Member of Parliament. Further investigation, however, showed that it had in fact been researched in Moscow by a KGB disinformation officer, Colonel Vassily Sitnikov, who had previously been chief of the KGB American Desk in Vienna.[1]

—A booklet published in Kanpur, India, in 1962, *CIA Over Asia*, accusing the agency of promoting American "imperialism" in the newly emerging nations.

—A pamphlet, *American Intelligence—This Is Your Enemy*, published in Egypt in 1964.

—A pamphlet, *Operation Boa Constrictor*, published in Ceylon in 1964. This and the Egyptian pamphlet state that through the CIA and American aid agencies, the U.S. is engaged in a conspiracy to dominate the Middle East, Africa, and Asia.

—The campaign accusing the CIA of backing the French Army officers' plot to assassinate De Gaulle. This story surfaced first in a far left Italian newspaper in April 1961. Further distributed by Tass, it was re-echoed by a French leftist journalist until it became a common theme of speculation throughout the press. Allen Dulles comments on the effectiveness of such disinformation in creating distrust of the CIA in other countries and on the difficulty of disproving such rumors.[2]

In a classic disinformation operation, the KGB fools a journalist into thinking he or she has stumbled across some hidden truth, manipulates the journalist into "investigating" the story along predetermined lines, then stands back and watches KGB propaganda emerge as a journalistic scoop under the reporter's by-line. Within a few years after Khrushchev took over, the Disinformation Department is estimated to have been producing more than 300 such deceptions annually around the world, many directed against the CIA.

Phase II—Propaganda from Within— 1965 to Date

As the Soviet disinformation operation became increasingly successful, by the mid-1960s more of the propaganda effort was beginning to come from American sources rather than directly from the Soviet media. The atmosphere in the U.S. was becoming increasingly radical and thus receptive to such agitation, with the country experiencing growing controversy over the Viet Nam War. Communist propaganda against our participation and American mistakes prolonging the war combined to create a heated climate favorable for attacks on many American institutions and the establishment in general. The CIA became one of the prime targets (along with the FBI and local police intelligence operations), all part of the Soviet objective of putting out the eyes and ears of its primary enemy, its *"glavny vrag."*

Though there is little concrete proof of direct Soviet influence on the Americans who led the campaign against the CIA, this chapter summarizes a large amount of circumstantial evidence. And several known Communists are sprinkled in key positions in the organizations leading the attack. These are all older persons identified as Communists by the FBI or Congressional committees in earlier years. On younger activists there is little such evidence since Congress and the FBI have been inhibited from investigating Communist propaganda activities in recent years.

Nevertheless, persuasive evidence of conscious or unconscious bias can be developed by the techniques used in the other chapters: *balance sheets* on the leading media personalities, and *case histories* the major propaganda campaigns. The attacks on the CIA covered so many aspects that it is impossible to summarize them in one case history. Instead, this chapter presents briefly four mini-case histories of campaigns that can now be seen to have been based so much on falsehoods or distortions that they must have been the result either of either pro-Communist inspiration or manipulation.

The campaign against the CIA and other American institutions began to get increasing support in the mid-1960s and early 1970s from the growing number of Far Left Lobby organizations that sprang to life in that period. For example:

—*The Fund for Investigative Journalism,* founded in 1969 by Philip M. Stern, president of the Stern Fund, has consistently financed projects to embarrass and hamper the CIA. Never has the Fund financed anything which might be remotely considered favorable to the CIA or unfavorable to Communist subversion. Some of the recipients of the Fund's grants include Patrick McGarvey for the book, *The CIA—The Myth and the Madness;* Victor Marchetti for the *CIA and the Cult of Intelligence;* Barton Osborne for "a probe of the role of U.S. intelligence agencies in political assassinations involving nationalist groups in post-war Germany"; and Winslow Peck for a study on the "possible involvement of an intelligence agency in the politics of a large American city." "Peck" is a pseudonym used by Perry Fellwock, who is active with the Communist-dominated Peoples Coalition for Peace and Justice and "research director" of the Fifth Estate, described more fully below.[3]

—*The Committee for Public Justice* was formed in 1970, principally by authoress Lillian Hellman, an admitted Communist sympathizer.

The Committee has sponsored a series of conferences and forums to "bring together leading experts on civil liberties" and to testify before Congressional committees on proposals to "reform and oversee" the CIA, FBI, and other intelligence agencies.[4]

—*The Committee for Action Research on the Intelligence Community (CARIC),* formed in 1972 to publicize confidential information on U.S. intelligence operations, merged in 1974 with another almost defunct organization which had been announced in 1973 by Norman Mailer at his 50th birthday party. Mailer said the purpose of his group was to investigate "various theories and possible crimes of our recent history and the relation of the Invisible Government to these capers." The outgrowth of this merger was something called *The Fifth Estate.* Four major projects of the Fifth Estate were

—The quarterly journal, *CounterSpy*.

—"Mass outreach," a speakers' program oriented towards college students.

—A research effort into the relationship between the CIA and organized labor.

—Construction of an Intelligence Documentation Center in Washington, readily available for research use, containing "books press clippings, debriefings, government reports, corporate reports, and stolen documents."

The Advisory Board of the Fifth Estate included the following anti-CIA activists:

Victor Marchetti

Anthony Russo (who cooperated with Daniel Ellsberg on the Pentagon Papers)

Winslow Peck

Philip Agee, CIA Defector, an admitted "revolutionary Socialist."

David Dellinger, one of the Chicago Seven

Frank Donner, an identified Communist, now head of the ACLU Political Surveillance Project

Mark Lane (later attorney for Rev. James Jones of Jonestown, Guyana)

Fletcher Prouty

Barton Osborn, one of the founders

Marcus Raskin, co-director of the Institute for Policy Studies

Kirkpatrick Sale, author of a history of the SDS

Margaret Van Houton, co-author of *The CIA as White Collar Mafia*

Rev. Philip Wheaton

Gareth Porter

In November 1975 *CounterSpy* published the names and positions of several CIA officers, including Richard S. Welch, station chief in Athens, Greece. In December Welch's name, home address, and phone number were published in *The Athens News*. On December 23, Welch was murdered by Greek leftists. *CounterSpy's* editor Tim Butz said, "It's not our fault," but Kirkpatrick Sale added, "The CIA is in the business of killing. Our job is the exposé of every clandestine agent until the CIA abandons its covert actions."

Reverend Wheaton said, "The CIA's Welches are serving a system and their crimes are of the most serious nature imaginable—the overthrow of a government." The implication is obvious. These people consider the CIA's clandestine officers "criminals." They want to stop this "criminal activity." If people have to die in the process, they won't be too sorry.

The Fifth Estate received financing from private donors and from the *Stern Fund* (Philip Stern was another member of the Advisory Board). In 1976 it merged into the *Public Information Project on the Intelligence Community* (PEPIC). Then in January 1977 this group in turn merged into the *Campaign to Stop Government Spying* (CSGS), a much larger organization founded by the National Lawyers Guild and described more fully below.

Sometime during 1976, many of the original staff left *Counter Spy* in a disagreement over policy. The magazine suspended publication but started again in 1979 under the editorship of John Kelly.

CounterSpy's attorney was Alan Dranitzke, a Washington lawyer with several far left connections who is a member of the firm of Forer and Rein in Washington. Forer was at one time a law partner of John Abt, the former head of the Soviet espionage ring known as the Ware Group and a member of the CPUSA Politburo. Dranitzke is a leader of the NLG Subcommittee on Cuba. His firm is the Washington branch of the New York law firm of Rabinowitz, Boudin, and Standard, which has represented Castro's Cuba since 1961.[4]

In 1978 Philip Agee at the Communist-sponsored World Youth Festival in Havana announced the start of a new magazine, *Covert Action Information Bulletin*, also to be published in Washington. The staff included many of the dissident members of the old *CounterSpy*.

In the U.S., the leader of the group is William Schaap of the National Lawyers Guild Washington office. Schaap has a long history of leftist affiliations before his work with *CounterSpy*. He was a law partner of Jonathan and David Lubell, who had been identified as Communists while at Harvard Law School. He also was one of the paid attorneys on the staff of the *Center for Constitutional Rights* in New York, a leftist law front for whom he represented many far-left clients including several member of the Communist Party USA front group, the Coalition to Fight Inflation, charged with disorderly conduct and criminal solicitation.[5]

In 1974 and 1975 Schaap and other NLG members had volunteered to provide legal aid to the Baader-Meinhof terrorist gang in West Germany.

The first issue of *Covert Action* declared that its purpose was to investigate and uncover CIA personnel and operations around the world. It appealed to its readers to send in any evidence of CIA activities, as well as U.S. diplomatic lists, embassy directories, and other data. Agee and Lou Wulf of *Covert Action* also prepared a book, *Dirty Work*, published in July 1978 by Lyle Stuart, Inc., which "describes in detail how to expose CIA personnel . . . and presents biographies of more than 700 undercover CIA and NSA personnel lurking in embassies in virtually every country on earth."

In the spring of 1980 Agee was known to have abandoned the radical Brazilian woman he had been living with in London and married a German, enabling him to retain a visa to live in Germany. He was living in Hamburg in a house owned by Kurt Groenewald, an attorney for the Baader-Meinhoff Terrorists.

The work of these burgeoning Far Left Lobby outfits and the Communist propaganda organs began to result in increasing attacks on the CIA during the 1960s by American media which should have known better. In the first years of the decade, criticisms by American sources mainly concerned the CIA's *competence,* including analyses of the U-2 incident, which had clouded a summit meeting between Eisenhower and Khrushchev, and critiques of the Bay of Pigs failure. But in 1964 the first book from a major publisher appeared criticizing CIA morality, *The Invisible Government* by David Wise and Thomas Ross, published by Random House. David Wise was a young journalist, a graduate of Columbia, and head of the *New York Herald Tribune* Washington office. Yale graduate Ross, another young New Yorker, was in the Washington bureau of the *Chicago Sun-Times.*

This pair had co-authored an earlier book, *The U-2 Affair* (1962), which was critical of the CIA's efficiency rather than of its philosophy. But with *The Invisible Government*, Wise and Ross launched a broad attack on the entire morality and philosophy of the CIA—the secrecy, the need for lying, and covert operations in general—thus echoing the major themes of the Communist anti-CIA campaign.

The book began to be quoted immediately in propaganda from the Soviet Union. In November the Communist magazines *Komsomolskaya Pravda* printed an attack on the director of the CIA, John

McCone, saying that the CIA had been transformed from just an "invisible government" into a government of U.S. oil monopolies, mainly Standard Oil, and its owners, the Rockefeller group.

In succeeding months the book was quoted frequently by Radio Moscow. As for David Wise, after 1964 he developed into a professional critic of the CIA, publishing three more books. The titles alone bespeak increasing stridency:

The Espionage Establishment (also with Thomas Ross) (1967)
The Politics of Lying (1973)
The American Police State: The Government Against the People (1977)

Thomas Ross continued to report from Washington after his final book with Wise in 1967. In 1976 he was appointed Assistant Secretary of Defense for Public Affairs by the Carter Administration at a salary of $50,000.[6]

In 1974 Philip Agee published his *CIA Diary* with assistance from the North American Congress on Latin America and members like Nicole Szulc, daughter of Tad Szulc. The book includes 26 pages of names of alleged CIA employees and contacts around the world. The reason for listing them, according to Agee, was to "expose these persons to interested revolutionary organizations." Also in 1974, Marchetti and Marks published *The CIA and the Cult of Intelligence*, an attack on the theory and morality of CIA operations even harsher than David Wise's earlier books.

The CIA has not been skillful in the face of such attacks. In the mid-1970s Colby started a policy of being as open as possible with the media and Congress. But the material he released only fueled the arguments of the CIA's enemies. Some senior CIA officers, both active and retired, bitterly resented what Colby did, even going so far as to accuse him of being a KGB "mole." But this seems farfetched. It is more likely that he is simply a liberal who underestimated the seriousness of the war with the KGB and the extent to which its propaganda had trickled through the Far Left Lobby to permeate the media, influence academic, church groups, and even Congress itself.

Four Case Histories

One of the "affairs" which Colby had a hand in revealing and which ultimately became a mainstay of anti-CIA propaganda serves well as the first of our mini-case histories.

The CIA in Chile

The story starts in 1970 when Salvador Allende-Gossens won the Chilean election for the presidency. Allende was a Socialist allied with the Communists. His party's platform in fact was as radical as that of the Communists, calling for a complete socialization of the economy and a concentration of power in the central government that would virtually eliminate democratic rights. His coalition won with only 36% of the vote. He was opposed by two other parties, the conservative Nationalists and the liberal Christian Democrats. Eduardo Frei, the popular incumbent president and leader of the Christian Democrats, was unable to succeed himself because of the Chilean Constitution. Allende's margin of 36% was actually *less* than he had gained in the previous election when he was defeated by Frei. And more than 64% of the population had voted against his coalition. Nevertheless, the Parliament, which had the constitutional function of deciding on the presidency in such cases where no candidate received a majority, was expected as usual to vote for the man with the largest vote.

Washington was extremely alarmed by the possibility of a Communist government taking power in Chile. Allende had been cooperating closely with Castro. The Communist Party was known to be importing arms, money, and foreign agitators on a large scale, through the Cuban embassy and with Soviet support. The possibility of a second Communist government in the south of Latin America with Castro in the north was considered extremely dangerous.

With other crises erupting in other parts of the world, several last minute and frantic efforts were made to mount some sort of measures via the State Department and the CIA in Chile that might head off an Allende election by the Parliament.

The U.S. approached the military on the subject of a coup. But the Chilean Commander in Chief, General Rene Schneider, was reluctant to move. The U.S. negotiated with one group of officers who were considering kidnapping General Schneider, removing him to Argentina, and launching their own coup. Though the U.S. decided this group was not worthy of support and specifically called off its backing, the group proceeded anyway with a kidnapping attempt. General Schneider resisted, and the man was shot. This "assassination" in which the U.S. was in no way involved later figures as one of the major crimes laid at the door of the CIA.

Allende took office and as expected immediately launched a Communist program of nationalization and of attacks on the press, broadcasting, and free labor unions. Money and agitators continued to pour in from foreign countries, especially Cuba. On a visit to Santiago, Castro gave strong support to the new government and warned Allende that he was probably not moving fast enough to control the military.

The U.S. through the CIA began to provide support to the free forces in Chile attempting to resist Allende's efforts to suppress democracy. These forces included the non-Communist labor unions, consumer groups, and media. Allende's policies were creating roaring inflation and economic chaos. As the influx of foreign agitators and arms grew, the military at last took action. On September 1973, the military overthrew Allende, who was reported to have committed suicide.[7]

The Communist propaganda organs immediately focused on American involvement in the coup. The keynote of the campaign was struck in the April 1974 issue of *Party Affairs*, a confidential, internal publication, issued only to U.S. Communist party members. In this the International Affairs Commission of the party addressed a directive to all members that a top priority task was "to involve Congressional leaders, to demand that investigations continue of the U.S. role in the coup, and to immediately cut off all forms of aid to the Junta." It added that party members should "continually exert pressure on Congress."[8]

Radio Moscow and Soviet print media took up the theme that the CIA was responsible for Allende's overthrow. This was the first time in history that a Communist party had taken over a country and then been thrown out of office, and the Soviets and their allies were furious. In line with their usual practice, however, they made a thorough study of their mistakes and then launched a major worldwide effort to overthrow the new Chilean government and restore a Communist regime. It has been estimated that the international Communist propaganda apparatus has devoted even more money and manpower to the campaign against the new Chilean government than it did to get the United States out of Indo-China.[9]

The campaign was soon reflected in American media, where tales of CIA activity behind Allende's overthrow began to appear. A series of stories by Seymour Hersh in the *New York Times* reported on this subject. In the U.S. Senate, the Committee on Multinationals under Frank Church began to investigate the role of I.T.T. in Chile. In the House, Congressman Michael Harrington of Massachusetts was the leader in demanding a probe of the CIA's role. (In

Chapter II, we noted that Harrington would attend a conference on Chile in Mexico City in February 1975 sponsored by the World Peace Council, an international Communist front, and that some of his expenses would be paid by Orlando Letelier and his IPS-Chilean network.)

Under pressure from Harrington, the House Intelligence Subcommittee called on Colby to testify. Harrington was not on this Committee, but he demanded his right to read the transcript as a member of the House and immediately leaked the contents of Colby's testimony to the *New York Times* in September 1974. (Harrington was later reprimanded by the House for this leak.) In his version he claimed that Colby had said the CIA was attempting to *"destabilize"* the Allende government. Colby immediately denied using this word, saying the CIA's mission was only to help democratic elements in Chile survive. But the word "destabilize" was picked up by the media and the Far Left Lobby. It became a major buzzword in future attacks on the CIA, which was accused of "destabilizing legally elected governments" in small countries around the world.

Soon after the appearance of Harrington's leak, Colby made the error of accepting an invitation to appear at a "conference" on "The CIA and Covert Action" sponsored by the Center for National Security Studies, a recently formed think tank with a staff of former members of the IPS, the NLG, and other Far Left Lobby organizations. (See Chapter III, p. 51.) This conference which brought together a large number of active opponents of the CIA in Congress, the media, and other elements of the Far Left Lobby, turned out to be a thoroughly hostile gathering. After Colby presented the case for the CIA, he was subjected to harangues by Michael Harrington and Senator James Abourezk on Chile, and by other participants on other subjects. (His acceptance of this invitation was another instance of his failure to appreciate the seriousness of the propaganda war against the CIA.)

The conference also provided a forum for Robert Borosage, director of the newly formed CNSS, formerly with the NLG and IPS, and John Marks, also of the CNSS staff, to present a paper on "Destabilizing Chile." This document summarizes the entire far left party line against the CIA's efforts to "destabilize" the Allende government, without once mentioning the massive ongoing Communist efforts to stifle democracy in Chile. The U.S. administration, the paper says, "obviously perceived the election of Allende, an avowed

Marxist, as somehow threatening America interests, and they were not about to stand by and let the people of Chile decide their own political future. Their response was, in part, to unleash the CIA."[10]

These efforts of the CNSS and the IPS-Letelier network, along with those of sympathetic journalists like Seymour Hersh and Legislators like Harrington, Church, and Abourezk, made the CIA record on Chile into a major issue, blackening the reputation of the CIA and the U.S. Government. The Far Left Lobby created the impression that the U.S. had acted only to support its "interests" in Chile: i.e., the property of "multinationals." This campaign ignored the fact that the U.S. was acting mainly to counter a much greater Communist effort to install a Marxist-Leninist dictatorship. Throughout this entire period, the CIA spent no more than $8 million, according to the later Senate investigation. The Communists over the years, however were spending vastly greatly sums. Victor Riesel, the labor columnist, reports on a visit to Chile in 1970 where he met with free labor leaders in a small unheated office. They asked him why the U.S. was not doing as much to support them as the Soviets were doing for the Communist labor unions: "All they asked for were a few autos so they could travel quickly north and south in their narrow land to compete with the Communist organizers who had a fleet of cars. I conferred with some 35 newspaper editions in Santiago. They wondered why the U.S. was so amateurish in battling Communist infiltration, Soviet subsidization of unions, and the press."[11]

The Letelier Papers, as described in Chapter III, lay bare the shocking insincerity of Letelier and his network of Cuban, Chilean, and IPS associates in claiming to be working for a liberal democracy in Chile. The correspondence reveals his contempt for liberals, and shows that in fact he was working to achieve a Communist dictatorship like "what has been done in Cuba." It also shows that he was actively working *against* Eduardo Frei, one of the true liberal democrats in Chile, as an alternative to the Junta.

An article by Letelier appeared on the Op-Ed page of the *N.Y. Times* on September 27, 1976, six days after he was killed. Entitled "A Testament" and headed by a patriarchal picture of Letelier by society photographer Richard Avedon, it speaks of "Chilean democracy that for 150 years constituted an example for Latin America and the world," and the Junta's attempt to destroy "the political parties that channeled the aspirations of the Chilean people, its trade union organizations, and its convivial way of life, based on the free play of ideas and respect for the human being." Comparing this article with the contents of the Letelier Papers, especially with Letelier's scornful remarks about "liberals" and his opposition to Eduardo Frei, reveals the almost sickening cynicism behind his use of the word "democracy." It is a striking example of the ability of pro-Communists to mask their designs under a mantle of words like "democracy" and "human rights."

The Chile story, then, became one of the major issues blackening the reputation of the CIA and leading to later congressional investigations and the emasculation of the agency. Like so many of the other attacks on the CIA it was based almost entirely on exaggerations and falsehoods with just enough kernel of truth to be believable to those who wished to think ill of our intelligence services.[12] It gained some credence from the fact that the Junta that succeeded Allende was more repressive than the U.S. would have wished. But this repression was also exaggerated by the Communist propaganda apparatus to a degree that could fill another chapter, and the anti-Junta agitators like Letelier hardly helped their credibility by opposing a truly liberal alternative to the Junta such as Frei.

The campaign had considerable impact on the media. The allegations against the CIA began to be covered heavily in the *Times* with Seymour Hersh's series, Harrington's leak, and similar articles in the *Washington Post*. To a large extent the major television networks are "edited" by the *New York Times* and the *Washington Post,* meaning that the directors of the network news operations turn to these supposed national "newspapers of record" to determine which stories are worth including in the evening news. Too frequently, the network news attitude is that if a story hasn't made the *Times* front page, it's not worth covering (and vice versa). And this surprising dependence of our media on a very few opinion leaders is one of the reasons the Soviets have been so successful with their propaganda campaigns. Once the *Times* and the *Post* decided the CIA in Chile was an important story, the networks followed suit.

An analysis of TV evening news performance during 1974 shows that out of 812 evening news programs, there were 92 items on U.S. and foreign intelligence activity. *The leading topic was CIA activities in Chile.* And like the print media coverage, there was virtually no mention of the activities of the KGB or other Communist subversion in Chile or elsewhere. Out of a total of 168 minutes devoted to intelligence matters, only 4% was devoted to the KGB or other foreign espionage.[13] Like the Far Left Lobby, the networks ignored the CIA's opponent, picturing the CIA as if it were shadow-boxing against a non-existent enemy.

Domestic Spying

Our second mini-case history provides an even clearer case of successful Communist manipulation of some of our leading media. The case starts with a December 1974 newspaper article that created a quantum increase in the heat of the war against the CIA. In *Honorable Men*, his memoirs, William Colby offers his version of how the episode began. He says he had a phone call December 18 from Seymour Hersh, who claimed to have a story "bigger than My Lai" about CIA illegal domestic activities. Colby says he was justified in in trusting Hersh because a year earlier when he asked Hersh to refrain from writing anything he learned about the Glomar Explorer project, Hersh "honored his request." So he trusted "Sy" to use his discretion in the present investigation and talked to him at some length, assuring Hersh that his information was only scattered exceptional misdeeds and activities that had been subsequently halted.

Colby was not aware that Hersh's earlier silence on the Glomar Explorer had not by any means been patriotic restraint. Hersh had simply not understood then that the project involved recovering a Russian submarine, and he was too busy at the time following up on Watergate to check further.

So Colby was rudely shocked by Hersh's reactions to his interview. As he says sadly, "Hersh did not see it my way at all."

On Sunday, December 22, the *Times* exploded a front page story with pictures of Colby, Helms, and Schlesinger and a three column headline: "Huge CIA Operation Reported in U.S. Against Anti-war Forces", with the lead paragraph starting, "The CIA, directly violating its charter, conducted a massive illegal domestic operation during the Nixon Administration against the anti-war movement and other dissident groups in the U.S., according to well-placed Government sources." Colby, naive to the end, had allowed himself to be used as a "well-placed Government source" in the propaganda campaign that almost destroyed the agency he was supposed to lead.

This was the final major breaking of the dam of media restraint in publishing any variety of leak, rumor, or slander that might be available. For the prestigious *Times* to give the story this sort of play opened the way for other media to join the campaign.

Hersh followed up with several more stories giving additional details. On at least one story he seems to have been the clear victim of a KGB disinformation agent. On December 29 he reported an elaborate "confession" by a CIA "ex-agent" who claimed to have worked for four years spying on radicals in New York City, not only infiltrating student activist groups but also participating in break-ins, wire-taps, and the use of a "boom microphone" to overhear distant conversations. This, incidentally was the only story by an actual participant in domestic spying to appear in the *Times*. But no such activities were ever confirmed by later *Times* checking, by the investigations conducted by the Senate and House Intelligence Committees, or by the Rockefeller Commission. And the *Times* was never able to produce the man to testify. Harry Rositzke, a former CIA officer, in his book, *CIA's Secret Operations*, says he was probably a disinformation "walk-in."[14]

Hersh already had a reputation as a leading investigative reporter based on his first big stories on My Lai and subsequent series on the CIA in Chile. From our present perspective, the striking conclusion after looking at an array of his major investigative projects is that almost all are on subjects that might aid and comfort the Communists, while none are on subjects that might harm Communist global policies. A balance sheet of his major works and a brief sketch of his background appear in the Appendix.

It is striking that in all of his work on the CIA, after which Hersh must have built up quite an expertise on intelligence matters, he has never made an effort to investigate KGB activities in the U.S., which should be a major subject for true investigative reporting.

Hersh's close connections with the Far Left Lobby may be partly or wholly responsible for the evident bias of his choice of stories.

His original work on My Lai had been partially financed by the Stern Fund and appeared first in the radical Dispatch News Service (which has also distributed stories by Gareth Porter and the Australian Communist journalist, Wilfred Burchett). He had also done work with the IPS and the CNSS.

When Hersh's story was later the basis for investigations by the Senate and the Rockerfeller Commission, it was found to be greatly exaggerated and overblown.

Hersh was nominated for the Pulitzer Prize but failed to get it. The *Times*, however, continued to follow up on the story. By giving such prominent play initiallly to this story of "massive domestic wrongdoing," the *Times* had maneuvered itself into a position of being committed to CIA misdeeds, so that no matter what the evidence later turned out to be, the *Times,* from Managing Editor Rosenthal on down, was committed to supporting his point of view. In fact after Hersh failed to get the Pulitzer and his article was criticized for being overblown, the *Times* and many of its columnists and reporters like Anthony Lewis and James McNaughton seemed to make a special effort to plead the case that Hersh had been right and his story "confirmed."

In any case the damage had been done. The Hersh story and its followers resulted in:

— consternation in the CIA and the Ford Administration.
— appointment by Ford of a commission under Nelson Rockefeller to investigate the domestic activities of the CIA.
— Senate establishment of a special committee to investigate the CIA under Senator Church.
— later follow-up in the House with an investigation under Otis Pike.

Colby calls the subsequent year of 1975 "The Year of Intelligence." It was a period when the CIA was hit by torpedoes from every direction. Colby, required to testify two or three or even five times a week during the year before the Rockefeller Commission and the various congressional committees, also had to attempt to maintain some sort of open relations with the media.

He made his first appearance before the *Rockefeller Commission* on January 13 and the *Senate Armed Services and Appropriations Committees* on January 15. He presented a frank and open summary of CIA activities with comments that illegal activities were minimal and had been terminated in earlier years. There was a sympathetic reception by both groups, but the Senate insisted on releasing his testimony. The *Times* published a front page Hersh article with two-page summary of Colby remarks, emphasizing misdeeds. Significantly, Colby started his statement with the phrase, "I flatly deny . . . ", but the Hersh lead begins, "Colby admits . . . " As usual, the *Times* treatment caused another sensation in the country and further furor in Congress and the media.

Assassinations

The third mini-case history concerns the furor over CIA assassination attempts and illustrates again the failure of high American officials, from William Colby all the way up to President Ford, to appreciate the adversary position of the media on intelligence matters. Ford himself was responsible for the initial leak on assassinations. On January 16, 1975, he hosted a luncheon for Arthur Sulzberger and the top editors of the *New York Times* at the White House. When subject of the Rockefeller Commission came up, Ford was asked whether its make-up of "conservative and establishment" figures did not detract from its credibility. He replied that he needed reliable men on the panel to insure that it did not delve into secrets that might "blacken the reputation of every U.S. president since Truman." "Like what?" asked *Times* Managing Editor Abe Rosenthal. "Like assassinations," said Ford, and then, realizing what he had said, he added, "That's off the record!"

Of course this remark leaked within two weeks and became a common topic of conversation in media circles. Daniel Schorr learned of it just shortly before an interview he had obtained with William Colby on February 27. He raised the subject towards the end of the interview in an off-hand way. Since the Rockefeller Commission's charter covered only activities within the U.S., he asked Colby whether the CIA had ever assassinated any one in this country. Colby was startled that Ford had mentioned such a topic and replied simply, "Not in this country." Schorr, startled, in turn realized that this meant the CIA had committed or at least attempted assassinations abroad. He asked Colby "Who?" but Colby refused to answer further questions. Schorr now thought he had a sensational story, which he proceeded to broadcast on CBS the following evening, that "President Ford has repeatedly warned associates that if current investigations go too far they could uncover several assassinations of foreign officals involving the CIA".[15]

This broadcast and the subsequent media follow-ups raised the furor against the CIA to another level of hysteria. The administration was obliged to widen the mandate of the Rockefeller Commission to include assassinations. The subject, of course, was added to the topics to be investigated by the Church Committee of the Senate.

For nine months, then, the subject of assassinations became another major subject of frequent headlines and sensational broadcasts, spearheaded by almost daily pronouncements by Daniel Schorr on CBS and leading to the further blackening of the reputation of the CIA and the American government. The investigations were secret, but they led to endless leaks and attempts of the media to catch witnessess before or after testimony. There was the involvement of the Mafia, participation by Howard Hughes's organization, evidence of European criminals being used in the attempt on Lumumba's life, and a remark half way through the investigation by Senator Church that the CIA had been "behaving like a rogue elephant out of control." This all provided endless material for sensational media treatment.

Daniel Schorr, one of the leading media figures in this and other campaigns against the CIA, had a background of ultra-liberal reporting dating back to the 1940s when he was in newspaper work in New York City.

The FBI claimed he was either a member of or a close sympathizer with the Communist Party and supported the Communist leadership of the New York Newspaper Guild in the 1940s, but Schorr denies both statements. In the early 1950s he was a free-lance journalist in Europe, stringing for the *New York Times,* the *Christian Science Monitor, Time, Newsweek,* and CBS. He was hired full time by CBS in 1953. Sent to Moscow for two and one half years in 1955, he was frequently cut off the air for broadcasting stories unfavorable to the Soviet regime, but he did succeed in arranging an interview with Khrushchev in 1957 that brought the Communist leader for the first time "into American living rooms," and he was criticized by President Eisenhower for spreading the Communist propaganda line.[16]

He became a CBS Washington correspondent in the 1970s. By 1974-75 he had become one of the most active critics of the CIA and the intelligence community.

The Church Committee issued its report on assassinations in November 1975. In summary, the committee concluded that the CIA had been "involved" in plots against only five foreign leaders. But a careful reading of its reports shows that the Agency in fact made efforts to assassinate only two of these: Castro and Lumumba. In the case of Castro, none of the attempts was successful. With Lumumba, the CIA preparations were haulted, and Lumumba was later killed by local rivals having no connection with the CIA. And in both cases it is apparent the CIA was acting only on directions from higher up and almost certainly with the knowledge of the Presidents.

In the other three cases—Ngo Dinh Diem of South Viet Nam, Rafael Trujillo of the Dominican Republic, and General Schneider of Chile—the CIA had nothing to do with assassination attempts. Though in touch with groups opposed to these leaders, the CIA neither advocated nor assisted in the assassinations. As in the case of General Schneider described above, the men were later killed by local groups without the aid or knowledge of the CIA.[17] The five cases are summarized in chart II.

Nevertheless, the assassination story was blown up out of all proportion by the media, Far Left Lobby groups, and the anti-intelligence forces in Congress. The *Times* story on the Senate report by Nicholas Horrocks under a front page three-column headline implied that the CIA was involved in assassination plots against "five foreign leaders". Only further down in the story is it evident that the Agency had nothing to do with the killing of three of these. Most other print media followed the example of the *Times*. TV throughout this period found the assassination story to be one of the most sensational subjects for broadcasts. The analysis of evening TV news by Georgetown University cited above shows that during 1975, "assassinations" became the second most common topic in broadcasts about intelligence, coming just after "domestic spying" (another subject still being blown out of all proportion). Out of 905 minutes of air time devoted to Intelligence by the three major networks, 18% was devoted to assassinations (and 23% to domestic spying). Even more striking is the fact that in 1975 the actions by the KGB and other foreign secret services dropped to less than 2% of TV news time devoted to intelligence.

This is another example of how the furor stirred up by the Communist propaganda campaign against the CIA and by those who cooperated in the Far Left Lobby, the media, and Congress was able to focus attention on U.S. misdeeds and obscure the fact that the CIA had been acting not for its own villainous reasons, but only in reaction to Communist aggressive actions. There is little treatment in the Senate report, and practically none in the media, of the real threat to the U.S. posed by Fidel Castro with his encouragement of Soviet installation of missiles and his on-going attempts to subvert other Governments in Latin America. (He now has welcomed an entire brigade of Soviet troops, may be installing missiles again in violation of the earlier Soviet agreement, and has 50,000 or more mercenaries occupying strategic countries in Africa.) Likewise, Lumumba at the time posed a real threat of another Cuba-type regime in that strategic country in Africa.

There is no question that there should have been some investigation of CIA assassination policy. But without the furor in the media, it could have been conducted in a more rational fashion, with more recognition of the reasons behind the policy and the fact that Helms,

Schlesinger, and Colby had all issued directives within the CIA against such policies in 1972 and 1973 well before any investigations started. A more measured investigation and report would have avoided the nine months of sensational headlines that further damaged the morale and reputation of the CIA, leading to its further emasculation in the future.

The assassination story is another case where all of the propaganda impetus came from American sources, wittingly or unwittingly following the Communist objective of attacking the CIA with the purpose of destroying it. The details were immediately picked up by Soviet media and played back all around the world. Communist propaganda in Latin America, Africa, India, and elsewhere made frequent reference to "CIA Assassination Teams" to cast doubt on American dipomatic efforts in those areas.

The Glomar Explorer

This fourth mini-case history of another campaign that damaged the CIA, and in fact American security in general, had its origin back in 1968. In February of that year, a Soviet "G Class" missile submarine left her pen in Vladivostok and sailed out into the Pacific. Somewhere in the mid-Pacific, she met disaster due to a malfunction which led to a series of explosions, rupturing her plates and causing her to sink out of control and at increasing speed until she hit the bottom more than three miles deep.

The U.S. Navy network of underwater monitoring devices tracking her progress detected the disaster and made a horrifying recording of the actual sounds of the fatal descent with fracturing plates and bodies and other objects slamming into steel bulkheads audible on the tape. The Navy was thus in possession of an exact fix on a wrecked Soviet submarine, and it realized that the Soviets were unaware of the accident and had no knowledge of the location of the vessel. Naval officials decided that the recovery of a Soviet missile submarine would yield priceless knowledge of Russian naval architecture, missile techniques, nuclear weaponry, code books, and other data. After several months of silence under strict security wraps, during which they determined that the Soviets had abandoned their efforts to discover the fate of the sub, naval officials started preparations in cooperations with the CIA for its recovery. Recovering a submarine of this size, possibly broken into several pieces and located at a depth of more than 17,500 feet was a technical problem of immense difficulty on a scale never before attempted.

The CIA and the Navy contracted with Howard Hughes' Summa Corporation and Global Marine Inc., a leader in the field of deep sea oil drilling, to carry out the operations. A large special vessel was built, the *Glomar Explorer*, under a cover story that it was to be used to mine mineral nodules from the ocean floor. Preparations were not completed until 1974, and in the summer of that year, the salvage operation was carried out in the Pacific.

There are conflicting reports as to how much of the submarine was recovered. The CIA later said that only about half was brought to the surface and that they planned another expedition in the summer of 1975 to recover the rest. Other reports say that the entire submarine was recovered, perhaps in three or more pieces. In any case, the operation was a tremendous intelligence coup. Most knowledgable comments say that the information gained on Soviet technology and codes was of incalculable value, worth far more than the several hundred million dollar cost of the project.

Security was tight but a few leaks started because of the thousands involved in different phases of the project. A few journalists, including Seymour Hersh, found out early in 1974 that the *Glomar Explorer* was preparing some important project, without learning its true purpose, but Colby persuaded them to drop the story because of its importance to national security. But early in 1975 the security began to come unstuck because of a bizarre burglary of the Hughes office in Los Angeles, during which documents about the project were stolen. The CIA was alarmed and requested the FBI, working with the Los Angeles police, to attempt to recover these papers from the burglars. When two police reporters from the *Los Angeles Times* picked up this story from the police, the newspaper printed it, but Colby learned of this leak and persuaded the paper to move it to a small item on a back page in later editions. Colby then made strenuous and successful efforts to get other media to hold off on the story. The reason he gave was that the CIA was planning to have the *Glomer Explorer* make another attempt the following summer to recover the rest of the sub. All media agreed.

Seymour Hersh now reentered the case. Having seen the item from the *Los Angeles Times* news service on a back page of the *N.Y. Daily News*, he told Colby that he was reinvestigating the story. In early 1974 Hersh had agreed not to follow up on the story, and Colby had complimented him on his patriotism, but in truth Hersh was showing no such restraint. He had simply not been interested in the case, first because he believed it involved only CIA attempts to recover ICBMs, and second because he was working almost full time on Watergate.

Hersh's colleague on the *New York Times*, Tom Wicker, gives a detailed account in his book, *On Press*, of how Hersh now went after the story. Though Wicker cites the *Glomar* affairs as an example of the press overly solicitous of "national security", his version actually reveals a reporter's surprising lack of regard for the elementary principles of his nation's security.

Hersh, he says, attacked the story with his usual "ferocity," flew to the West Coast, and within a week had a "complete" story which Hersh said was worth six columns in the *N.Y. Times*. Colby meanwhile had appealed to the *Times* management, and Sulzberger and Abe Rosenthal, the managing editor, agreed that the story would be held up until Colby said it was no longer crucial, or until another medium broke it. This restraint infuriated Hersh, who wrote a series of angry memos to Rosenthal.

Rosenthal, who had considerable experience covering disarmament conferences, said he had a gut feeling that the *Glomar Explorer* did in fact represent a true case of a national security issue.

Elements of the story were now common among journalists, but the final break came from a rather sinister combination of events. Wicker says that Charles Morgan, Jr., head of the Washington office of the American Civil Liberties Union and a lawyer who Wicker says would make a "great reporter," learned that the *Glomar Explorer* was involved in some secret work more important than its public cover story. A Law of the Sea Conference had started in Geneva that week, and Morgan was convinced that the U.S. was attempting to steal a march on the rest of the world in deep sea mining.[18] This is one more instance of the tendency of the ACLU and the Far Left Lobby in general to think the worst of U.S. actions. The U.S. Government, of course, was making no such efforts to "steal a march on the rest of the world," and it might be asked why Morgan and his colleagues should continue to have this attitude after the amount of aid that the U.S. has given the rest of the world since the Marshall Plan, the Truman Doctrine, the Point Four Program, the Alliance for Progress, and the Agency for International Development.

Morgan was active in the Far Left Lobby, being a member of Lillian Hellman's Committee for Public Justice, (described more fully above), along with such Communists as Jessica Mitford and Far Left liberals like Morton Halperin, Orville Schell Jr., and Philip Stern. [19]

Morgan telephoned Jack Anderson, the columnist, to alert him to the story and see if he had further facts. Anderson's assistant, Les Whitten, then called Hersh to determine whether he knew anything. Wicker says that Hersh gave Whitten "suggestions on further sources." Whitten called Hersh back that afternoon to say that Anderson had enough information to break the story and would broadcast it that night, March 18, 1975.

So this triple play, Morgan to Anderson to Hersh, caused the release of this story, which in retrospect can have only done grave injury to a major valuable enterprise by the CIA.

It is still not clear from reports available to the public whether the CIA did in fact plan to go back the following summer, or whether this was simply a cover story used by Colby to persuade the media to hold off, to conceal from the Soviets that we had recovered the entire vessel. In either case, by blowing the project, the Morgan-Anderson-Hersh combination did considerable harm to national security. If it prevented the CIA from completing the project the following summer, we lost an opportunity to gain a great amount of additional data at a marginal cost.[20] If in fact the CIA *had* recovered most of the sub the first summer, this information had now been leaked to the Soviets, thus diminishing its value considerably.

The media enlarged upon the *Glomar* incident for several months, making many attempts to use it to show the CIA in the worst possible light. Some media even implied that the entire exercise was an attempt to create good publicity for the CIA and that in fact there had been no real effort to recover a sub. Other reporters, like Wicker himself, who had no technical expertise, attempted to claim that the entire attempt had been a waste of money, with Colby's efforts to maintain security simply ploys to cover up CIA waste. These stories implied that the submarine was "old" (built before 1968) and the code books, nuclear warheads, etc. were "out of date."[21] Most neutral observers with any technical background, however, agree that the recovery of an entire Soviet submarine, even one built seven years earlier and having with "old" code books, nuclear missiles, and other machinery and equipment, would be an intelligence coup worth hundreds of millions of dollars.[22]

This episode was one more example of the Far Left critics of the CIA mounting a campaign that did further serious damage to the Agency, giving additional ammunition to its opponents in the media and Congress who wished to limit its scope. All this paralleled the Soviets' objective of crippling American intelligence.

Further media manipulation in 1975

The fall of Saigon at the end of April 1975 provided a new stimulus for attacks on the CIA.

The defeat of our ally after years of American support created many problems for the CIA in attempting to withdraw in an orderly fashion. And as with all defeats, individuals and organizations involved tended to blame others, with the media in general active in handing out blame to all sides, especially to such vulnerable targets as the CIA. The attitude was typified by Peter Arnett, a correspondent for AP during the closing months in Viet Nam. "It seems to me," he said in a talk at the Air War College in February 1975, "that this is going to be the year that the 'spooks' get theirs, or they have to start answering questions .... Many reporters that I know are starting to go to Washington and trying to find all the security people, all the discontented CIA officers and others who could feed the grist for the mill to find the story of what went on ...."[23]

Many organizations in the Far Left Lobby were becoming active in this effort of searching out such disgruntled officers and exploiting them, as described more fully below.

When the *Senate Intelligence Subcommittee* under Frank Church started hearings on May 21, the CIA hired Mitchell Rogovin, partner in Arnold and Porter and one of Washington's best known civil liberties lawyers, as a legal advisor. The move shocked and surprised many of the Far Left Lobby, who regarded Rogovin as a traitor for accepting the assignment. Rogovin is counsel to IPS and Common Cause, and was representing liberal journalists Neil Sheehan and Tad Szulc in suits against the Government. A story by Hersh in the *Times* on Rogovin's appoinment quotes Marcus Raskin, a director of IPS, who unwittingly blurted out a comment that revealed the true attitude of the Far Left Lobby towards the CIA. "I'm just shocked and very deeply disturbed", Raskin said. *"Not even Mitchell Rogovin can save the CIA,* and let's pray to God that the CIA doesn't destroy Mitchell Rogovin." In plain terms this inadvertent comment illustrates that Raskin and his associates are not interested in *reforming and preserving* the CIA but in *destroying* it.

The *Rockefeller Commission* issued its report and ceased activity in May 1975. The report was a generally reasonable summary of CIA activities as Colby in turn had summarized them. One tragic incident, however, was revealed: the death of Frank Olson after CIA experiments with LSD in 1953. His family had been given financial support usual for a line-of-duty death but never notified of the true facts. President Ford extended government regrets, and Colby met with the family personally.

The Far Left Lobby seized upon the case and exploited it further. In September 1975 David Kairys and David Rudovsky of the *National Emergency Civil Liberties Committee* filed suit in behalf of the Olsen family. Both are also members of the National Lawyers Guild, Rudovsky now is national vice president and Philadelphia representative for the Center of Constitutional Rights. (See Chapter III.)

The Far Left Lobby and the media exploited the CIA drug experiments out of all proportion, completely failing to recognize that these were conducted towards the end of the Korean War when Communist techniques of brainwashing were causing deep concern in the administration, and as other incidents such as Cardinal Midzenty's behavior on trial in Hungary, indicated that the Communists might have developed mind-influencing drugs.

In September 1975 Colby appeared at an open hearing of the Senate Committee with a poison dart gun developed by the CIA, which in fact had never been used. Picked up and examined by Senator Church and other Senators in the full glare of television floodlights, this gun caused another sensation in the media.[24] The episode was a further example of Colby's excessive volunteering of information, and it provided the media and the Far Left Lobby with one more item to be added to the catalogue of CIA "crimes."

The New York Subway Poison Story, which emerged the same day as in the Senate hearings, was another example. A harmless chemical had been sprayed in parts of the New York Subway system *by the Army* several years earlier in an experiment to determine whether an enemy could saturate the subways with poison. After reports of this experiment in CIA files were dredged up at the hearing, many in the media and the Far Left Lobby seized on the incident and accused the CIA of spreading poison in the New York subways. For example, in *The Lawless State* by Halperin, Berman,

Borosage, and Marwick (Penguin Books, 1976), these members of the Center for National Security Studies blame the CIA for this harmless *Army* experiment.

Throughout this difficult year, the CIA was attempting to carry out its regular duties and coping with several major crises and challenges, including:

—the Mayaguez incident off Cambodia.

—the attempts to bolster anti-Communist forces in Angola against the pro-Communist forces under Neto, which were getting massive Soviet and Cuban support.

—support for the Kurds in Iraq.

Colby says the CIA during 1975 was required to report these and other activities and covert operations to no less than eight Congressional committees because of the new rules, and *every one of the operations leaked*. He cites this as reason for a change in the rules to limit disclosure to a smaller number of responsible committees and individuals.

Colby was fired by Ford on November 2, 1975, probably because of excessive openness, but consented to stay on until George Bush, his successor, could be confirmed and sworn in.

A final blow to the CIA in 1975 was the assassination of Richard Welsh, Station Chief in Athens, on December 23. Welsh's name had been printed in *CounterSpy* magazine and later reproduced in a radical Greek newspaper. This tragedy shocked the country. President Ford, Henry Kissinger, and Colby attended the memorial service for Welsh. There began to be something of a reaction among the public to the attacks on the CIA and the leaks from Congress and the Executive branches.

The House and Senate Investigations— Leaks and Distortion

By January 1976 there was further evidence that the Communist campaign against the CIA and the efforts of the Far Left Lobby were having more impact on the media and on Congress than on the general public. As happened in other cases described in this book, the American people seemed to have a reserve of common sense that resisted the exaggerations in the propaganda. The House Committee investigating the CIA completed their report in January 1976, but immediately launched into a controversy about its release. The CIA and the Executive Branch had furnished large quantities of information with the understanding it would not be made public. President Ford and George Bush at the CIA now were pressuring the Pike Committee to release only a summary of the report. After several days of controversy, the House voted by the large margin of 264-124 to keep the report confidential. When Daniel Schorr met Speaker of the House Tip O'Neill at an Israeli reception that evening and asked him the reason for this "surprising development," O'Neill answered that his colleagues were "getting a lot of flak about leaks, and they're going to vote their American Legion posts." Thus the public began to register some reaction against the anti-CIA hysteria, and this in turn began to affect the Congress.

But the people's will, as expresed by the House, was to be frustrated again by a leak. A copy of the entire report was given under the table to Daniel Schorr. Schorr decided that his "journalistic duty" obliged him to have the entire report published, in spite of the House of Representatives' vote that it should remain confidential. He first unsuccessfully attempted to have his employers at CBS sponsor a book. Through an intermediary, he then succeeded in finding a buyer, the *Village Voice*, the trendy left wing weekly edited by Clay Felker.[25]

The Village Voice published major portions of the report in its issue of February 16, 1976, with a large headline covering the entire front page, "The Report of the CIA that President Ford Doesn't Want You to Read."

This leak provoked another uproar in the country and the House of Representatives, but this time in the form of some backlash against the continuing leaks and harrassment of the CIA. Schoor was subpoenaed by the House Committee and there was a move to have him declared in contempt of the House, which might have resulted in a jail sentence. But after a lengthy investigation, the House was unable to discover the source of the leak, and Schorr refused to name it, invoking freedom of the press. Schorr was defended in a press conference by several leftist and ultra-liberal journalists, including Dan Rather, Mary McCrory, Carl Bernstein, I. F. Stone, and Schorr's friend and neighbor, Seymour Hersh. The House Committee in the end voted not to hold him in contempt. But Schorr was discharged by CBS, although this was not made public until after the House hearing. For more than two years, Schorr's throaty, gloating voice had come over the air almost every evening describing CIA "misdeeds." His campaign must have aggravated many supporters of America's defense efforts. It evidently aggravated William Paley, President of CBS, who had distrusted Schorr since 1964 when Schorr made a broadcast from Germany with a distorted claim that Goldwater, soon after his nomination for President, was going to visit German right wingers (by implication pro-Nazis) in Berchtesgadan, Hitler's former retreat.[26] Paley ordered Schorr's discharge.

The conclusions of the House Committee were almost lost in the controversy over the report's handling and the leak. The report confined itself to the CIA's overseas covert activities in an effort to add something to the work already done by the Senate and the Rockefeller Commission. One of its most important conclusions, apparently a slight dig at Senator Church and his Committee, was that the CIA had *not* been "a rogue elephant out of control." All evidence in hand suggests that the CIA, far from being out of control, has been utterly responsive to the instructions of the President and the Assistant to the President for National Security Affairs." The report added that almost all recommendations for covert paramilitary operations had come from outside the CIA. In many cases the CIA had expressed misgivings, but was then summarily ordered to proceed.

The report, however, was highly critical of the effectiveness of the CIA, describing failures to predict crises that had occurred in Viet Nam (the Tet offensive), the 1968 Soviet invasion of Czechozlovakia, coups in Portugal, the Mid East war, and crises in Cyprus and India.

The CIA itself called the report "biased, pejorative, and inaccurate." Colby in his last news conference before leaving office denounced the "bursting of the dam protecting many of our secret operations." Kissinger, in testimony before a Senate committee, said the Pike Committee "used classified information in a reckless way, and the version of covert operations they have leaked to the press has the cumulative effect of being totally untrue and damaging to the nation."

So although attacked from every side for irresponsibility and inaccuracies, the House Committee report remained as another array of CIA "crimes" that would give American opponents of the Agency further ammunition in the future in urging its emasculation, and Soviet propaganda organs further material for quotation.

The Senate Intelligence Committee released its final report at last in installments during April 1976. This was a lengthy document reflecting compromises between the pro- and anti-intelligence members of the staff. Colby calls it more reasonable than might have been expected when the Committee was first formed, and a justification for his open policy. Like the House report, the Senate report rejected the notion that the CIA was "out of control" and said that American intelligence agencies "have made important contributions to the nation's security, and generally have performed their missions with dedication and distinction." While highly critical of many CIA actions in the domestic field, the *facts* as presented in the report did not add up to a serious indictment.

Nevertheless, the *Times* and many other media played up the report as further documentation of CIA crimes. And as usual, the findings were widely reported by Soviet media with critical comments, mainly from American sources.[27]

After the Investigations: 1976-78

This Senate report marked the end of the phase of major investigations of the CIA. Colby and others in favor of a strong intelligence agency then relaxed to some extent, assuming that Congress and the Executive Branch would proceed with reasonable reform measures. But the Far Left Lobby did not relax. Their friends in the media kept up a continuing barrage. The war against the CIA went on and now with more ammunition.

As though there were not enough pressure groups in the field already, several large new organizations sprang up to agitate against American intelligence:

The American Civil Liberties Union joined with the Center for National Security Studies (CNSS) in a *Project on National Security and Civil Liberties,* directed by Morton Halperin. In November 1976, this group published *The Lawless State: The Crimes of the U.S. Intelligence Agencies* cited above, a 328-page pseudo-scholarly hatchet job on the CIA, FBI, NSA, and IRS, edited by Halperin, Borosage, Jerry Berman, and Christine Marwick, with the assistance of others in CNSS and ACLU, and partly financed by the Fund for Peace and the Field Foundation. A *New York Times* review by Thomas Powers, another perennial critic of American intelligence, praised the book.

This joint project also instituted a 1976 lawsuit, *Hawkins vs. Richard Helms,* which the ACLU annual report said is "a promising avenue for discovering the top secret operations of the National Security Agency and the CIA."[28]

198

Then in January 1977 several Far Left Lobby groups cooperated in the formation of a large organization that was to spearhead the drive against American intelligence from then on: The Campaign to Stop Government Spying (later given the more prestigious title of the Campaign for Political Rights). This was launched at a National Conference on Government Spying on January 20 through 23 in Chicago.

While there is no evidence of direct connection between this and the Soviet propaganda organs, there were several Communists or probable Communist fronts among the founders. The National Lawyers Guild was the organizer, and other cooperating groups included the American Friends Service Committee, the American Civil Liberties Union, the Center for National Security Studies, the National Emergency Civil Liberties Committee, and the Political Rights Defense Fund, a front of the Trotskyite Communist Socialist Workers Party (SWP). The three featured speakers were Frank Donner, Frank Wilkinson, and Morton Halperin. Donner and Wilkinson have been identified several times as Communists by witnesses before congressional committees. Donner is also director of the Political Surveillance Project of the ACLU. In 1980 he published, *The Age of Surveillance,* which attacks the CIA, FBI, and police antisubversive work. This was cited favorably in the *New York Times* and given a favorable review in *The Washington Post* by David Wise, the veteran CIA critic without any mention of Donner's Communist background.[29]

Wilkinson has been a long-time agitator against the House Un-American Activities Committee and other government efforts to combat subversion. In 1956 and '58 he refused to answer questions about his Communist Party membership before HUAC and was cited for contempt. He was convicted by a Federal Court in Atlanta and after his appeal was turned down by the Supreme Court in 1961, he served nine months of a one year sentence in jail.[30]

The Campaign for Political Rights is now housed in the same building on Massachusetts Avenue as Women Strike for Peace. It has grown into a coalition of more than 80 far left or well-meaning liberal organizations including those listed above and Friends of the Earth, ADA, Black Panthers, the Center for Constitutional Rights, the Church of Scientology, and the Women's International League for Peace and Freedom. Other staff members include Margaret Van Houten, formerly on the staff of the Fifth Estate, which spawned *CounterSpy* magazine, and Esther Herst, once an organizer for the National Committee Against Repressive Legislation, whose directors were Wilkinson and Harvey O'Connor, both identified Communists. Halperin and these staff members are in frequent touch with congressmen and senators with advice on intelligence matters. Halperin has appeared as a witness at almost every hearing of the House and Senate Intelligence Committees during their investigations and their later deliberations on legislation to regulate U.S. intelligence agencies.[31]

The Campaign also has a speakers' bureau which includes such far left activists as Eqbal Ahmad, Jerry Berman, Robert Borosage, and John Marks.

Halperin has emerged as probably the leading "expert" on intelligence matters among the Far Left Lobby groups. He and his organizations have had a consistent record of advocating the weakening of U.S. intelligence capabilities. His organizations are also notable for ignoring the activities of the KGB or any other foreign intelligence organization. His criticisms of American intelligence misdeeds would give the impression that our agencies have been committing these crimes simply for their own villainous reasons in a world where the U.S. faces no external enemies whatever. A balance sheet analysis of Halperin's writings and testimonies in the Appendix gives Halperin a score of 100% on the side of output favorable to the Communist line and 0% on any output opposed to the Communist line.

The American Friends Service Committee also came out openly against the CIA and FBI during this period. In 1976 it organized a Task Force on Government Surveillance and Citizens' Rights, under Spencer Coxe, who is also Executive Director of the ACLU in Pennsylvania. In 1976 and 1977 this Task Force produced a mass of material on FBI, CIA and local police "repression." In April 1976 the AFSC issued a report authorized by its board of directors saying "The AFSC unhestitatingly adds its voice to those who say the CIA and the Internal Security Division of the FBI must be *abolished*." (emphasis added.)[32]

The Institute for Policy Studies Government Accountability Project (GAP), under Ralph Stavins, cooperated with the Center for National Security Studies and its Director, Morton Halperin, in "whistle blowing" projects, in which government executives are encouraged to blow the whistle on activities with which they disagree. This became part of a major effort by IPS, CNSS, and others in the Far Left Lobby to recruit dissatisfied CIA or FBI personnel to leak information that can be used to attack these agencies. The most notable recruit is John Stockwell, formerly head of the CIA task force in Angola, who resigned and cooperated with IPS in producing a movie, *The Case Officer*, attacking the CIA role in Angola. Director of this movie was an IPS "Fellow," Saul Landau, and the cameraman was Haskell Wexler, a former film expert for the Weather Underground.[33] The CNSS also assisted Frank Snepp, the former CIA officer in Viet Nam who resigned from the CIA and published a book, *Decent Interval*, denouncing CIA activities during the last months before the fall of Saigon. Mark Lynch, Counsel to the CNSS and the ACLU, represented Snepp in the suit brought by the Justice Department. After more than a year of trial and appeals, this suit resulted in a ruling that Snepp's royalties should be impounded as "ill gotten gains" derived from a book in which he violated his oath of secrecy. But meanwhile, Snepp's book and newspaper and TV interviews provided another rich source of ammunition for the Agency's enemies to attack its morality and efficiency.[34]

John Stockwell's 1978 book, *In Search of Enemies*, an account of American policy in Angola, virtually ignores Soviet and Cuban backing of Communist groups and distorts American intentions in supporting the other side. The book jacket says it is a "description of CIA's efforts to start another war as the Viet Nam war is closing down." Stockwell acknowledged help from Stavins, Wexler, Peter Weiss (of NLG and Rubin Foundation), John Shattuck of ACLU, and Saul Landau of IPS. A two-column front page article by Hersh in the *New York Times* announced the release of this book.

Saul Landau, a "fellow" of IPS, who figured prominently in this anti-intelligence activity and elsewhere in the work of the Far Left Lobby described earlier, is hardly a typical think-tank scholar. Most of his experience has been in propaganda movie production and in agitation for various Far Left causes. A revealing glimpse of his true motivations is provided by the Letelier Papers, which also uncovered much of the truth about other IPS internal workings. In a letter to a friend in Cuba, which he had given Letelier to deliver, Landau says, "I think that at age 40 the time has come to dedicate myself to narrower pursuits, namely, making *propaganda* for *American Socialism* . . . we cannot any longer just help out third world movements and revolutions, although obviously we shouldn't turn our backs on them, but get down to the more difficult job of bringing the message home." (emphasis added.)[35] A balance sheet of the movies Landau has produced and of his other political activities appears in the Appendix and indicates that his work has been heavily weighted on the side of projects that would give aid and comfort to Communist causes, with none that might harm the Communists.

Spurred by these pressure groups in the Far Left Lobby, many in the media kept up a continuous anti-CIA barrage even after the conclusion of the Congressional hearings and the evidence that the new Carter Administration was making a vigorous effort at reform. It was apparent that many such people were not interested in *reform* but in *total destruction*, as we have seen hinted by Marcus Raskin of the Institute for Policy Studies and stated explicitly by the AFSC.

A major example of the continuing anti-CIA media vendetta was the investigative reporting on the CIA's use of journalists and book publishing. This was raised partially by the Senate investigation, and covered extensively in an article by Carl Bernstein (of the Woodward-Bernstein team) in *Rolling Stone* in September 1977. *The New York Times* took up this theme and assigned a team of reporters who "devoted three months" to the investigation. For three days running the *Times* carried front page, two column stories with full pages inside, though the stories were generally a rehash of earlier information.

Testimony by Colby and others before a House Subcommittee under Les Aspin generally defended most such practices. Again Colby justified CIA actions, but the *Times* headlines read "Colby Acknowledges . . ."—another case of guilt by exaggeration.[36]

Reading these articles from the perspective of a few years afterward, one is struck by their exaggerations and distortions. The CIA's use of journalists is played up as though it would inevitably cause them to distort their own reporting to the U.S. There is no recognition of the fact that the CIA was using such persons in a contest with a much larger and stronger enemy, the KGB and the world-wide Communist propaganda and subversion apparatus. Colby and the journalists who appeared before the congressional committees testified that in fact the CIA connections had no influence on their own accuracy of reporting.

The CIA's encouragement of various news services, research projects, and book publishing was similarly distorted. Almost without exception these activities were devoted to promoting dissemination of *the truth*, that is, an accurate picture of events to counteract the much more extensive Communist propaganda which was attempting to distort the news to the Communists' advantage. And yet these activities were pictured in the *Times* and other media and in the Congressional hearings as efforts to deceive the public.

The pressure of this agitation caused the Carter Administration and the Congress to forbid any CIA use of journalists in the future. As this was added to prohibitions of the use of people in other occupations, it caused David Phillips, the former CIA Latin American chief, to say ruefully at a Congressional hearing, "The only professions you are leaving to us to recruit are pimps and prostitutes." An even more cogent criticism was voiced by John Maury, who pointed out that while the CIA was prohibited from using journalists, there was *no on-going investigation of the KGB's use of American journalists.* It is now even true that while it is illegal for the CIA to use foreign journalists, it is doubtful whether it is illegal for American journalists to work for the Soviet propaganda apparatus!

By 1979 there were no less than 10 magazines devoted exclusively to campaigns against American intelligence and law enforcement organizations. In addition to *CounterSpy* and *Covert Action Information Bulletin* described above, these included:

—*Organizing Notes,* published by the Campaign for Political Rights, Morton Halperin's group in Washington (the same address as Women Strike for Peace).

—*Police Spying in Michigan,* Michigan Coalition to Stop Government Spying, Detroit.

—*Quit Snoopin',* Mississippi Surveillance Project, American Friends Service Committee, Jackson, Mississippi.

—*The Public Eye,* Repression Information Project, Washington, D.C.

—*First Principles,* Center for National Security Studies (also directed by Halperin), Washington, D.C.

—*Clandestine America,* Assassination Information Bureau, Washington, D.C. Editor: Carl Oglesby (former SDS President).

—*Spotlight on Spying,* American Friends Service Committee, Philadelphia.

—*State Research Bulletin,* Independent Research Publications, London, England.[37]

The motion picture industry was also affected by the anti-CIA bias. At least five major movies in recent years slandered the CIA:

—*Executive Action* with Burt Lancaster, written by Dalton Trumbo, one of the Hollywood Ten and an admitted Communist, and based on a story by Mark Lane, the left-wing lawyer who has been making a career out of questioning the Warren Commission report. In this film the Kennedy assassination was portrayed as the result of a plot by "Big Businessmen" with undercover assistance from the CIA. This was precisely the line being promoted by Communist propaganda organs after Kennedy's death.

—*All the President's Men*, which implies at the end that Woodward and Bernstein were in danger of assassination by the CIA, a falsehood not included in their own book on Watergate.

—*Three Days of the Condor*, with Robert Redford, generally showing the CIA in a bad light.

—*Scorpio*, also with Burt Lancaster, portraying the CIA as the villains.

—*Hopscotch*, a comedy starring Walter Matthau and Glenda Jackson, attempts to make the CIA (and the FBI) look like blundering fools. Matthau, the hero, is shown sympathetically as writing a book revealing CIA secrets, to be published in England (thus parallelling the Agee case). The CIA is pictured as threatening to blow up the publisher's office. The only KGB agent to appear is no more villainous and much smarter than the CIA men.

There have been no American movies in the past two decades critical of Communist secret police, only occasional mentions in movies like *Topaz* and then not in a particularly bad light. And TV thrillers like *Mission Impossible* seldom show the good guys fighting Communists. Villains nowadays are almost always unidentified Fascist-type dictators.

The book publishing industry also gradually developed the same tilt. Since the death of Ian Fleming, there have been few novels casting the KGB as the villains. John Le Carré's spy thrillers are notable for portraying British and American intelligence as plagued by politics and disillusionment and scarcely less unscrupulous than their Soviet counterparts. Another notable example is Robert Ludlum, who in *The Matarese Circle* paints the KGB as a rather friendly group who cooperate with the CIA to defeat the real villains, a sort of international Mafia organization.

Television continued to show the same strong bias after the end of the Congressional hearings as it had exhibited in 1974 and 75. The analysis of TV evening news by Dr. Ernest Lefever and his department at Georgetown University shows that the percent of unfavorable references to U.S. intelligence dropped between 1974 and 1976 but still remained much greater than that of the favorable mentions. Unfavorable mentions in 1976 were 60% while only 15% were favorable and 25% neutral. The balance improved only slightly in 1978. Even more striking was the fact that in 1976 and 1977 less than 5% of the mentions of intelligence referred to the KGB or other foreign activities. Taking its cue, as is usually the case, from the print media, TV virtually ignored the KGB and pictured the CIA as engaging in "crimes" simply for its own purposes.

In 1978 there was some increase in the TV coverage of foreign espionage. Such subjects jumped to 33% of the total mentions. But these referred almost entirely to news items about a few sensational spies—the Kampiles CIA case and the two young men in California who sold American satellite secrets to the Soviets—rather than any treatment of the problems of KGB and Soviet propaganda subversion as a whole. Dr. Lefever's report comments that this "was probably a temporary aberration rather than evidence of a decision to provide adequate information on the hostile environment in which U.S. intelligence is forced to operate."[38]

In fact one strategy of Communist propaganda may be to promote this impression that the only threat of the KGB in the U.S. is an occasional "spy" who in any event is apt to be caught by the FBI. A few headlines about Colonel Abel 15 years ago or the two young men in California in 1978 give the impression that such military spying is the extent of KGB efforts. This myth does much to lull Americans into ignoring the full dimensions of Soviet infiltration and subversion. At the Accuracy in Media Conference in November 1979, when I asked Seymour Hersh why he and the *New York Times* had never reported on KGB activities during all of their work on *American* intelligence misdeeds, he answered, "Assuming the KGB is operating illegally and is always trying to buy off people—so what? That is what we expect. That gets reported quite often. People get caught—pinched."[39]

The Carter Administration—1977-80

When Carter took office in 1977, the war against the CIA was widened to an entirely new battlefront. Carter himself and his associates had no preconceived ideas about further limiting American intelligence. But in order to unify the Democratic Party, he made many concessions to the McGovern wing and their sympathisers, including his own Vice President, Walter Mondale. Large numbers of appointments in the new administration went to ultra-liberal and radical followers of this group, including Anthony Lake, who took charge of Carter's transition team for the State Department, and David Aaron, who became second in command of the National Security Council under Brzezinski. Lake had close ties to the Institute for Policy Studies, and Aaron had been on the Board of the Center for International Policy, one of the Fund for Peace radical think tanks. William G. Miller, another former CIP Board member, was already staff director of the Senate Intelligence Committee and continued in this influential post throughout Carter's term in office.

Carter gave Mondale most of the responsibility for overseeing the reform of the intelligence community. Mondale had been a member of Frank Church's Senate Intelligence Committee, where his assistant had been David Aaron. On the National Security Council, Aaron took over the main responsibilities for reorganizing American intelligence.

He was joined there later by others from the Senate Intelligence Committee Staff, including Karl Inderfurth and Gregory Treverton, who had been among the most aggressively anti-CIA in the Senate investigation.

Under the guidance of such officials during the first few years of the Carter administration, a further dismantling of the CIA took place, with more wholesale firings of over 800 people, mainly in the covert intelligence and counter-intelligence branches. Counter-intelligence virtually went out of existence, and covert intelligence, said one veteran, lost the equivalent of thousands of years of experience.

The Administration also promulgated a series of executive orders further restricting the activities of the CIA, limiting its power of surveillance and its ability to gather covert information and counter-intelligence.

Meanwhile, Congress and the Administration were struggling to devise legislation, a "Charter" that would formalize the new regulations for the CIA and the intelligence community. This effort proceeded in an atmosphere of increasing controversy and doubt from 1977 onwards.

Mondale and Aaron were backed up by elements of the Far Left

Lobby, including Halperin's Center for National Security Studies and his Campaign for Political Rights, the ACLU, and Lillian Hellman's Committee for Public Justice. Halperin and others from these groups testified regularly at intelligence hearings on Capitol Hill. A draft charter that emerged in 1978 had close parallels to the recommendations of these Far Left groups.[40] Their efforts were constantly spurred on and supported by the media campaigns described earlier.

But by late 1978 these efforts to further hobble the CIA were being overtaken by events. Even President Carter was becoming alarmed at the breakdown of our intelligence capability. Early in his administration he had decried "the inordinate fear of Communism," but by 1978 his administration had experienced several intelligence disasters:

—The failure to forecast the revolutions in Afghanistan.

—Complete misinformation on the upheavals in Iran.

—Angola's invasion of Zaire. Carter accused Cuba of helping to train and command the Angolan forces and then was unable to produce adequate evidence supporting this charge— a major embarrassment for the U.S. in the UN and before World opinion.

—Detection of a Soviet brigade in Cuba.

On November 11, 1978, Carter sent a hand-written note to Admiral Turner, with copies to Vance and Brzezinski, saying, "I am dissatisfied with the quality of political intelligence," and followed this up with an icy directive to "correct the situation." To compound the irony of the security breakdown in Washington, this note itself immediately leaked to the press.

Further disasters followed in late 1979 and 1980: the excesses of the Khomeini regime in Iran and the seizure of the hostages, and then the Soviet invasion of Afghanistan. Carter said that his ideas on Soviet aims had changed more in the two weeks following this invasion than in his entire previous career.

By the spring of 1980, then, Carter was demanding a stronger intelligence capability. The general public appeared to approve of such an objective, and, as we have suggested, it seems probable that it would have supported this point of view all along. As noted above, back in 1975 at the height of the scandals over the House Intelligence Committee Report on Covert Operations, the House was said to be "voting their local American Legion Posts" in deciding to keep the report confidential. As we have seen in other case histories, the American public often seems to have a reservoir of common sense that enables it to resist the effects of Communist propaganda and the work of the Far Left Lobby and the media to a greater degree even than the Congress and the national administration. Politicians and Washington officials are likely to be more directly affected by propaganda filtering through the eastern prestige media or through lobbying groups than are the people back home.

So by the spring of 1980 Congress abandoned efforts to write a new charter for the CIA. In effect American intelligence was going to be allowed to rebuild some of its strength with a congressional policy of looking the other way.

The *New York Times* wrote an indignant editorial on this Congressional abandonment of the Charter and Tom Wicker and other ultra-Liberal journalists wrote similar blasts.[41] Tad Szulc contributed a disapproving article in the *New York Times Magazine* on April 6, 1980, on "Putting Back the Bite in the CIA," concluding that "The general talk of unleashing the CIA suggests that Congressional oversight is about to vanish. . . . For many in Congress who have lived through agency adventures in the past, the reduction in oversight makes for a threatening future." (He did not say *who* in Congress feels that lifting restrictions on the CIA will lead to a threatening future.)

Summary

To summarize the nature and effects of the Communist propaganda war against the CIA:

—The Soviets set the overall objective: *destruction of the CIA,* as part of their goal of crippling the eyes and ears of the United States, their "main enemy." In the early years they carried out most of the propaganda implementation themselves, through Soviet media or disinformation placed in foreign media.

—By the mid-1960s, however, the design and implementation of the propaganda had shifted almost entirely to Americans— agents or sympathisers working in Far Left Lobby organizations, the think tanks or citizens committees, and their friends in the media. These Americans were able to tailor the campaigns more effectively to appeal to American opinion, and to devise the tactics for stimulating investigations of the Agency that would most damage its reputation.

There is no proof of a direct link between these Americans and

Soviet propaganda organs, but there is much evidence that they were either sympathisers or being manipulated. For example:

—There are many Communists or former Communists among the groups most active in attacking the CIA: for example, Frank Donner and Frank Wilkinson associated with the Campaign for Political Rights and the American Civil Liberties Union, Lillian Hellman with the Committee for Public Justice.

Many others have declared their allegiance to "Revolutionary Socialism," including Saul Landau of the Institute for Policy Studies, and Philip Agee, supporting the *Covert Action Information Bulletin* from his exile in Germany.

—Others in the media or in influential think tanks have not declared their political beliefs but an analysis of their output shows that this has been almost 100% on the side of attacking the CIA and virtually zero on the side of investigating the KGB. These include journalists like Seymour Hersh, David Wise, and Daniel Schorr and think tank officers like Morton Halperin. Hersh has not only failed to investigate the KGB during his years of reporting on intelligence matters, but actually claims that the KGB represents no internal threat to the U.S.

—By the late 1970s these Far Left Lobby organizations and their sympathisers in the media had been able to mount a large number of serious accusations against the CIA, resulting in investigations by Congress or major campaigns in the media. Over time almost all of these accusations were found to be vastly overblown or simply false. They can be summarized as follows, in comparison with the true facts behind them as revealed in the Congressional or Rockefeller probes:

1. *Domestic Spying.* Negligible. Vastly exaggerated by the Hersh *Times* articles and resultant other media coverage. (See Chart II)

2. *Mail Openings.* The evils of this effort were greatly overblown. It started during the uneasy armistice of the Korean War and covered just three Communist countries (the Soviet Union, China, and North Korea). Mail openings have been customary in wartime, and it could be argued that the Korean Armistice period, and many years after, were in fact a "cold war" era in spite of the attempts at detente. Only about 7,500 letters per year were opened. The practice was discontinued after CIA's own investigation a year before

the press story. No Americans suffered unjustifiably from this operation, while it did assist Counter-Intelligence and the FBI.

3. *Drug Testing*. Some major abuses, but stopped in the 1950s after five years. This should be evaluated in terms of conditions at the time when there was a real possibility that Soviets were developing drugs which could have disastrous effects on American security.

4. *CIA use of Media and Book Publishing*. Abuses greatly exaggerated. Most of what was criticized was legal under the CIA charter.

5. *Assassinations*. CIA involved in only two programs (Castro and Lumumba, both unsuccessful), not in the others implied by the media and Congressional investigators. The Castro and Lumumba programs were both at the orders of higher authorities, almost certainly with the knowledge of Kennedy or Eisenhower.

6. *Covert operations*. Nothing illegal found by probers. Criticized only alleged inefficiency and overemphasis.

So in total, when accusations are examined in detail and media exaggerations are analysed, the CIA was found to be guilty of very few violations of its charter. And most of the abuses ended long before press reports or Congressional probes.

—This one-sided offensive by the media and Far Left Lobby and the hemorrhaging of classified information did immeasurable harm to:

... the morale of the CIA.

... possibilities of recruiting foreign agents in future.

... relations with allied foreign intelligence operations.

... CIA operations in general (examples: *Glomar Explorer* and many instances of electronic monitoring operations blown).

The propaganda also succeeded in causing overreaction by Congress and the administration, probably going beyond the opinions of the American public. At least one foreign expert, Brian Crozier, a former editor of *The Economist* and the director of the Institute for the Study of Conflict in London, said that the CIA was no longer an effective instrument of American foreign policy (in his latest book, *Strategy of Survival*).

Thus the campaign started by the Kremlin and carried forward in later years mainly by sympathisers or agents in the U.S. succeeded in almost completely crippling the CIA. Up until the middle of 1980, the Soviets appeared to be close to their goal of total destruction. But by that time a popular reaction had set in and even President Carter was having second thoughts. The 1980 election reflected this backlash even more clearly. The new administration and Senate majority, working with like-minded representatives in the House, will have an enormous task to restore the Agency to its former effectiveness.

Perhaps the most frightening lesson of all of this experience has to do with the ease with which our media have been manipulated. The KGB and its propaganda apparatus have learned to get our "free press" to do their work for them in destroying the eyes and ears of the USSR's "glavny vrag." In their one-sided tendency to seize on CIA faults and distort them out of all proportion, while ignoring the pervasive activities of the KGB, some journalists were probably acting out of innocent laziness: it's much easier to find out what a U.S. government agency is doing than it is to discover the secrets of a foreign power, especially with Congress leaking like a sieve. Other journalists may have been operating out of mistaken but sincere beliefs in Far Left causes. And still others may have been carried away by their natural journalistic desire to get at the truth, an investigative fervor particularly intense in newspapers beaten to the Watergate story by the *Washington Post* (though this does not explain why the same desire does not seem to operate when KGB activities are concerned). The most sinister possibility of all, of course, is that some highly respected journalists may be conscious agents of the USSR, an especially frightening possibility in light of the way our media tend to follow each other like sheep in their treatment of news. There is no concrete evidence of KGB agents in our media, but with our investigative agencies crippled, how could there be? In any event, the Russian propaganda apparatus seems to understand the ways our media operate better than does the American public, and it uses this knowledge with frightening efficiency in crippling our government's ability to counter Soviet aggression.

CONCLUSIONS
AND RECOMMENDATIONS

While many observers in the U.S. and abroad have been alarmed and mystified by America's loss of will during the past decade, virtually no one has identified Communist propaganda as a principal cause. A notable exception is Andrei Sakharov, the great Russian dissident. In his latest book, *My Country and the World,* he speaks of the loss of will among elites in the West due to "an unrelenting stream of mendacious propaganda aided and abetted by fellow-travelling intellectuals."[1]

The case histories in previous chapters were designed to show the effects of such propaganda in affecting American media and hence public opinion and even government policy. We selected these to illustrate crises in American policy where media treatment of the issues can now be shown to have been based so clearly on *falsehoods* and at the same time *to have followed so closely the Communist line* that the treatment must have been executed either by Communist agents or sympathizers or by well-meaning people being manipulated: the portrayal of the Cambodian Communists as "gentle people" when in fact they were among the most brutal tyrants of modern history; the whitewashing of the North Vietnamese as sincere nationalists trying to bring about a "government of national reconciliation" when in fact their tyranny was driving hundreds of thousands of their fellow citizens to face starvation and drowning as refugees; gross distortions of the humanitarian work of AID; vast exaggerations of CIA activities; misinformation about the effects and purposes of the neutron bomb; and so forth. These are only a few of the typical case histories that could be developed to demonstrate the pervasive effects of Communist propaganda on American media and in turn on the way we and our goverment have per-ceived the world.

These eamples illustrate two revealing phenomena, *Zig-Zag Parallelism* and *The Double Standard*, both of which also furnish strong circumstantial evidence of Communist manipulation. In *Zig-Zag Parallelism*, persons in the media or public life show a sud-den radical shift in their opinion which exactly parallels a shift in the Communist party line. Such a 180 degree turn occurred among certain American politicians and journalists in 1978 when Viet Nam began to prepare for the invasion of Cambodia. These people flip-flopped from support of the Cambodian Communists to strong attacks on them, echoing what had been said all along by more dis-interested observers, but incidentally paralleling a new party line by Viet Nam and the Soviet Union.

Illustrating the *Double Standard* symptom, certain journalists and public figures were vocal opponents of American policy in Viet Nam and constant critics of "tyranny" by the South Viet Nam gov-ernment. Yet after the Communist victory, when the evidence of brutal repression by the North Vietnamese became overwhelming and the flood of boat people mounted into the hundreds of thou-sands, such people refused to admit the facts. Not only did they try to deny the repressions, but many of them actively opposed the ef-forts of true liberal humanitarians to appeal to the North Vietna-mese to reform their policies.

Similar double standards appear in other case histories. Many critics of the CIA, for example, have never attempted to investigate the activities of the KGB, which represents a true threat to Ameri-can democracy. And organizations agitating against nuclear wea-pons, such as Women Strike for Peace, demonstrate militantly against American nuclear preparations, but refuse to criticize such flagrant Soviet actions as their breaking of the nuclear moratorium in the early 1960s. These case studies show a large degree of syste-matic bias by almost the entire "northeastern press" and the major TV networks.

Who are the agents behind such bias or manipulation? There is little firm evidence, because of the inhibitions placed in recent years on FBI investigation of subversion and the dismantling of the Congressional Internal Security committees in the 1970s. In coun-tries where the security agencies are allowed to conduct investiga-tions, such as Singapore and Malaysia, they have unearthed large networks of agents influencing media performance and government policy, as described in Chapter IV.

There is no direct evidence of actual agents in American media. But certainly the biases shown in the foregoing case studies and in the balance sheets in the Appendix indicate that even if there are no agents, at least there has been massive manipulation of sympathizers. When new employees apply, few media now check their prospective journalists for Communist affiliations. Such checks, in fact, would now be considered "McCarthyism," as is illustrated by current attitudes toward the CBS practice of the 1950s of assigning an executive to check employees for possible Communist backgrounds. In his new history of the U.S., William Manchester suggests that this practice is reprehensible. But CBS has long since dropped the practice anyway, according to the network's chairman, William Paley. When queried on the subject by Reed Irvine, director of Accuracy in Media, at a recent stockholder's meeting, Paley said the network no longer checks employees' Communist affiliations. Given the KGB's proven efforts elsewhere, it seems an excessively naive demonstration to trust in Communist good intentions to assume the Soviets would make no attempt to infiltrate such an influential medium.

The only identified Communists in American media and the Far Left Lobby are those of the older generation named in the 1960s or earlier when the FBI and the Congressional committees were still active. These include Communists or former Communists like the writers Frank Donner and Lillian Hellman, Australian journalist Wilfred Burchett, and long-time American intelligence opponent Frank Wilkinson. All have been prominent in the efforts described in the foregoing Case Histories. Several other notable agitators, though not identified as Communist agents, are self-proclaimed "Revolutionary Marxists." These include Saul Landau of IPS and Philip Agee, who guides the *Covert Action* campaign against the CIA from exile in Germany. The late Laurence Stern, managing editor of *The Washington Post,* was a Trotskyite Communist in his youth. There is no evidence on his beliefs in later life, but certainly during his tenure, the *Post* showed some of the most extreme evidences of bias, a few of which are outlined in the foregoing case studies, including its suppression of the horrors of Cambodia and the inaccurate attacks on the neutron bomb.

A third type of media personality includes those who apparently favor some type of "Communism with a Human Face" or the "right kind" of Communism. These people may dislike Soviet tyranny, but they nourish the hope that Communism could be carried out more justly by some other regime in the future. These include the Bristish journalist, William Shawcross, who expressed these beliefs frankly in his book on Dubcek. Also in this group are those who have favored the Maoist Chinese as providing some sort of "just" Communism. These include Elizabeth Becker of the *Washington Post* and Richard Dudman of the *St. Louis Post Dispatch,* who accompanied the late British Maoist, Malcolm Caldwell, in his ill-fated visit to Peking and Cambodia during the rule of the murderous Pol Pot regime.

How is the Communist propaganda effort organized? Again there is no firm evidence of the structure in the United States, but from indications given in the foregoing case studies and other sources we can arrive at some estimates. The most important conclusion is that a major portion of the effort is now implemented by Americans working within this country. Before World War II and up through the early 1960s, the major portion of the propaganda emanated directly from Communist media such as Radio Moscow or Peking, Soviet printed media, speeches, cultural exchanges, and so forth. But beginning in the 1960s an increasing part of this was being carried out by American agents and sympathizers working within this country. In the case studies of Cambodia, the North Vietnamese, AID, and the CIA, for example, we can see that most of the slogans and the tactics for stimulating Congressional investigations and recommendations for new legislation, were devised by Americans in the Far Left Lobby or the media. They were following, knowingly or unknowingly, major objectives laid down in Moscow (or Peking), but were adding to them their expertise in how best to influence American opinion.

So from this circumstantial evidence we can hypothesize a flow of influence on propaganda as follows:

Overall broad objectives are set in Moscow (or Peking), for example: "Get the U.S. out of Viet Nam," "Destroy the CIA," "Stop the Neutron Bomb." These are decided on by the Politburo, and transmitted through the International Department under Ponomarev and the Information Department with its propaganda office under Zamyatin. These organizations get advice and assistance from the KGB, especially its Disinformation Directorate, and from the Institute of the U.S. and Canada under Georgi Arbatov, who has been showing increasing expertise in tailoring propaganda for American audiences.

But the greater part of the resulting propaganda no longer is channeled through Soviet media as it was in former years. Books published in the U.S. on Communist propaganda up through the 1960s, mainly, describe such direct techniques. This book, however, describes the much more subtle and ultimately dangerous Soviet practice of getting Americans to create and disseminate the propaganda themselves, a practice which became much more important in the 1960s and which until recently has gone unnoticed or been deliberately ignored.

It is striking to compare the output of Radio Moscow and digests of the Soviet press in the 1950s and 60s with similar output in the 1970s. In the earlier years, there is a large amount of direct Soviet attacks on American policies or interests. By the 1970s, however, almost all such output consists of *quotations from American sources,* paralleling the Communist line. This indicates that the bulk of the propaganda implementation is now being carried out by Americans. It also illustates the tactics described by Aleksandr Kaznacheev, the KGB propaganda agent who defected to the Americans in Burma and described this technique of stimulating comment in local media and then playing it back in Soviet publications.

The Communists can stimulate such activity through several channels in the U.S. The pro-Soviet Communist Party U.S.A. is an obvious channel but today is less important than in the past. In the 1940s it operated through the Pro-Cells described by Herbert Philbrick, made up of professional party members, journalists, lawyers, advertising executives, and others able to exert influence on public opinion and policy. But though the number of card-carrying members of the party is low today, there may be more people cooperating with party objectives without formal membership.

The Soviet embassy and the UN delegation also include several representatives assigned to cultivate media people, front groups, and other opinion leaders. Far Left Lobby organizations, working for Communist objectives either wittingly or unwittingly, have proliferated so greatly in recent years that they have taken on a life of their own, and many are plunging along with only occasional or indirect stimulation from the Soviets. Some were organized without direct Communist backing, but are now encouraged and assisted by the Communists, sometimes without their being aware of the source of the help, under the Soviets' "franchise system." And

217

many of them maintain close relations with the Communist international fronts, which operated under the direction of Ponomaraev's International Department. (The most important of these relationships are summarized on Chart I in Chapter II.)

According to the estimates outlined in Chapter I, there may be 4,000 or more Communist propaganda agents working within the U.S. and spending more than $240 million annually.

It is time that this vast activity be investigated more thoroughly and brought out into the open. While the public and the Congress have been awakening to the increasing Communist *military* menace, there should be an awakening to the *propaganda* menace. It will not be sufficient to counter the Communists on the military front if we continue to let them win battles on the propaganda front. We can be strong militarily, but it will be to no avail if we allow them to bore from within, and we crumble, as Lenin predicted, like a beam eaten by termites.

There *are* Communists under the bed, as Eldridge Cleaver said, but it is not necessary to prove that specific individuals are agents. The most important task is to demonstrate to the American public that this campaign is going on, and that American media have been overly influenced by it. This may arouse cries of "McCarthyism", but such accusations should be met head on. The epithet "McCarthyism" itself, was probably created by the Communist propaganda apparatus as a means of discouraging *any* investigation of subversion. An expert on Communism infiltration, Robert Morris, formerly chief counsel to the Senate Internal Security Subcommittee, says that one of his early assignments in 1950 was to trace the origin of the term. He found that it had first been used in *The Daily Worker,* the Communist newspaper.[2]

If we can bring this propaganda out into the open and neutralize it, there is no reason why the United States and the free world should continue to suffer the defeats we have experienced in recent years. It is not true that the U.S.S.R. is the Sparta and the United States the Athens of the present age, as some pessimists believe. We are not a decadent people who are destined to be conquered by the more "disciplined" people of Russia with their superior morale. Actually, the morale within the Communist countries is abominable, and is in fact their greatest weakness.

Refugees from the Soviet Union like Navrozov, Solzhenitsyn, and countless others less prominent, are unanimous that the majority of people hate the system and that intellectuals no longer take

Communism seriously as a doctrine. Humor is often an accurate gauge of true political feelings, especially in a dictatorship where other frank expression is forbidden. Numerous jokes have emerged from the Soviet Union which reveal the disillusionment with Marxism-Leninism.

Examples:

Q. *What is the difference between Communism and Capitalism?*
A. Capitalism is the exploitation of man by man, and Communism is the opposite.
Q. *Is it possible to build Socialism in one country, for example, Holland?*
A. Certainly, but what have you got against Holland?
Q. *Comrade, why weren't you present at the last meeting of the Communist Party?*
A. No one told me it would be the last.

One of the most striking anomalies of recent history is that this system, which is disliked or hated by most of its own citizens, has been succeeding in gradually slicing off large parts of the free world, even where the people prefer freedom to dictatorship. A system that is working poorly inside its own borders is still able to expand around the world, mainly by the trickery of skillful propaganda, but ultimately by military force.

Dr. Fred Schwartz, who heads the Christian Anti-Communist Crusade, and is an assiduous student of Communism, has a striking metaphor which helps explain this phenomenon. Schwartz, a medical doctor, compares Communism to a cancer. A cancer, he says, may grow into a large mass, yet it cannot produce the blood vessels and nerves to sustain itself, so it begins to die and rot on the inside. But even while the cancer dies internally, it grows and invades healthy tissues in the rest of the body.

Thus today we have a striking irony: Communism is widely hated in its own lands. Democracy, on the other hand, is generally liked within its borders, although its citizens are continually complaining (and have the unique right to do so).

The Communist line sounds convincing to many in theory (production for use, not for profit, attacks on "imperialism," "monopoly," "racism," etc.), but it works badly in practice. Democratic free enterprise sounds bad to many in theory (the profit motive, free markets, etc.) but works well in practice. These twin and connected anomalies account for the fact that Communist propaganda

219

can be so effective outside its borders in underdeveloped countries where people have had little experience with either system.

As a result Communism is a great system for political analysts to recommend *for other countries.* We see scores of scholars, commentators, and reporters, happily producing favorable reports on Cambodian and Vietnamese Communists, recommending that they be allowed to take power or to join in "governments of national reconciliation." These experts, however, continue to live comfortably in the United States, winning literary prizes and earning royalties, while the Cambodian and Vietnamese people—those who have not already perished—are left to suffer under Communist tyranny.

Conclusions

So the conclusions of this study can be summarized in just 9 points:

1. The Communists' drive for world domination has been making relentless progress since World War II. In 1945 the Soviet Union controlled 7% of the earth's population. Following the latest takeovers, Communist governments now dominate more than 33%. Americans should be concerned about the survival of the free world if this trend continues, but recent Communist victories have been virtually unopposed.

2. The Communists have been succeeding by subversion and propaganda as much as by military means. Throughout history, from Lenin and his successors, they have regarded propaganda as being as important a weapon as physical force in gaining power.

3. There are more than three million people, "agit-prop cadres", *within the Soviet Union* engaged full time on propaganda directed *at the Soviet population.*

4. There are more than a half million Communist propaganda agents working around the world outside the Soviet Union, spending more than $3 billion a year on propaganda.

5. The United States is the number one target, "Glavny Vrag," the main enemy.

6. A substantial percent of these half million agents are operating within the United States, at least 4,000 and possibly many more, spending over $240 million annually on propaganda

7. There are several levels of propaganda agents. Their activity can be classified from high to low as follows:

220

— Russian (or other Communist country) agents in the U.S.

— American agents (usually not party members).

— Opportunists who follow the Communist line for the sake of their careers.

— Idealists being manipulated, often without their knowledge.

8. Many journalists have been following the Communist line. The same is true of persons in other influential organizations, especially the legal associations, citizens committees, think tanks, and foundations described in chapter III. Only a few of these individuals have been identified as Communists, and these are almost all in the older generation. The reason is that American intelligence agencies have been crippled in recent years and the Congressional internal security committees have been dismantled. So there have been no government authorities capable of determining who may be agents.

Instead this study has used two other techniques: a) the Balance Sheet Method, to assess the output of major media personalities and show the degree of Communist influence—summarized in the Appendix, and b) the Case History Method. Seven case histories are presented to illustrate Communist campaigns that can now be seen to have been based primarily or wholly on falsehoods. In turn these case histories show that major media passed along these distortions to such a degree that the media people responsible must have been either agents or unknowingly manipulated by agents. In recent years while overall propaganda *goals* have been set in Moscow (or Peking), the implementation has been carried out by American organizations and individuals, including devising slogans, designing campaigns, and concocting tactics for causing Congressional investigations and legislation.

These propaganda activities have been having a devastating effect in undermining America's will power abroad, causing defeats in such areas as Viet Nam and Cambodia; distorting public attitudes towards American institutions like the CIA, the FBI, and the Agency for International Development; and weakening our defense and intelligence efforts.

9. Propaganda is the only area where the Communists are superior to the Free World. In economics, internal morale, human freedoms, scientific development, and weapons (at least until recent years), we surpass them. But if the trends of the past thirty years persist, the Communists may succeed in taking over the world by subversion and propaganda, backed by their eventual use of force,

even though the majorities of the peoples are against them.

Recommendations

The key to defeating propaganda is to expose it as such. In order to expose it, we Americans should do at least the following:

1. We must restore the FBI's authorization to investigate subversive activity, and reactivate the internal security committees of the Senate and House of Representatives. The disastrous gap in the Government's investigative functions must be closed.

As part of their new duties there should be an investigation of Communist propaganda activities in the United States. This has already been recommended in a CIA study of Communist propaganda *abroad*, submitted to the House Select Committee on Intelligence by the CIA on July 3, 1978. Admiral Turner's covering letter pointed out that an investigation within the U.S. was beyond the CIA's scope, but he urged that it be conducted by other Government organs, presumably including the FBI.

Senator Gordon Humphrey's office, in following up Admiral Turner's recommendations, found that the FBI was not monitoring Soviet propaganda efforts in the U.S. and did not feel authorized to do so. (See p. 3, Chapter I.) The FBI should be directed to begin this activity.

2. Valuable work can be done by private organizations. Some useful studies are being carried out now on details of the total propaganda picture by organizations like the Church League of America, Accuracy in Media, the American Security Council, and *Information Digest*. But we need a much larger activity of this sort.

3. The results of both private and public investigations into propaganda and subversion should be made public if at all possible. There is little purpose in investigating Communist activities if the findings remain buried in the files. It is not generally known that the FBI has no power to publish its results or to bring in indictments. That can only be done by the Justice Department using FBI findings. One valuable function of the Congressional investigating committees was to publicize evidence of Communist subversion that the Justice Department was unable to prosecute.

4. It is not enough to expose falsehood. One must also tell the truth. Therefore, the government's own information agencies should be strengthened. The ICA, the Voice of America, Radio Liberty, Radio Free Europe, and other organizations, which have been cut back drastically in recent years, should be greatly strengthened.

5. These organizations should become more vigorous in drawing attention to aggressive Communist behavior around the world and in defending American policies. The new U.S. information agency (International Communications Agency or ICA) as reorganized under the Carter Administration in 1978, has a rather bland charter which declares as its purpose "to encourage the sharing of ideas and cultural activities among the people of the United States and peoples of other nations." It has a staff of 8,000 and a budget of more than $400 million, less than a fifth of the estimated Soviet budget of $2 billion (which itself is probably vastly understated). Even with these resources the ICA's broadcast and magazine producers have become little more than a government-sponsored press association, with conscious efforts to avoid criticizing the Communist countries for fear of harming "detente" and sometimes a surprising amount of radical or critical matter about the United States. (For example, in January 1980 the Voice of America carried the left wing feminist, Betty Friedan, on a program about the future of the American family. Ms. Friedan predicted that by the year 2000 the traditional American family will be almost non-existent.)

6. There is a need for more control of the media. This raises the difficult question of whether there should be any Government control of news contents.

Perhaps there is enough competition in print media so that no control is needed. But the influence of the three major TV networks is another matter. This near-monopoly has become so powerful in opinion formation that national survival demands some assurance that they will not free to disseminate the misinformation and distortions that have occurred in recent years. The Fairness Doctrine is already on the books. But this law passed to guard against propaganda from the *right* has proved to be ineffective against propaganda from the *left*.

This is an age when the President of the United States blames one commentator, Walter Cronkite, for swinging American opinion against the Viet Nam War. And when, after the networks grossly exaggerated the dangers of the Three Mile Island accident, the President of RCA, who presumably should know something about engineering, admitted that he had no idea that an atom-bomb type explosion in a nuclear reactor (as hinted in one scare shown on NBC) is an impossibility. In a word, TV news has become much too important a matter to be left to TV newsmen.

A preliminary recommendation for a solution to this problem is to require an ombudsman for each major network (such as now exist on some newspapers), but appointed by an independent outside body such as the FCC. This individual would be responsible for a continuing audit to see that the Fairness Doctrine is followed. Another of his important functions would be to ensure that the networks are employing adequate expert advice on any major national policy issues arising in the news. As the world becomes more complex, more expert advice is required — on issues like the neutron bomb, nuclear power, or our policy in Indo-China. An ombudsman could prevent the situation that happens so frequently now when the only TV comments on such large, difficult questions are provided by news commentators without specialized knowledge, or by one or two "experts" with doubtful credentials.

What Private Citizens Can Do

The above recommendations were for Congress and the federal government. But the United States is a democracy, and some of the most powerful work to counter the Communist propaganda offensive can be done by Americans themselves working as individuals or in non-governmental groups. Herewith are some recommendations for private individuals or for citizen-group action:

1. You can monitor your own local media. Make your own mental or written balance sheets of the most popular columnists or broadcast commentators in your area. Do they tend to show a heavy tilt towards policies that parallel the Communist line? If so, ask them to explain, and also write editors, news directors, and media owners for explanations. And remember that radio and television stations are licensed by the Federal Communications Commission and must periodically renew their licenses. Broadcasting stations must keep your letters on file for review at license renewal time: this is one of the most powerful tools we citizens have for controlling the electronic media.

2. Monitor the national organization of your church or temple. What are its political policies? If this is not made clear to your local church, make sure someone writes to national office for a statement of their political policies. If the organization is active politically, do a balance sheet of its major policies. If here again you see a distinct tilt towards the pro-Communist side, have your church or temple demand an explanation and also review its contribution policies.

Does your church contribute to the National Council of Churches, which in turn contributes to the World Council of Churches? Are you familiar with the many leftist policies of these organizations? Write for literature if necessary, and have your church make known its opposition if the congregation disagrees.

3. Monitor the votes and speeches of your Congressman and Senator. Do a balance sheet of these if necessary. If you are in disagreement, write. If you fail to get a satisfactory explanation, work for an opposing candidate in the next election.

4. Also monitor any Congressmen and Senators from your state who are on the Foreign Affairs, Intelligence, Justice, or Armed Services Committees. Do their policies tend to strengthen the U.S. or the reverse? Write if you disagree. (It is less effective to write to legislators from outside your state.)

5. Try to keep abreast of the major decisions before Congress and the Administration. Write to your Senator and Congressman to support those policies that seem to strengthen the U.S. Never underestimate the power of letters to politicians and the media.

6. Consider joining citizens' organizations active in working for a stronger America. Veterans organizations, the Coalition for Peace Through Strength, and Young Americans for Freedom come to mind. Most labor unions have also been notable for resisting Communist infiltration and working for a stronger defense policy.

7. If you are in a profession, consider joining or forming a professional organization to offset pro-Communist activities. If you are an attorney, you could join or form some type of public service law group to counter the activities of such radical organizations as the National Lawyers Guild. You might be able to contribute towards preserving the capabilities of your local law enforcement organizations and preventing their emasculation, as has happened in so many communities from the actions of the radical groups like the NLG. The American Bar Association's Standing Committee on Law and National Security is doing valuable work.

If you are a scientist you could consider joining one of the groups that have been springing up around the country to provide reliable scientific advice to the media and public authorities to counter the activities of radical crazies who have been disseminating erroneous scare facts on subjects like nuclear power, carcinogens, and pollution.[3]

8. Finally, it is possible for private citizens and private organizations to have considerable effect in countering the Communist propaganda offensive in other countries. Everything you can do as a

private individual in travelling or doing business abroad has some effect on America's image and the impression of the U.S. as a free enterprise democracy. You and your business or your trade association may be able to cooperate in helping promote America's cause in foreign countries.

9. Lastly, there is one area where it is even possible for you to have a direct influence behind the Iron curtain—that is, in assisting those in Communist countries who are attempting to excercise their right to worship as they please. Several organizations in the U.S. and Europe are carrying on campaigns to send bibles into Communist countries and in other ways to help believers there worship the way they see fit. The Soviet Union and other Communist countries claim to allow freedom of religion, but in fact they cruelly prosecute those who are not following the stringent rules governing religious exercises. Among the organizations active in this work are: the Christian Anti-Communist Crusade and the Eastern European Bible Mission.[4]

This is only a bare outline of recommendations for countering the Communist propaganda campaign. Such propaganda is the one superior weapon the Communists wield in their offensive against the Free World. One reason it is so powerful is that it is so little known. If it can be brought out into the open and publicized, if the people in the U.S. and other countries can be awakened to this danger, it can be neutralized and defeated. The truth is on our side. On the Communist side is all deception and fakery. They talk of "Democracy" and "Human Rights" when in fact within their inner circles they are laughing at liberals ("You know how Liberals are"), and working for dictatorship and the rule of the Communist elite.

In his speech after winning the Nobel Prize for Literature (which he was unable to deliver in person), Solzhenitsyn quoted an old Russian proverb, "One word of truth outweighs the whole world."

The truth about Communist designs for world conquest and their methods of gaining this end through propaganda and subversions can outweigh the advantages they now have in this field. If we can unmask the propaganda offensive, if we can overcome this one advantage the Communists have over the free world, we can arrest the continual retreat, we can stave off defeat, and turn it into a victory—and we can do it without a nuclear war.

The American people have a reserve of common sense and patriotism that will withstand the onslaught of the Communist propaganda campaign if it can be unmasked and reversed in time. A defector from the Czech KGB described his organization's secret evaluation of Americans. Josef Frolik, testifying before the Senate Committee on the Judiciary on November 18, 1975, said, "The patriotism of the average American citizen is evaluated as being extremely high . . . . The [KGB] intelligence officer should not permit himself to be misled by the apparent indifference shown by the average American . . . . The American masses are referred to as 'the sleeping giant,' who always requires a shock before he comes to his senses, but thereafter is merciless."[5]

In fighting two world wars against other brands of tyranny, the United States perfomed as the Arsenal of Democracy. A top architect of that mobilization in World War I and an influential elder statesman in World War II was Bernard Baruch, who had a favorite quotation in commenting on these victories. "There is nothing more powerful," he said, "than the spontaneous cooperation of a free people." If Americans can overcome this superior weapon of the Marxist-Leninists, the other superior qualities of our system should prevail, and we should be able to go forward to the future of a free democratic society that most in the West had assumed would be ours.

APPENDIX

This Appendix is an approach to measuring the degree of the influence of Communist propaganda lines on some prominent figures in the media. It employs the Balance Sheet method in which the individual's output—magazine and newspaper articles, books, public statements, etc.—is arrayed according to whether the information and rhetoric is favorable to the Communist line or opposed. If the Debits—statements in harmony with the Communist line—heavily outweigh the Credits—statements opposed to the Communist line—this is persuasive evidence that the individual is at least being strongly influenced by Communist propaganda, consciously or unconsciously, or has views closely approximating it, if not an actual agent.

In many cases the Debits are based partially on the truth. The Communists are skillful in hooking their propaganda campaigns to causes that have some element of believability (such as corruption and incompetence in the Cambodian Government of Lon Nol). But if the individual in question has written only about such "truths" and *never* about the anti-Communist truths, he is as suspect as those whose output consists totally of falsehoods.

Following are balance sheets on four individuals and two think tanks that figure prominently in this volume, all scoring 100% on the Debit side and 0% on the Credit.

Seymour Hersh

Graduate, University of Chicago. Worked for various news services in Chicago and the Midwest before joining AP in Washington in 1965. Resigned after one year to free-lance.

Debits

1967—Articles on U.S. chemical and biological warfare in *New Republic*:

"Just a Drop Can Kill," May 6.

"Germs and Gas as Weapons," June 7.

"Gas and Germ Warfare," July 1.

"But Don't Tell Any One I Told You," December 9.

1968—*Chemical and Biological Warfare: America's Hidden Arsenal,* published by Doubleday. Publisher later claimed this was major influence in U.S. decision to halt production of these weapons. (It is now apparent that the Soviets continued to produce these weapons in violation of the Biological Warfare Convention signed with the U.S. in 1975 outlawing their use. See the report, "Soviet Biological Warfare Activities," by the House Committee on Intelligence, June 1980.)

—Press Secretary to Senator Eugene McCarthy for his presidential primary campaign, during which McCarthy opposed the U.S. effort in Viet Nam and recommended lower defense spending. Hersh resigned from McCarthy's staff after campaign and criticized McCarthy for being 'nothing but a liberal" with no feeling for "the revolution."[1]

1969—Article, "On Uncovering the Great Gas Cover-up," *Ramparts,* June. (Here Hersh is already using phrase, "cover-up.")

—"20,000 Guns Under the Sea," *Ramparts,* September.

—Learns that the Army is trying Lieutenant Calley for the My Lai incident, and begins an investigation. (At this period the Communists were facing a major potential propaganda problem in the Hue massacre, which had occurred during the Tet Offensive, in which more than 2,000 leading citizens of Hue were killed by the North Vietnamese and thrown into mass graves. There are indications that the Communists saw the My Lai affair as a possible distraction. Hersh received backing for his My Lai research from the Stern Foundation and a new Fund for Investigative Journalism founded by Philip Stern and headed by James Boyd. The Stern-Boyd team assisted in Hersh's investigation and arranged for an almost moribund small press syndicate, the Dispatch News Service, to distribute Hersh's stories. The My Lai industry was launched, and the Hue massacre was virtually ignored by the media.)[2]

—*My Lai,* published by Random House.

—Institute for Policy Studies publishes *The Pentagon Watch-*

ers: Student Reports on the National Security State, a book based on summer work by students under the guidance of Hersh, NACLA, and others.

—Joins Advisory Board of Fund for Investigative Journalism.

1972—*Cover Up,* on My Lai, published by Random House, still pushing this subject four years after the incident and two years after his first book.

—Joins Washington Bureau of *New York Times.*

1973—Front page article in *Times* on U.S. "secret" air raids against Cambodian sanctuaries in 1970, quoting cable from Sihanouk from his haven in North Korea saying he did not know of raids, an obvious untruth. (See chapter on Cambodia, p. 77)

1974—*Times* articles with leak of Congressional testimony on CIA's activities in Chile before Allende's overthrow. September.

—Front page three-column article in *Times* on CIA's "massive illegal domestic spying." December 22. Followed up by almost daily articles containing highly exaggerated, often inaccurate information. Hersh nominated for Pulitzer prize but failed to get it because articles considered overblown and poorly researched.

1975—*Glomar Explorer,* secret project to recover sunken Russian nuclear submarine in Pacific, blown by leaks caused mainly by Hersh, Jack Anderson, and Charles Morgan of ACLU.

1977—Favorable review of Arthur Sampson's book, *The Arms Race,* in *New York Times,* July 24. Sampson blames multinationals, the Pentagon, and careless western governments for creating the arms race, with no mention of the Communist build-up which brought on the race.

1978—Front page story in *New York Times,* March 17 on CIA recruitment of blacks in 1960s to infiltrate Black Panthers and other radical groups in U.S. and abroad.

—Front page story in *Times* May 8 announcing John Stockwell's book, *In Search of Enemies,* attacking CIA's policies in Angola.

—Article June 1 on lapses in monitoring of CIA's covert actions by Congressional Oversight Committees. (Representative Edward P. Boland, Chairman of House Committee on Intelligence, writes in June 8 issue to say that Hersh article is misleading.)

—Front page article July 16 on leaked Senate Intelligence Committee report concluding that Colby and Kissinger mislead Congress on U.S. role in Angola. CIA and Kissinger deny charges.

1979—*Times* article January 7 by Hersh says CIA rejected warning on Shah. Former Iran analyst interviewed by Hersh says Shah was a "pipsqueak" and a "megalomaniac."

—In August, Hersh is one of few American journalists to be allowed to visit Viet Nam. During and after a 10 day visit, he writes a series of six articles for the *Times* which generally pass along the North Vietnamese propaganda line, including:

... After six hours of interviews with Vietnamese Foreign Minister, Hersh quotes him as blaming U.S. for failure to "normalize" relations with Viet Nam.

... There has been no bloodbath.

... The "reeducation camps" are austere, but there is no starvation or cruelty. One "reeducated" inmate, a physician, is quoted as having enjoyed the labor.

... Refugees are simply those who had cooperated with the Americans, became used to the easy life with American assistance, and could not get accustomed to austere life under Communism.

... The Government is not extracting money from the refugees.

... Horrors exist in Cambodia (Hersh describes these at length). As described in Chapter V, it is now a major theme in Vietnamese propaganda to stress the horrors of the Pol Pot regime and thus justify the Vietnamese conquest of Cambodia.

... The Soviets are not seeking military bases in Viet Nam. (Contrary to Hersh's report, intelligence is now overwhelming that the Soviet Navy is making use of Cam Rahn Bay and Danang harbor, although the Russians may not yet have set up their own "bases" there.)

... The New Economic Zones have been having some minor problems, but in general the people are content there. (By coincidence, one of the same issues of the *Times* that carried a Hersh story from Viet Nam also ran a short news item with directly contradictory evidence. It said that Viet Nam had cancelled a scheduled visit by nine American Congressmen because one of the nine had "slandered" Viet Nam. They were referring to a statement by Robert F. Drinan, Democrat of Massachusetts, that the New Economic Zones amount to "concentration camps" and that "Viet Nam is engaged in one of the most fundamental violations of human rights that we have seen in this century." Drinan is an ultra-liberal, was one of the most active opponents of the Viet Nam war, and is not one to attack Communist Viet Nam without consideration.)

... There is a relatively free press. One of Hersh's six articles is entirely devoted to an interview with a newspaper editor in Ho Chi Minh City (formerly Saigon), who said he is able to publish almost anything he pleases with only mild "guidance" from the government. Hersh must be incredibly naive—or something worse—to accept this propaganda as truth.

1980—Op Ed *Times* article May 1 on Iran rescue mission says "Perhaps the failure of the operation will be as instructive for Jimmy Carter as was the Bay of Pigs for John F. Kennedy in 1961." In other words the advice of the intelligence and military communities cannot be trusted.

Credits

No articles can be found that could be considered against the Communist line. For example, in all his voluminous writings on My Lai, there is no mention of much greater massacres by the Communists, of which Hue was only one. His 1979 series of articles on his Viet Nam visit contains nothing about the reported horrors in the reeducation centers, the suppression of free press and free religion, the Americans missing in action, growing Soviet influence, and other problems.

Likewise, he has produced *no* articles on the activities of the KGB, which represent a vastly greater threat to American liberties than his favorite target, the CIA. In fact he has expressed exactly the opposite view, that the KGB represents no threat. At the Accuracy in Media conference in Washington in November of 1979, at the end of a question period he was asked the following:

Q: *Mr. Hersh, this conference is entitled "The Media and the*

*Present Danger." Do you believe there is a danger, and if
so, what is it?*

Hersh: There is no danger. I don't believe it. There is no danger of the KGB penetrating the U.S. to the point where our
institutions are at stake. (Laughter.) I consider that a James
Angleton fantasy. I really do. I think we are in terrific
shape.[3]

Gareth Porter

PhD. from Cornell. On faculty of Center for International
Studies, Cornell, 1964-68 Joined Indochina Resource Center, 1970
(one of leading organizations in opposition to Viet Nam War; see
page 55).

Debits

1968—"People As the Enemy," *New Republic*, February 2. An
attack on U.S. policy in Viet Nam.

1969—"Diemist Restoration," *Commonweal*, July 11. An attack
on South Vietnamese government.

—"Vietnam: The Bloodbath Argument," *Commonweal*, No-
vember 11. Asserts that South Vietnamese need not fear a
Communist takeover and that stories of bloodbath in North
Vietnam after their victory there are false.

1971—Correspondent and "bureau chief" in Saigon for the leftist
Dispatch News Service. (See above under Seymour Hersh.)

1970-74—Voluminous publications from Porter at Indochina Resource Center opposing U.S. efforts in Viet Nam, painting
North Vietnamese and Viet Cong as patriotic nationalists,
and urging government of "national reconciliation."

1975—"Pressing Ford to Drop Thieu," *New Republic*, February 8.

—"Viet Nam; Reconciliation Begins," *Christian Century*, July
11.

—*A Peace Denied: the U.S., Viet Nam, and the Paris Peace
Agreement*, Indiana University Press. The thesis of this
book is that "from the beginning of its involvement in Viet
Nam up through the last days, the policies of the U.S. were
the cause of the war and the major stumbling block preventing a negotiated settlement.... It was the kind of war in
which dishonorable and ultimately futile deeds (by the
U.S.) were always clothed in the rhetoric of peace." This
book has been assigned reading in courses in U.S. Inter-

national Relations in several leading universities.

1976—Porter gives principal speech at meeting in Union Theological Seminary welcoming Ieng Sary, Foreign Minister of new Pol Pot Cambodian Communist government, on his arrival in New York for UN session. No mention of reports of massacres by Communists in Cambodia.

—"Viet Nam's Long Road to Socialism," *Current History*, December. A highly optimistic account of the new Vietnamese government's attempts to build "socialism."

—As evidence of tyranny in Viet Nam grows, many humanitarians, formerly active in anti-Viet Nam War movement, compose a letter to Vietnamese government appealing for more human rights and an open society. Letter sponsored by Fellowship of Reconciliation. Signers include Daniel Ellsberg, Daniel Berrigan, Joan Baez, etc. Porter not only refuses to sign but *actively campaigns against release of letter*.

1977—Porter, representing Indochina Resource Center, testifies before House Subcommittee on International Relations investigation of "Human Rights in Cambodia." Says reports of massacres are false, exaggerated like "earlier reports of bloodbath in North Viet Nam after Communist takeover in 1954."

—Indochina Resource Center becames Southeast Asia Resource Center, moves to Berkeley, California. Porter leaves and joins Institute for Policy Studies in Washington, a key organization in the Far Left Lobby. (See p. 44.)

—"Healing the Wounds of War; Justice, not Peace for Viet Nam," *Christian Century*, March 2.

—"Kissinger's Double Cross for Peace," *Nation*, April 30.

1979—Viet Nam invades Cambodia (ignoring the UN), overthrows Pol Pot, and sets up puppet government. Porter in telephone interview with author says Vietnamese invasion of Cambodia is justified. "A typical way a nation will react to protect its interests when a small neighbor allies itself with another powerful neighbor (China) providing a significant threat." Justifies Viet Nam's keeping people in "reeducation centers" because of the "near famine" conditions in Saigon and other cities. "Government fears unrest if more people are released."

1980—Joins the Center for International Policy, another organization active in the Far Left Lobby. (See p. 48.)

Mentioned as an unpaid volunteer working for John Anderson's campaign for the presidency as an independent.

Credits

No record of any Porter writings contrary to the Communist line on Indo-China. Defended the brutal Pol Pot regime up until it became permissible to attack Cambodia in order to justify the Vietnamese invasion. Continually opposed U.S. policy in Viet Nam. After the fall of Saigon, gave a steady optimistic picture of developments. In spite of his background in Vietnamese affairs and access to good sources, failed to criticize the tyranny that was becoming more evident, and in fact tried to suppress others' attempts to do so.

Morton H. Halperin

Ph.D. Harvard. On staff of Harvard Center for International Affairs, 1960-65.

Debits

1961—An early advocate of unilateral American disarmament.

—*A Proposal for a Ban on Nuclear Weapons,* published by Institute for Defense Analysis, suggests that U.S. should disarm even if Soviets do not and that inspection is "not absolutely necessary."

1966-68—In Defense Department, rising to Deputy Assistant Secretary. Member of group reporting to Leslie H. Gelb, responsible for preparation of Pentagon Papers, critical of U.S. role in Viet Nam.

1969—Hired by Kissinger for National Security Council staff in Nixon administration.

—FBI names him as most likely suspect for having leaked story of secret bombing of Cambodian sanctuaries. Kissinger takes him off list of those allowed to see top secret documents. He is one of first to have phones tapped by "Plumbers" operation, designed to curb serious government leaks. (No evidence was found that he was the leaker.) Later resigns from National Security Council.

1972—Testimony before House Appropriations Committee recommends series of drastic progressive cuts in defense expenditures, a limit of $68 billion for fiscal 1972, $8 billion below Administration's request, and "declining limits for succeeding years." Recommends eliminating multiple warheads on missles, Minuteman III, the Trident submarine, and several advanced fighter planes including the F-14 and F15. Also said that eventually we could eliminate two out of our three legs of the three-legged defense system, i.e. bombers and land-based missles, leaving only nuclear submarines.

1974—Joins Center for National Security Studies, a far left think tank in Washington (see p. 51 for details).

—"Covert Operations, Effects of Secrecy on Decision-Making," paper presented at Conference on Intelligence sponsored by the Center for National Security Studies. Recommends removing secret classification from U.S. satellite reconnaisance operations and National Security Agency communications intercepts, and a greatly reduced covert operations role for CIA. Paper later published in *Society* magazine and in a book, *The CIA File*, by Viking Press.

1975—"Most Secret Agents," *New Republic*, July 21.

"Led Astray by the CIA," *New Republic*, July 28.

"CIA Denying What's Not in Writing," *New Republic*, October 4.

"Activists at the CIA," *New Republic*, November 8.

1976—Appointed Director of Project on National Security and Civil Liberties, a joint operation of CNSS and ACLU. Concentrating on investigating and reducing the role of FBI, CIA, police departments, and other internal security organizations.

—Co-author of *The Lawless State: The Crimes of the U.S. Intelligence Agencies*, a report of the CNSS published by Penguin Books.

—"Did Richard Helms Commit Perjury?", *New Republic*, March 6.

—"Public Secrets," *New Republic*, November 20.

—Board member of the Committee For Public Justice, organization started in 1970. Principal organizer was Lillian Hellman, who has never renounced her support of Stalinist Russia. (Other Board members include admited Communist Jessica Mitford.)

1977—Campaign to Stop Government Spying founded with backing of National Lawyers Guild. Halperin is Chairperson. CNSS is a cooperative organization, along with 33 other groups. More coordinated effort to restrict role of U.S. internal security organs.

—Frequent testimony before Congressional commitees on

237

legislation to govern operations of CIA, FBI, and other security organizations, generally favoring strict limits.

1978—Testimony before House Committee on Intelligence regarding the Foreign Intelligence Surveillance Act. Recommends no surveillance be permitted unless there is *prior evidence of criminal activity* (which most security experts say would cripple investigative process).

—Becomes Director of CNSS.

—Co-signer of letters to Justice Department, as head of Project on National Security, opposing all wire-taps except with prior evidence of criminal activity.

Credits

No record of any writings or statments that might be against the Communist line. All the "studies" of "national security" conducted by the Center for National Security Studies and other organizations he has directed have dealt voluminously with the CIA, FBI, and other U.S. security organizations, and heve generally attacked their methods and recommended drastic restrictions. But his organizations have *never* mentioned the KGB or other Communist subversive activities.

Saul Landau

Landau is one of the most active associates of the Institute for Policy Studies and has been Director of their subsidiary, the Transnational Institute, since the former director, Orlando Letelier, died by bombing in 1976. Despite his prominent positions with IPS, he is not a typical think-tank scholar. Most of his background has been in left-wing agitation or in film production, mostly far-left, propaganda documentaries. (For further details on IPS and TNI, see the chapter on the Far Left Lobby.)

Born in 1936, he graduated from the University of Wisconsin and obtained a Master's degree in History. In the early 1960s he held various teaching and social work jobs in California.

Debits

1959—Join editorial board of *Studies on the Left*, a radical magazine.

—Collaborated with C. Wright Mills a writer prominent in Far Left and pro-Castro causes in the 1950s and 1960s, and accompanied Mills on trips to Cuba and Europe.

1961—Speaks as a representative of the Fair Play for Cuba Committee January 28 at an American-Cuban Friendship Rally in New York City sponsored by Advance, a youth organization of the Communist Party. (The Fair Play for Cuba Committee went out of existence in 1964 when Lee Harvey Oswald was revealed as a member.)

1962—Featured speaker at pro-Castro rally in October at University of California, Berkeley, sponsored by Trotskyite Socialist Workers Party, and at similar rally at Stanford University the following day.

1963—In May, joins with about 100 leftists in the formation of a new movement of the left called "The San Francisco Opposition" or "The Opposition"[4].

1964—In October, fired from his hospital social work job for promoting the showing of *Un Chant D'Amour*, a French film about homosexual love produced by Jean Genet, the French homosexual and ex-convict. Film co-sponsored by SDS, "The Opposition," and SLATE, a radical student group at Berkeley. (Landau eventually took his case on the banning of this film to court, and in 1966, the California District Court of Appeals handed down a decision saying that the film was nothing less than hard-core pornography and should be banned. The judge said it was devoid of theme, plot, or character development. *Time* Magazine described the film as "a silent 30 minute portrayal of a sadistic prison guard alternately beating and spying on four convicts engaged in homosexual acts."[5] This was Landau's first highly-publicized entrance into film distribution or producing.)

1965—Active in Students for a Democratic Society (SDS) affairs, including speaking at SDS benefits, serving as an instructor in the SDS's "New School" in San Francisco, and speaking at SDS Regional Conference in December.

—Joins staff of *Ramparts*, the radical magazine.

1966—Becomes active in the North American Congress on Latin America (NACLA), the new radical organization formed by former SDS members who were becoming too old to be considered "students." Objectives are research and action on "the real forces shaping U.S. policy in Latin America—corporations, government agencies, foundations, churches, and unions."

1967—Becoming active as a film producer. Attended an International Cultural Congress in Havana as a film maker. Landau's wife, Nina Serrano Landau, attends Communist Youth Festival in Moscow and then travels to Red China, in violation of State Department regulations.

1969—Produces two propaganda films about Cuba: *Report From Cuba* and *Fidel.*

1970—Film, *Que Hacer,* ("What Is to Be Done"), on "revolution" in Chile

—Joins editorial board of *Socialist Revolution,* a new pro-Communist magazine published in San Francisco.

1971—Produces film, *Brazil—A Report on Torture.* Co-producer is Haskell Wexler, the radical film maker who accompanied Jane Fonda on one of her trips to North Viet Nam and has produced films for the National Lawyers Guild and other far left organizations.

1972—Film, *Robert Wall—Ex-F.B.I. Agent.* "Confessions of a former FBI agent who describes how he spied on the IPS, Stokely Carmichael, and others."

—Film, *The Jail,* a trip through the society of "prisoners and jailers, tranvestites, murders, drunks, and sadists."

—Film, *An Interview With Allende,* co-produced with Haskell Wexler.

1973—Film, *Song for Dead Warriors,* "examines the reasons for the Wounded Knee occupation in the Spring of 1973 by Oglala Sioux Indians and members of the American Indian Movement".

1975—Film, *Cuba and Fidel,* a "film picture postcard of Cuba with interviews of Fidel on socialist law, the difference between Russians and Americans, and Cuba before and after the Revolution."

1976—Film, *Land of My Birth,* on "Jamaica's charismatic Prime Minister, Michael Manley, in the midst of his election campaign."

—Letelier killed by a bomb blast under his car in Washington along with IPS associate Ronni Moffitt. Letelier papers found in his brief case include a letter from Landau to be delivered to a friend in Cuba saying "I think at age 40 the time has come to dedicate myself to narrower pursuits, namely making propaganda for American Socialism . . . . we cannot any longer just help out third world movements and revolutions, although obviously we shouldn't turn our backs on them ....." (For further details see the chapters on the Far Left Lobby and the CIA.) Landau takes over the operation to handle the publicity on Letelier's killing and the campaign to get the maximum propaganda value against the Chilean Government. He later succeeds to Letelier's position as "Director" of the Transnational Institute.

1978—Film, *In Search of Enemies,* co-produced with Haskell Wexler, based on John Stockwell's book attacking CIA role in Angola.[6]

—Landau article in *Mother Jones,* the radical magazine partially funded by IPS, "Behind the Letelier Murder," blames the CIA for a part in the killing because of its encouragement of the Chilean intelligence organization. No word in here, or any other Landau IPS output on Letelier about his receiving money from Cuban Intelligence.

1980—Book, *Assassination on Embassy Row,* by John Dinges and Saul Landau, continues propaganda campaign against Chile, CIA, and U.S. government, based on Letelier killing. Receives a moderately favorable review in *New York Times,* although reviewer says "the main actors in the drama are superficially and sometimes clumsily portrayed....We are expected to believe that the first word spoken by Letelier's infant son, Christian, was 'Allende'."

Credits

There is no record of any of Landau's films or published works that could be considered critical of Communist aggression, subversion, or tyranny.

The Center for National Security Studies

This organization was founded in 1974 through the initiative of the National Lawyers Guild and the Institute for Policy Studies. It was funded initially by the Fund for Peace and the American Civil Liberties Union Foundation. (For further details see the Chapter on the Far Left Lobby.)

The following balance sheet of its published works is taken from its "Publications" for March 1980:

Debits

—*The Lawless State: The Crimes of the U.S. Intelligence Agencies* by Halperin, Jerry Berman, Robert Borosage, & Christine

Marwick. Covers the activities of the CIA, FBI, IRS, military intelligence, and "politically motivated" grand juries, and details such operations as the overthrow of the "democratic government" of Chile.

—*The CIA File,* edited by Borosage and John Marks. Papers presented at the 1974 CNSS Conference on the CIA, entirely by CIA opponents except for William Colby, who was subjected to an hour and a half harangue during the question period. (See page 51 for further details.)

—*FBI Charter Legislation Comparison.* Compares the proposed FBI Charter Act of 1979 with other recommendations, including Attorney General Levi's guidelines, the Church Committee proposals, and recommendations by opponents of the FBI like the ACLU and the Committee for Public Justice.

—*The CIA and the Freedom of Information Act: Report on the Proposal for an Exemption.* This criticizes the CIA's testimony that the present FOIA is crippling the Agency's ability to maintain foreign agents and gain the cooperation of foreign intelligence services.

—*From Officials' File: Abstracts of Documents on National Security and Civil Liberties Available from CNSS Library.* Catalogue of materials in CNSS files, available for researchers. Documents have been obtained by FOIA releases and discovery processes in law suits, most formerly classified. Many obtained "only after a courtroom struggle." Includes such items as: transcripts of Kissinger's off-the-record press conferences on Middle East and SALT, FBI surveillance of J. Robert Oppenheimer, DOE Report on uranium diversion and theft, documents on intelligence operations by state and local police, etc.

—*Comparison of Proposals for Reforming the Intelligence Communities,* by Berman, Mark Drooks, Halperin, and Barbara Pollack. Compares the Church Committee report, Carter's Executive Order and the Senate Intelligence Committee 1978 and 1980 bills.

—*Nuclear Power and Civil Liberties,* by Allan Adler and Jay Peterzell. "Critics of nuclear power have said it presents a major risk to civil liberties because the nuclear materials provide a powerful justification for surveillance of protesters and other measures."

—*Operation Chaos* by Jay Peterzell. Comparison of Church Committee account of CHAOS with other later information gained through FOIA and lawsuit by ACLU.

—*Freedom vs. National Security* by Halperin and David Hoffman. 600 page "sourcebook" on cases and statutes on such topics as Pentagon Papers, CIA, Viet Nam, and Watergate.

—*The Federal Bureau of Investigation.* A pamphlet that "reviews the Bureau's history and lays out recommendations for reform . . . . The FBI's long-term apparatus for surveilling American citizens and targeting movements for social change have not been put under control."

—*National Security and Civil Liberties* by Morton Halperin. Deals with wiretap law.

—*The CIA Corporate Shell Game* by John Marks. On CIA proprietary companies such as Air America, which "are another area of unregulated clandestine operations."

—*The Grand Juries: An American Inquisition,* by Judy Mead.

—*Top Secret: National Security and the Right to Know,* by Halperin and Hoffman. Case studies of "several of the country's biggest secrecy snafus—the Pentagon Papers, the bombing of Cambodia, the Angolan intervention."

—*Documents: A Collection from the Secret Files of the American Intelligence Community,* by Christy Macy and Susan Kaplan. Reproduces "a selection from the paper trail left behind by improper intelligence agency programs."

—*FOIA Litigation Manual* edited by Christine Marwick. Technical manual for attorneys on "all aspects of Freedom of Information and Privacy Acts."

—*Using the Freedom of Information Act: A Step by Step Guide.*

Credits

There is no record that the Center for National Securities Studies has conducted any "studies" of the threat to American "security" posed by the KGB or Communist propaganda or subversive activities. The CNSS statement of purpose says that it was founded "to reduce government secrecy, to limit the surveillance of Americans by intelligence agencies, to prohibit surveillance or manipulation of lawful political activity, and to protect the rights of Americans to write and speak on issues affecting the national security." The organization has never attempted to study the degree of surveillance of American citizens or American defense or industrial activities by *Communist* intelligence agencies. One hundred percent of its studies have been aimed at the CIA, FBI, and other American agencies. It has ignored the well-documented evidence of Communist espionage and surveillance; for example, the interception of American telecommunications traffic and the massive and growing activities in espionage and propaganda in the U.S. by the KGB and other Soviet organs.

Institute for Policy Studies

This section arrays the published output of the IPS, classified as to whether it is for or against a Communist line. Further details on the IPS are given in the chapter on the Far Left Lobby, page 44.

The following balance sheet is based on the Fall 1979 IPS Catalogue and a supplement for Summer/Fall 1980. These provide the titles and brief descriptions of 80 publications and 14 films. Ten of the films were directed by Saul Landau and were described earlier in this appendix. The remaining four films and 80 publications are the subject of this section.

Out of these 84 items, 68 are found to be closely parallel to the Communist line in their main subject matter and orientation as described in the IPS Catalogue. For example, many advocate unilateral American disarmament, attack the U.S. intelligence community, or analyze the American economy from a "class conflict" point of view. The remaining 14 might most charitably be called neutral. Although not necessarily paralleling a Communist line, even these are generally critical of American institutions, including such titles as *Whistle-Blowers' Guide to the Federal Bureaucracy, Industrial Exodus* ("a classic study of strategies for preventing plant closings and run-away shops"), and so forth.

This section does not describe all 84 items in the IPS Catalogue, but presents a sampling of typical titles and quotes from the descriptions given in the catalogue. (Emphasis has been added in some of the descriptions.)

Debits

—*The Politics of National Security* by Marcus Raskin. "This historical analysis of the *national security state* traces its evolution from a planning instrument to ensure national stability, *mute class conflicts,* and secure the domestic economy to the basis for overt and covert *imperialism.* The debacle in Indochina, *the genocidal nature of the arms race . . . . etc.*"

—*The Search for 'Manchurian Candidate': The CIA and Mind Control* by John Marks.

—*The Lawless State: The Crimes of the Intelligence Community*" by Halperin, Borosage, Berman, and Marwick.

—*The Counterforce Syndrome* by Robert C. Aldridge. "How 'counterforce' has replaced 'deterrence' contrary to what most Americans believe . . . ."

—*Dubious Specter—A Second Look at the "Soviet Threat"* by Fred Kaplan.

—*The Rise and Fall of the "Soviet Threat"* by Alan Wolfe.

—*Resurgent Militarism* by Michael T. Klare. "An analysis of the growing militaristic fervor which is spreading from Washington across the nation . . . ."

—*NATO's Unremarked Demise* by Earl C. Ravenal. "A critique of the Atlantic Alliance . . . . This study refutes two assumptions of the post WWII era: that the defense of Europe is required for the balance of power, and that 'interdependence' is required for our national security. A drastically changed international system invites American disengagement from Europe."

—*The Economy of Death* by Richard J. Barnet. ". . . . . this trenchant analysis of the defense budget exposes how the military-industrial complex manipulates public expenditures to squander vast sums in useless hardware . . . . Social costs of this waste require a program of national conversation to an 'Economy of Life' achieved by citizen action in defiance of this threat."

—*Intervention and Revolution* by Richard J. Barnet. "A classic study of American intervention in developing nations. This lucid work refutes the Cold War tenets of U.S. foreign policy and document the *history of repressive military intervention.*"

—*The Sullivan Principles: Decoding Corporate Camouflage*, by Elizabeth Schmidt. "An analysis of the Sullivan Principles, the fair employment code devised by American corporations in South Africa to deflect public criticism of investment in that country." (Actually this code was not developed by American corporations but by the Rev. Leon H. Sullivan, pastor of the Zion Baptist Church, the largest church in North Philadelphia, and one of the most respected black ministers in the U.S. Sullivan devised these principles as a means of allowing the blacks in South Africa to have the benefits of employment by American corporations without the corporations being parties to encouragement of apartheid.)

—*How the Other Half Dies* by Susan George. "This examination of multinational agribusiness corporations explains that the roots of hunger are not overpopulation, changing climate, or bad weather, but rather control of food by the rich."

—*The Dead Are Not Silent.* Film produced by Studio H&S of Communist East Germany, describes the overthrow of the Allende government in Chile as told by two women—Isabel Letelier and Moy de Toha.

Credits

No publications are listed that could be considered to oppose a Communist line in any respect. In none of the many studies of U.S. defense policies is there any recognition of the danger of the Soviet arms build-up. In fact many of the books specifically discount this threat. There is no mention of the work of the KGB or Soviet propaganda organs. While there is considerable treatment of American multi-nationals and "monopolies", there is nothing about the problems of Communist monopolistic practices in such areas as grain purchasing or the setting of shipping rates, which is now causing grave problems for free world shipping.

DEDICATION, ACKNOWLEDGEMENTS, AND WHY THIS BOOK WAS WRITTEN

Dedications usually appear at the beginning, but this one has been placed at the end for a special reason. Readers should appreciate its significance much more fully after having read (at least partially) the book itself.

This book is dedicated as a small tribute to the hundreds or even thousands of Americans serving in AID, the CIA, and other American agencies who devoted their careers to encouraging the spread of Democracy and combatting Communism and who have remained unsung and even vilified, largely as a result of the propaganda of that same Communism.

I met several such AID workers during a trip to Viet Nam in 1972. There was Dr. Daniel Hays, who had spent seven years in charge of the AID education program in the Mekong Delta and had adopted three Vietnamese girls as his daughters. This was only the latest in a series of hardship or hazardous posts during his career. Dr. Norman Hoover had given up a position at the Mayo Clinic to head the AID-American Medical Association team advising the Saigon University Medical School (started from scratch in 1954 and the first medical school in South Viet Nam.) The school was graduating 200 doctors a year by 1972. Dr. Hoover married a Vietnamese, one of the country's few physiotherapists.

Bill Williamson, a burly former agricultural agent from Texas, spent six years in the field as a senior advisor in the AID agricultural program, assisting the Vietnamese to launch the "Green Revolution" which more than doubled their productivity in rice and other grains and was doing much to put them back on a self-sufficient basis in food production. Williamson spent most of his time not in a Saigon office but out in the 95 degree heat of the rice paddies, orchards, and hog farms, literally getting down to the grass roots to implement the program. "You take me away from the farmers—you've lost me," Williamson said to me during a rough jeep ride out into the Delta rice country.

Robert Mueller was a former English teacher who had served in the Navy off Viet Nam and then got himself assigned there as a civilian with the U.S. Information Agency. He spent five years in the country, learning fluent Vietnamese and travelling all over the South. During his tour in Saigon he refused to live in the air conditioned bachelor officers quarters, but rented an apartment in a neighborhood inhabited only by Vietnamese to get to know the people better. He married a Vietnamese and when Saigon fell, he was one of the last Americans to leave.

Such people and many like them had made tremendous progress in helping the Vietnamese help themselves as they emerged from colonialism and attempted to fight off an aggressive enemy. All of this work, of course, was swallowed up when the Communists won the military and propaganda war in 1975.

I had devoted my "vacation" to go to Viet Nam in October 1972 at my own expense to investigate civilian developments in education, medicine, agriculture, and land reform. Two magazines had expressed interest in my story suggestions. I did not intend to pose as an instant expert after a three-week visit, but I was able to interview a large number of true experts, Americans with many years experience and Vietnamese of many political beliefs. These included three Cabinet officials; the head of the largest labor confederation, Mr. Tran Quoc Buu (See Chapter X), who was opposed to Thieu but greatly preferred his government to the Communists; several refugees who had fled the Communist "Easter Invasion" of 1972; and various Third Force politicians opposed to the South Vietnamese Government.

I was surprised at the progress of civilian development in spite of the fact that South Viet Nam had become independent only in 1954 and had been fighting a guerilla war for ten years.

The influence of Communist propaganda first struck me when I returned from this trip in November 1972. It was a great shock to be exposed again to the coverage of Viet Nam provided by most of the American media—the TV networks and the "northeastern liberal press." The South Vietnamese Government was generally portrayed as a dictatorial tyranny with no popular support, propped up only by its own army and large police force and the American military. American involvement was pictured as a vast mistake from which we were now wisely withdrawing. The contributions of the of the U.S. to helping the Vietnamese defend themselves from Communist aggression and our contributions to civilian progress were completely ignored.

My own opinions were well expressed by another man who had visited Viet Nam in October 1972: Dr. Sheldon Penman, Professor of Biology at M.I.T. He wrote a letter to the *New York Times,* which appeared soon after my return:

> It is impossible for me to reconcile your editorial stand on Vietnam, as expressed on October 11, with the reality I perceived on a recent visit to that country. I found a lively, vital, and relatively open society that has made impressive strides in education, medical care, land reform, etc. against what seems insuperable obstacles . . .

> I went to South Viet Nam as a private citizen to learn as much as possible in a brief visit about higher education, medical training, and the society in general. For background information I had, of course, the benefit of the efforts of some 400 reporters covering a country the size of Florida.

> I might as well have gone to the moon for all the information our media carry on these subjects . . .

> South Viet Nam can be freely entered by the news media and by private citizens. In contrast, North Viet Nam is accessible only to politically reliable visitors. As a consequence, as great an institution as *The Times* concludes that there is little worth supporting in the open society, and by implication, the closed one should be permitted to carry out its aggression.

Dr. Penman's letter struck a responsive chord in many other *Times* readers, and he received several letters, including the following from David Lilienthal, former director of the Tennessee Valley Authority:

> Your letter in the *N. Y. Times* of November 12 encouraged me to believe that there are many others like yourself who know enough about South Viet Nam to sense that the affirmative story of that nation's efforts to build their country has rarely been told.

> At the urgent request of President Johnson, a technical staff from my firm spent some three years working jointly with a group of Vietnamese from the Vietnamese private sector studying the postwar development prospects of that country. Our report, delivered in May of 1969, was published in English by Praeger. Of what has happened in that country since the com-

pletion of that report I have no firsthand knowledge and, therefore, read your own observations with particular interest."

Some of the distortions in American media during this period seemed so drastic that they must have been more than simply the result of bias by liberal humanitarians concerned about the supposed evils of an "unjust" war.

I have not attempted in this book to debate the pros and cons of American involvement in the war. That controversy became so complex and has not yet been resolved. In fact I do not deal at all with the propaganda campaign against American participation in the war. There is one chapter on the campaign to whitewash the North Vietnamese *after* their conquest in 1975. But it is sufficient to say here that the distortions in American media in 1972 were enough to arouse my concern that much of this might be the result of Communist propaganda efforts. This in turn led me to begin to study Communist propaganda as a whole and how it might be influencing American media, public opinion, and government policy.

One of the first thing I discovered was that there had been very little study of this subject for almost 10 years. During the 1950s and early 60's there had been extensive research by such scholars as Harold Lasswell, Frederick Barghoorn, Phillips Davison, and Ithiel Pool, but after 1965 the subject seemed to fall out of favor with academic and government scholars, probably as being out of style during a period of "Detente." Many knowledgeable people assured me, however, that it was worth a new study. Dr. Frank Trager, professor of International Affairs at New York University and director of research at the National Strategy Information Center, was the first to give me some advice. I began an effort that has taken up a large part of my spare time (nights, weekends. and vacations) for the past five years. Others who have given valuable advice include Frank Barnett, also of the National Strategy Information Center, and many on the staff of the American Security Council, including Elbridge Dubrow and Charles Murphy. Charles Wiley, director of the National Committee for Responsible Patriotism and a long time expert on Communist propaganda, provided some extremely valuable suggestions and co-authored Chapter XI on the Neutron Bomb. Invaluable assistance was also provided by Accuracy in Media Inc., the organization in Washington dedicated to monitoring TV and the press, and especially Reed Irvine, Bernard Yoh, and Cliff Kincaid. The back files of their *AIM Report* were an indispensible source on media performance. Publications of the Church League of

America were also very valuable.

William Henderson of the American-Asian Educational Exchange provided some productive leads in the early stages.

Mr. and Mrs. Sidney Jaffe of the Institute of Propaganda Analysis in Chicago had many suggestion.

Three energetic young people in Darien, Connecticut also provided help on research: Priscilla Williams Bercovici, Vivianne Carley and Larry Casey.

NOTES TO CHAPTER I

1. Brian Crozier, *Strategy of Survival* (New Rochelle, 1978).

2. Speech at the session on "Media Coverage of Closed Societies," Accuracy in Media Conference, Washington, D.C., November, 1979. He has expressed similar ideas in articles in *Commentary, National Review,* and the Rockford Institute's *Chronicles of Culture.*

There was an ominous undercurrent of such concern at the Republican Convention in 1980. It was often noticeable that when a speaker turned to foreign policy, the delegates were apt to fall silent, mute the cheers, and listen with worried attention. Reagan, Bush, and the other leaders generally did not go into details, probably to avoid creating a negative atmosphere. But Senator Goldwater was the frankest, saying in his address, "This may be the last convention of the Republican Party or any other party, if we do not turn this country around."

Many other American experts on Communist policies who are equally knowledgeable but less well known to the public have expressed similar views:

—Philip C. Clarke, a journalist with 20 years experience covering American military and political affairs in the U.S. and abroad for AP, Newsweek, and Mutual Broadcasting, said in early 1980 that if we do not reverse the present trend to cripple American intelligence agencies and halt the decline of U.S. military strength within the next year, "it's all over." (Clark is the author of *National Security and the News Media,* America's Future Inc., New Rochelle, N.Y. 1979.)

—Charles Wiley, a foreign correspondent and expert on Communist propaganda for 25 years, has visited more than 100 countries and covered six wars. In 1979 he was one of the first Americans to be given a tour of the Chinese-Soviet border by the Chinese military. "We have one more year to reverse our military and intelligence decline," he says, "or we've had it." (Wiley co-authored Chapter XI in this book on the Neutron Bomb. For further details on his background, see the notes to that chapter.)

—William J. Clements, Jr., governor of Texas and former deputy secretary of defense, says, "We in the United States face greater danger today than we did in December, 1941, after Pearl Harbor."

—General Lewis W. Walt, former Assistant Commandant, Marine Corps, in his recent book, *Eleventh Hour,* states, "No generation of Americans has ever before been so recklessly placed at the mercy of so pitiless and powerful an enemy. At the current rate of Soviet military growth, they may soon be in a position to offer the U.S. an ultimatum to either surrender or be incinerated in a nuclear holocaust....the alternative of fighting a thermonuclear war we cannot win or handing over the American people to an oligarchy of tyrants whose viciousness and brutality have no match in the long, bloody history of man's cruelty."

—The 1979-80 edition of *Jane's Fighting Ships* (London) says that the U.S. and other non-Communist powers have allowed their naval power to decline to a point where they will soon be vulnerable to Soviet blackmail.

—The American Security Council in Washington, though its monthly *Washington Report* and in press conferences and seminars, has disseminated the views of several senior retired military officers that the U.S. is in a disastrously weak position. These include Lt. General Daniel O. Graham, former chief of the Defense Intelligence Agency; Major General George Keegan, former Air Force chief of

Intelligence; Admiral Thomas Moorer, former chairman, Joint Chiefs of Staff; and Major General John Singlaub, former chief of staff of the Army Forces Command, who resigned over a disagreement with U.S. policy in Korea.

3. Correspondence between Senator Gordon Humphrey and FBI and Justice Department personnel, August 22 through November 27, 1979.

4. This simple method was suggested as long ago as 1967 by Suzanne Labin, the French expert on Communism, in *The Techniques of Soviet Propaganda* (Washington: Government Printing Office). Dr. Igor Glagolev has also pointed out that we can detect pro-Communist journalists by simply examining how much of their output is pro or anti the Soviets. (Quoted by John Rees in *Infiltration of the Media by the KGB and Its Friends* Washington, 1978).

NOTES TO CHAPTER II

1. "The Soviet and Communist Bloc Defamation Campaign," *Congressional Record*, Sept. 28, 1965.

2. John Barron, *KGB: The Secret Work of Soviet Secret Agents* (New York, 1974), p. 166-174.

3. *New York Times*, 21 and 29 July, 1963; 7 and 8 July, 1964. *Newsweek*, 7 October 1963.

4. Leo Bogart, "Premises for Propaganda," USIA Report completed in 1954, published for the first time in 1976 (New York).

5. "Soviet Covert Action and Propaganda," presented to the House Committee on Intelligence, by the deputy director for operations, CIA, February 1980.

6. *Newsletter*, East European Bible Mission, Roosendaal, The Netherlands, February/March 1979.

7. 11 March, 1977.

8. Hedrick Smith, *The Russians* (New York, 1976).

9. Edward J. Epstein, *Legend: The Secret World of Lee Harvey Oswald* (New York, 1978). Epstein quotes evidence that Oswald had attended a school for agit props in Minsk, that he later claimed to be experienced in "street agitation," and that he was said by friends in Dallas to have some skill in political argumentation.

10. Herbert Philbrick, *I Led Three Lives* (New York, 1952), pp. 10 ff.

11. Alexander Kasnacheev, *Inside a Soviet Embassy* (Philadelphia, 1962), pp. 101 ff.

12. Quoted by Anthony Cave-Brown, *Bodyguard of Lies* (New York, 1975), p. 268.

13. A. Doak Barnett, *Cadres, Bureaucracy, and Political Power in Communist China* (New York, 1967), pp. 200-201.

14. See, for example, a speech by the late Eric Chou, a Chinese defector formerly with the Chinese propaganda apparatus and editor of a Communist newspaper in Hong Kong, in "Media Coverage of Closed Societies," Accuracy in Media Conference, Washington, November, 1979.

15. Victor Riesel, "The Red Star of Peking," column, 25 August 1977.

16. Allen C. Brownfield, "Is Pro-Peking Effort Red Made?" *Human Events*, 7 May 1977.

17. Adam B. Ulam, *The Bolsheviks* (New York, 1965), p. 176.

18. Quoted by John Rees, *Infiltration of the Media by the KGB and Its Friends*, Washington: Accuracy in Media Inc., 1978.

19. House Subcommittee on Oversight, "The CIA and the Press," Statement by John H. Maury, 27 December 1977.

20. Frederick G. Barghoorn, *Soviet Foreign Propaganda* (Princeton, 1964), pp. 22-26.

21. Philbrick, *Three Lives*.

22. Kaznacheev, *Inside*, p. 101.

23. See also House Subcommittee on Intelligence report, "Soviet Covert Action (The Forgery Offensive)," 16 February 1980.

24. Howland H. Sargeant, *Soviet Propaganda* (New York: National Strategy Information Center, 1972.)

25. Henry Kissinger, *White House Years* (Boston, 1979), p. 112. Dr. Franz Gross, Professor of Political Science and Dean of the Faculty at the University of New

Haven, is a student of Soviet policy and has had frequent contact with Arbatov and the U.S. Institute, most recently at the Moscow Conference on Social Science in August 1979. He says that there are several scholars in that institute who are more knowledgeable about American affairs, but Arbatov is the most skilled at communicating with Americans. Analysis of foreign countries for purposes of advising on propaganda and subversion is a major industry in the USSR. The Academy of Sciences has several institutes in addition to the U.S., including a large force working on Africa.

26. *Newsweek* gave Arbatov an entire page for an "exclusive" article, 28 May 1970 on why the Russians want the SALT II treaty and "what the Soviet response would be to Senate-imposed changes." On 13 July 1979 the *New York Times* ran an article on the Op-Ed page by one of Arbatov's subordinates, Genrikh A. Trofimenko, entitled "Too Many Negotiators," arguing that if the Senate amends the treaty the world will wonder "who exactly in the U.S. can speak on international relations." The Galbraith scene was cited by Mrs. Mimi Jaffe of the Institute of Propaganda Analysis, Chicago.

27. Miles Copeland, *Beyond Cloak & Dagger: Inside the CIA* (New York, 1975), Afterword.

28. "European Security and the Soviet Problem," Institute for the Study of Conflict, *Bulletin*, London, January 1972.

29. Interview with Mr. Ray Wannall, 9 February 1979.

30. *New York Times*, 9 October 1977. *Situation Report*, Washington: Security & Intelligence Fund, March 1979.

31. Senate Subcommittee on Internal Security hearings, 1965.

32. Subcommittee on Internal Security, 18 November 1975.

33. Bruce Cook, *Dalton Trumbo* (New York, 1977), and John T. Flynn, *While You Slept — Our Tragedy in Asia and Who Made It* (Old Greenwich, 1951, reprinted several times as late as 1971). Contrary to Trumbo's statement, Flynn says that more than 30 films made in Hollywood in the 1930s and 40s promoted Soviet ideas in one way or another.

34. Barron, *KGB*. The entire manual is reprinted starting on p. 346.

35. Copeland, *Beyond Cloak and Dagger*. See especially the Afterword of the paperback edition, which was written after the massive attacks on the CIA in the media in 1974 and 1975 and contains information Copeland had considered too confidential to discuss earlier.

36. Tomas Schuman (formerly Yuri Besmenoff), Seminar on "KGB and Novostii Tactics in Canada," Hart House, University of Toronto, 3 April, 1978. "No 'Novostii' is Good Novostii," by Tomas Schuman, *World Peace and Freedom Monthly* (Toronto, June 1978.)

37. Douglas Waples, in *Public Opinion Quarterly* (Spring 1956).

NOTES TO CHAPTER III

1. Francis M. Watson, *The Movement: Role of U.S. Activists*, Conflict Studies #80 (London: Institute for the Study of Conflict, February 1977).

2. The American Security Council has named many of these groups "The Anti-Defense Lobby." See *Washington Report*, December 1978. Dr. Ernest W. Lefever and Roy Godson of the Ethics & Public Policy Center of Georgetown University describe the role of many of them and call them "The Anti-Intelligence Lobby" in *The CIA and the American Ethic* (Washington, 1979).

3. See *Foreign Broadcast Information Service* and *Digest of the Soviet Press*.

4. Research Department, Church League of America, *Protecting Traitors, Spies, and Terrorist* (Wheaton, Ill., 1978), pp. 42, 56, etc

5. Church League, *Attorneys for Treasons, The True Story of the National Lawyers Guild* (Wheaton, 1975), pp. 12, 21, etc. See also the Senate Internal Security Subcommittee report, January 1975.

6. *AIM Report*, January 1979 II.

7. Senate Internal Security Subcommittee, 25 October 1951; 31 August 1960. HUAC Annual Report, 9 September 1960. Rabinowitz's wife, Marcia, also refused to answer such questions.

8. The Lubells, twin brothers with the Biblical names of David and Jonathan, pleaded the Fifth Amendment when asked about CP membership before the Senate Internal Security Committee in March 1953. They were identified as Communists by an undercover agent of the FBI testifying before HUAC in March 1958.

9. *Attorneys for Treason*, p. 42. *Human Events*, 4 December 1976, 4 February 1978. *Information Digest*, 29 September 1978. William Buckley column, 7 April 1980.

10. Gluck was identified as a Communist by an undercover informant for the N.Y. Police Department, testifying before the House Un-American Activities Committee on May 3, 1955. In appearance before the Committee on November 14, 1962 he invoked the Fifth Amendment.

O'Connor was identified as a Communist by former Communist, Benjamin Gitlow, before HUAC on September 13, 1939.

Wilkinson was identified as a Communist by an undercover operative of the FBI testifying before HUAC on December 7, 1956. On the same day and again in July 1958, he appeared before HUAC and refused to answer questions about Party membership. In 1958 he was cited for contempt, convicted by a Fedeal District Court in Atlanta in January 1959, and sentenced to a year in jail. In 1961 the Supreme Court upheld this conviction. He served nine months of the one year sentence. (HUAC Annual Report, 1962.)

Stavis invoked the Fifth Amendment when asked about Communist Party membership before HUAC on February 28, 1956.

For further details on the pro-Communist activities of these individuals, see "The Nationwide Drive Against Law Enforcement Intelligence Agencies," report of the Senate Internal Security Subcommittee, 11 July, 1975, and *Protecting Traitors*.

11. *Protecting Traitors*, p. 23. Center for Constitutional Rights, *Docket Report* 1979/80. *Say 'No' to the FBI*, C.C.R. (1979).

12. *Protecting Traitors*, pp. 18, 55. "Campaign to Outlaw U.S. Foreign & Domestic Intelligence," Rep. Larry McDonald, *Congressional Record*, 27 April 1977. *Information Digest*, 29 September 1978.

13. Obituary of Rubin by Carey McWilliams, *Nation*, 6 January 1979. The ambergris incident was described by Sam Baron, an American correspondent in Spain during the Spanish Civil War for the Socialist newspaper, *The Call*. Baron went to Spain as an enthusiastic backer of the Republican Government, but became disillusioned by the extent of Communist domination of the Loyalist cause. Arrested by the Communists and almost executed, he returned to the U.S. to denounce Communist manipulation of the Republican Government and their assassination of Loyalist opponents. He broke with Norman Thomas in the Socialist Party, who preferred to overlook Communist excesses in Spain in order to maintain the united front against Fascism. (HUAC Hearings, November 1938, pp. 2522 ff.)

14. Joseph Shattan, "Why Breira?", *Commentary*, April 1977. For an example of pro-PLO efforts by Breira see Arthur Waskow article in *New York Times* 28 June 1975. Breira's monthly letter, *Interchange*, contains much thinly-disguised anti-Israel material and attacks on U.S. pro-Israel policies. The name, *Breira*, means "alternative," which in itself is something of a needle into Israel, since the Israel motto is "Ein Breira," which freely translated means, "We have no alternative." Breira ceased operating in 1980, perhaps because of growing unfavorable publicity.

15. *Protecting Traitors*, p. 61.

16. Ibid., p. 45.

17. *New York Times*, 17 June 1980.

18. *Protecting Traitors*, p. 27 *Information Digest*, 7 April 1978, 21 April 1978. Rep. Larry McDonald, "Eurocommunism in America—Grassroots Organizing," *Congressional Record*, 8 February 1978.

19. McDonald, *Congressional Record*, 10 September 1975.

20. Allen C. Brownfield, "Carter's Radical Fringe," *Human Events*, 11 November 1978.

21. *Wall Street Journal*, 21 September 1978.

22. *New York Times*, 28 August 1980.

23. Paul Dickson, *Think Tanks* (New York: Atheneum, 1971), p. 276. (Written under a grant of the University Fellowship for Reporting from the American Political Science Association at George Washington University.)

24. *Foreign Affairs.*

25. John Rees, "Infiltration of the Media by the KGB and Its Friends," paper presented at Accuracy in Media Conference, April 1978.

26. *Information Digest* 21 April 1978; Heritage Foundation, Report on Institute for Policy Studies, May 1977; *Protecting Traitors,* p. 47.

27. *AIM Reports* from January 1977 through January 1978 give a complete account of how the leading media completely failed to report the contents of the Letelier Papers, one of the major coverups of recent history. A good analysis of the significance of the Letelier Papers and Letelier's real role in a Communist propaganda network appears in "The Mysterious Letelier Affair: Another Rush to Judgment" by Virginia Prewett, Special Report of the Council for Inter-American Security, September 1978. Prewett is a journalist who has won Columbia University's Cabot Award and the Overseas Press Club's Citation for reporting on Latin America. Many of the Letelier papers were inserted in the *Congressional Record* of 23 June 1977 by Congressman Larry McDonald.

28. CIA Report on Propaganda, Appendix B of "The CIA and the Media" Hearings of the House Committee on Intelligence, April 1978.

29. *Far Eastern Economic Review,* 4 November 1977. *News World,* 23 August 1978.

30. *Congressional Record,* 23 June 1977, p. H6441.

31. See testimony of Major General George Keegan, Jr., before the National Committee to Restore Internal Security, Washington, D.C., Feb. 15, 1980, published in the *Hearings of the N.C.R.I.S.,* 305 Fourth St. N.E., Washington, D.C. 20002.

32. *Protecting Traitors,* p. 27; Borosage and Marks, *The CIA File* (New York, 1976); Halperin, Borosage, Berman, and Marwick, *The Lawless State: The Crimes of the U.S. Intelligence Agencies* (New York, 1976).

33. William A. Colby, *Honorable Men* (New York, 1978), p. 381.

34. "CNSS Publications," March 1980. For further comments on the CNSS see the CIA chapter and the Appendix.

35. Church League, *Headquarters for Destruction,* 1972.

36. *Foreign Report,* 10 August 1977.

37. *Human Events,* 28 May 1977; *AIM Report,* May 1977.

38. *Human Events,* 16 April 1977.

39. Church League, *Wild William Turner,* May 1972; *Protecting Traitors,* p. 34.

40. *Protecting Traitors,* pp. 29, 42, 49. AIM Conference on the Media, April 1978, Session on "Infiltration of the Media," statements by Francis McNamara, former Director of the Subversive Activities Control Board, and John Rees.

41. From "Jane: An Intimate Biogaphy of Jane Fonda" by Thomas Kiernan (New York, 1973), quoted in "Betraying America—the Jane Fonda-Tom Hayden Axis," Church League, 1980.

42. This information on the activities of the Riverside Church has been taken from its own publications and the announcements of the Connecticut conferences. In 1974 according to *The Pink Sheet on the Left* for November 3, 1980, the Rev. Coffin endorsed Joelle Fishman for Congress in Connecticut's Third District. Fishman, a Communist and an atheist, was the candidate of the Communist Party (USA).

NOTES TO CHAPTER IV

1. Leonard R. Sussman (Director of Freedom House, New York), "Developmental Journalism—A Backward Idea Whose Time Has Come," *Quadrant* magazine (Sydney, Australia), November 1976.

2. Ronald Reagan, "Taking A Look at UNESCO," *Human Events,* 7 January 1978.

3. CIA Report on Communist Propaganda of 3 July 1978, appendix to "The CIA and the Media," House Committee on Intelligence, 1978, pp. 600-603.

4. See for example, "Media Unfair to Developing World," speech by Carlos Romulo, Philippines Secretary of Foreign Affairs, in *South China Morning Post,* 8 April 1977 and *Far Eastern Economic Review,* 8 April 1977. Also "A Call to Broaden the News" by Mustapha Masmoudi, Chairman of the Intergovernmental Council for the Coordination of Information in the Non-Aligned Countries, Op-Ed

TARGET AMERICA

Page, *New York Times*, 8 June 1977.

5. Sussman, "The 'March' Through the World's Mass Media," *Orbis*, Winter 1977, and "The Rage to Regulate the Press," *Freedom At Issue*, September-October, 1979.

6. For some of the opposition see *Wall Street Journal* 7 September 1978; *Christian Science Monitor*, 26 October 1978; *The Economist*, 1 December 1978; *Far Eastern Economic Review*, 8 December 1978. The complete UNESCO Compromise Declaration appears in the *New York Times*, 23 November 1978.

7. Sussman, "Press Licensing, Penalties for 'Error' Proposed Anew at UNESCO," *Freedom at Issue*, May-June 1979; "Press Freedom in 1979," *Freedom At Issue*, January-February 1980.

NOTES TO CHAPTER V

1. See Sir Robert Thompson, *Defeating Communist Insurgency*, New York, 1966. (The recent history of Malaysia is complex. The territories on the Malay Peninsula were named "Malaya" when they were granted independence by the British in 1957. After Sarawak and Sabah, former British colonies on the north coast of Borneo, were added to Malaya in 1963, the entire new country was renamed "Malaysia." To avoid confusion, the latter name is used throughout this chapter, although some of the events occurred before 1963.)

2. *Far Eastern Economic Review*, 17 September 1976.

3. *New York Times*, 28 May 1976.

4. *F.E.E.R.*, 25 June and 24 September 1976.

5. *F.E.E.R.*, 25 February 1977.

6. Singapore Government Press Statements, 11 and 16 February 1977.

7. *F.E.E.R.*, 5 January 1979. There was a more recent indication that the late Malcolm Caldwell's associates are still showing sympathies for the China-Pol Pot side of the Communist split in Asia. On January 25, 1980, *F.E.E.R.* published a letter from a Brian Maurice in England attacking the British Government for discontinuing recognition of the Pol Pot regime. Maurice had been a student of Caldwell's in London, who went to Singapore in 1972 to teach at the International School. Caldwell recommended him to Raman as a "liberal with leftist leanings." (Statement of G. Raman, Singapore Government, March 1977.) He was expelled by the Singapore Government later in 1977.

8. Singapore Government Press Statements, 19 February 1977 and 12 March 1977.

9. Singapore Government Press Statements, 11, 16, and 19 February 1977 and 12 March 1977.

10. *F.E.E.R.*, 25 June 1976 and 24 September 1976.

11. Statements of Arun Senkuttuvan, 28 February 1977, and G. Raman, 3 March 1977, Ministry of Home Affairs, Singapore. Singapore Government Press Statement, 16 March 1977.

12. Addendum to Ministry of Home Affairs Press Release, 26 March 1977.

13. *F.E.E.R.*, 17 September 1976.

14. *F.E.E.R.*, 31 December 1976. "The Prussians of Southeast Asia: Can They Be Stopped?", Frank Mount, *Asian Affairs*, July-August 1979.

13. "The KGB in Asia—Part II," *F.E.E.R.*, 31 December 1979. John Barron, "KGB—The Secret Work of Soviet Secret Agents," New York 1974, p. 399.

14. The F.E.E.R. for 8 April 1977 quotes the U.S. State Department annual report on human rights in 82 countries receiving foreign assistance. The paragraphs on Singapore read in part, "Access to legal guarantees for violations of rights is available, except for persons detained under the provisions of the Internal Security Act (ISA).... The right to a fair trial is scrupulously observed except for persons detained under the ISA.... As of September 1965 about 65 persons were detained under this act.... The Prime Minister has stated publicly that they have not been released because they refuse to agree not to use force to overthrow the Government and not to support the MCP."

15. Thompson in "Defeating Communist Insurgency" describes several cases where witnesses had given evidence of Communist murders and other subversive

acts but then refused to testify in open court after threats of reprisals.

16. AIM Report, August 1980 I. CIA Study: "Covert Action and Propaganda," February 6, 1980, in "Soviet Covert Action." Hearings Before the Subcommittee on Oversight, Permanent Select Committee on Intelligence, House of Representatives, February 6, 19, 1980, p. 59 ff. *Hearings of the National Committee to Restore Internal Security,* Vol. 5, "Soviet Disinformation, Testimony of Arnaud de Borchgrave," Oct. 1980.

NOTES TO CHAPTER VI

1. Kenneth M. Quinn, "Cambodia, 1976," *Asian Survey,* January 1977. Edith Lenart articles in *Far Eastern Economic Review,* 5 May, 28 May, and 28 June 1976. "Black Paper—Facts and Evidences of the Acts of Aggression and Annexation of Viet Nam Against Kampuchea" published by Democratic Kampuchea, September 1978. Although a publication of the Pol Pot regime is not to be considered reliable, the facts given in this booklet about Vietnamese ambitions do provide some indications and have been born out by later Vietnamese success in installing puppet regimes in Laos and Cambodia.
2. Douglas Pike, "Cambodia's War," *Southeast Asian Perspective,* March 1971.
3. *Newsweek,* 6 August 1973.
4. *Human Events,* 23 September 1973.
5. Pike, p. 42.
6. *Time,* March 14, 1977, p. 80.
7. Henry Kissinger, *White House Years* (Boston 1979), p. 460 ff.
8. Kissinger, p. 467.
9. See map in Kissinger, p. 471.
10. Kissinger, p. 507. Frank N. Trager, "After Vietnam: Dominoes and Collective Security," *Asian Affairs,* May-June 1975, p. 271 ff.
11. *F.E.E.R.* 10 September 1969, 10 October 1970, 5 August 1971, 25 February 1974. *Newsweek* 11 September 1972, p. 80. A note on Buddhist monks still assisting anti-Communist Cambodians in the refugee camps in Thailand in 1977 appears in *F.E.E.R.* of 30 September 1977.
12. Pike, p. 42.
13. Foreign Broadcast Information Service.
14. Digest of the Soviet Press.
15. *AIM Report,* 15 January 1977.
16. *Behind the Lines,* transcript of "The Back Page War," WNET Channel 13, 31 January 1975.
17. Quoted in Bruce Herschensohn, "The Gods of Antenna," (New Rochelle, 1976).
18. *F.E.E.R.,* 7 January 1977, 14 January 1977, etc.
19. "Sideswipe," *The Economist,* 4 August 1979, p. 79.
20. For more details on this visit to Cambodia by Dudman and Elizabeth Becker of the *Washington Post,* see Chapter VIII.
21. Foreword to "Sideshow."
22. "Dubcek," p. 223.
23. 13 January 1977, 3 May 1979, 1 June 1979, 31 December 1979, etc.
24. WNET Channel 13. Educational Broadcasting Corp. 30 October 1979, 8 P.M.
25. 23 July 1979.
26. Kissinger, p. 512.

NOTES TO CHAPTER VII

1. For a discussion of the statement, "We should not be the policeman of the world" and its possible source in Communist propaganda, see "Influence on U.S. Media by the KGB and its Friends," AIM Conference Session, 21 April 1978. Speakers: Francis McNamara and John Rees. Available on tape or transcript.
2. Foreign Broadcast Information Service, "Digest of the Soviet Press" 1975-76.
3. The issue of the *New Yorker* where this statement occurred contained ads for

imported Tanquerey Gin, hand-woven Khalabar rugs, Estée Lauder Copper and Bronze make-up, Trevira knits at Lord & Taylor, Ispansky fine china figurines at $450, English Leather Cologne, the 914 Porsche roadster, and 25 other pages of ads for similar examples of "decadent individualism."

Frances FitzGerald was a student of Paul Mus, a French scholar who developed the theory that Communism followed more closely in the Vietnamese tradition than did French culture. This may have some validity during the period of French colonial rule when most nationalistic Vietnamese felt oppressed by French imperial practice. But it does not apply to more recent times when the Vietnamese were attempting to gain independence from both the French *and* Communist imperialism. Stephen Young, who spent six years in Viet Nam with U.S. AID and reads and speaks fluent Vietnamese, wrote an article in *Orbis* of August saying that Communism and even Confucianism is contrary to ancient traditional Vietnamese mores, which put more stress on individuals' rights to self expression and self-improvement. Confuscianism was actually a veneer imposed on the Vietnamese with the Mandarinal system by the Chinese. He says that FitzGerald, who does not read Vietnamese and did not use native Vietnamese sources, never understood this.

4. House of Representatives, Subcommittee on International Organizations, Hearings on "Human Rights in Viet Nam," testimony of the Rev. Andre Gelinas, 16 June 1977, p. 28, and Theodore Jacqueney, pp. 55-60.

5. Carl Gershman partially summarizes these religious persecutions in "After the Dominoes Fall," *Commentary*, May 1978. Gershman is executive director of Social Democrats, U.S.A., and as such could hardly be considered a conservative hawk.

6. Washington Area League for Human Rights in Viet Nam and the Institute of American Relations, "Charter 78: An Appeal to the Human Conscience from the Suffering People of Viet Nam."

7. Theodore Jacquenay and Mrs. Jacqueline Lee (Tuyen's daughter), telephone interviews, 7 July 1979. Press release of Democracy International (Jacquenay's organization, 28 April 1979. *AFL-CIO Free Trade Union News*, September 1977. A late notice of Tuyen's death appeared in the *New York Times*, 11 July 1978. Jacquenay's original article on the prominent Third Force leaders in prison appeared in the *New York Times* 17 September 1976.)

8. Subcommittee on International Organizations Hearings, p. 57.

9. Reports on a Paris press conference 29 May 1978 held by the Khmer-Lao-Vietnamese Committee for the Defense of Human Rights in "Charter 78."

10. Ibid.

11. "Charter 78" includes a map of the identified prisons and prison camps in South Viet Nam as of May 1978. See p. 15.

12. *Worldwide Magazine*, p. 9. April 1977. It is impossible to summarize the available evidence on the horrors of the Vietnamese gulag in one or two pages. Another example is the following excerpts from a description by Nguyen Van Coi, a member of the Hoe Hao Buddhist sect who had been a representative in the provincial assembly of Quang Duc province in the Mekong Delta. He was arrested in August 1975, but after imprisonments in two prisons and a forced labor camp, he escaped and got out of Viet Nam by boat in October 1976. He also testified at the Subcommittee Hearing, p. 73.

"Our camp didn't have surrounding walls, no roof to cover us when it rained or snowed. It's capacity was only six people, living around the base of a tree trunk. At night our feet were chained to the tree just like chaining a dog. There were many animal groups like ours at the U Minh farm, and every group was provided a tree as a camp. The Communist government didn't want our labor and production. There was no purpose of re-education but the purpose was to beat and investigate us... Therefore, the people who supported the old regime were shipped away with the myth of studying and eventually they will die in the jungle... Many people died because of inadequate food and inadequate medicine. When a person died, the Communists threw the body in a big hole and covered it with dirt. There was no tombstone, no grave, and the relatives were not informed... They shined the light in my eyes, hung me upside down, and poured fish sauce in my nose, etc. I was not lucky because the Communists continued to beat me after I was unconscious, but I was luckier than anybody else because they did not want me to die, they wanted me to stay alive for more information."

13. Hearings, p. 8.
14. The 800,000 estimate was reported in the prestigious liberal French newspaper, *LeMonde*, which had been sympathetic to Hanoi during the war. *LeMonde* sent a team of reporters to Viet Nam at the invitation of the Communists. This team was able to gather enough evidence to return with a very negative impression of conditions under their hosts' regime. Reported in *Christian Science Monitor*, 10 October 1978. The estimate was also reported by William Dowell, Paris correspondent of *Time-Life* News Service. He based the estimate on refugee testimony. Reproduced in *Human Events*.
15. A colleague of Schurmann on the America's Third Century project and the Pacific News Service was T. D. Allman. Allman has authored several articles for the *New York Times Magazine, Harper's*, and the *Far Eastern Economic Review* with a far left bias.
16. Hearings, pp. 8, 21, etc.
17. Detailed transcripts of the TV cameramen's and producers' accounts of this incident and the AP story are found in *Big Story* by Peter Braestrup, published by Westview Press for Freedom House. These include several witnesses' testimony that the man was found armed during a battle outside the An Quang pagoda. pp. 460-462, 501, 503.
18. Hearings, p. 48.
19. Hearings, p. 61.
20. Accuracy in Media conducted several analyses of media reporting on the repression in Viet Nam. See *AIM Reports* for March 1976, September 1976, and July 1977.
21. *Human Events*, 6 November 1976, p. 3. Nat Hentoff, "Vietnam 1977: Is It Any of Our Business?", *Village Voice*, 8 February 1977.
22. Hentoff, *New York Times*, 30 December 1976.
23. Hentoff and telephone interviews with members of F.O.R. and SANE and with Theodore Jacquenay.
24. *Vietnam News*, (Vietnam Information Bureau, Cheverly, Md.) 20 October 1977.
25. Hearings, p. 148.
26. Hearings, p. 151.
27. "The Silence the World Calls Peace", *AIM Report*, March 1976, and *AIM Report*, September 1976 (Part I) and July 1977 (Part I).
28. *Far Eastern Economic Report*, 10 August 1979, p. 8, and 1 February 1980, p. 14.
29. See *AIM Report*, September 1980 (Parts 1 and II) for analyses of TV reporting on human rights, by country.
30. Taped recordings of four such programs were supplied to me by Robert Mueller, formerly with U.S. AID in Viet Nam and later on the staff of the House Committee on International Relations. These include *Far From Vietnam*, '67, a documentary by French pro-Hanoi activists, PBS, 2 January 1978; *Vietnam: Picking up the Pieces*, pro-Hanoi documentary produced by John Alpert, 11 April 1978; *Vietnam, 30 Months After the War*, PBS, 20 April 1978; and NBC Three-Part Series on Vietnam by Dan Oliver, March 1978.
31. *N.Y. Times*, 30 May 1979. Telephone interviews with members of F.O.R. and Joan Baez.
32. *Human Events*, 7 July 1979.
33. Quoted by Michael Ledeen in "Europe — The Good News and the Bad", *Commentary*, April 1979. A few others have made similar apologies for biased reporting. Uwe Siemon-Netto, a Vietnam corespondent & former Managing Editor of West Germany's largest Social Democratic daily, spoke at the AIM awards banquet on November 3, 1979 and wrote in the *International Herald Tribune* 15 June 1979, "I am now haunted by the role we journalists played in Vietnam. Those of us who wanted to find out knew of the evils of the Hanoi regime. We knew that after the division of the country, more than 1 million had fled south. Many of us had seen the tortured and carved up bodies of men, women, and children executed by the VC in the early phases of the war. And many of us saw in 1968 the mass graves of Hue... Why, for heavens sake, did we not report about these expressions of deliberate North Vietnamese strategy at least as extensively as of the My Lai mas-

sacre and other such isolated instances that were definitely not part of U.S. policy? What prompted us to make our readers believe that the Communists, once in power, would behave benignly? What made us belittle warnings by U.S. officials that a Communist victory would result in a massacre? . . ."

NOTES TO CHAPTER VIII
1. Including the International Mine, Mill, and Smelter Workers, the United Office and Professional Workers; Harry Bridges' International Longshoremen — West Coast; and the International Leather and Fur Workers. These examples were suggested to me by Murray Baron, President of Accuracy in Media, who at that time was Vice President of the International Leather and Plastics Goods Workers, and later a consultant on labor relations.
2. Including Herbert Philbrick, a young pacifist who had joined the Cambridge Youth Council, an anti-war group, in 1940. When this Council switched to support the war, Philbrick was so disillusioned that, suspecting manipulation, he talked to the FBI and became one of the most effective undercover agents in the Communist Party. See *I Led Three Lives*.
3. Foreign Broadcast Information Service.
4. *AIM Report*, April 1977, Part I; July 1977, Part I.
5. Catalogue of Center for International Policy reports. At the time of Goodfellow's article this was called the Institute for International Policy. The name may have been changed to avoid confusion with the Institute for Policy Studies, with which it has close relations.
6. *New York Times*, 15 June 1975. At a press luncheon in August 1975, Schanberg modified his opinions enough to admit that he and the *Times* had been wrong about the Khmer Rouge. He complimented the *Times* for its courage in admitting it. The *Times* had done so in their editorial mentioned above, but their news pages and Op Ed page continued to reveal a strong bias giving the Khmer Rouge the benefit of the doubt. Schanberg received the Pulitzer Prize for his reporting from Phnom Penh, presumably for his courage in staying behind after the fall, if not for his accuracy.
7. "Newswatch," *TV Guide*, 30 April 1977. Dr. Lefever is Director of the Center for Ethics and Public Policy of Georgetown University, which has made a number of major studies of media performance on public questions. In March 1981 he was nominated Assistant Secretary of State.
8. Vanderbilt TV Archieves.
9. For several years the *Times* editorial page under John Oakes showed a more sober appreciation of the Communist menace than most of the rest of the *Times*. Oakes has since retired to an advisory position.
10. *AIM Report* November 1977, Part I; December 1977, Part I.
11. *New York Times*, 11 September 1976.
12. House Subcommittee on International Organizations, Hearings on "Human Rights in Cambodia," 3 May 1977. Barron and Paul's descriptions of the eye-witness accounts of the horrors are beyond the scope of this book. *Murder of a Gentle Land* was published by the Reader's Digest Press and distributed by Thomas J. Crowell Inc .(New York, 1977).
13. Foreign Broadcast Information Service.
14. *AIM Report*, March 1980, Part I.
15. *Wall Street Journal*, 31 August 1978.
16. *AIM Report*, March 1978, Part II; June 1978, Part I. Miss Becker showed similar bias in October 1978 in her *Post* story on a press conference by Lon Nol, who was appealing for international help for his suffering people. The Becker story said that his visit to Washington was "an embarrassment" and his plea was "hopeless." See *AIM Report* for October 1978, Part I.
17. *AIM Report*, January 1979, Part II.
18. *F.E.E.R.*, 28 December 1978.
19. *F.E.E.R.* and *New York Times*, 25 December 1978 and 29 December 1978.
20. Quoted in *AIM Report*, January 1979, Part II.

NOTES TO CHAPTER IX
1. Frederick C. Barghoorn, *Soviet Foreign Propaganda* (Princeton, 1964), p. 59.

For similar attacks on the U.S. Information Agency, see Theodore Sorenson, *The Word War*, pp. 156 ff.

2. Interview with Jerry Rosenthal, Chief Publications Division, AID, January 1975.

3. *AIM Report*, September 1974, February 1975, and November 1976, Part I.

4. Dr. Ernest W. Lefever, "Romanticizing Terrorism," *Near East Report*, 27 June 1973; and article distributed by North American Newspaper Alliance, appearing in *Boston Globe*, 9 September 1973, and elsewhere.

5. Lefever and David Reed, "The Tupameros," *Readers Digest*, September 1973.

6. Canby in 1977 wrote a favorable review of the movie *Hearts and Minds*, an artful but savage attack on American policy in Viet Nam. Canby said it should be the one thematic movie for America's Bicentennial Year. In 1980 Canby followed with a highly favorable review of a movie on the Hiss case, which portrays Hiss as innocent. Canby thus placed himself and the movie producer as among the few liberals who still believe in Hiss's innocence after the exhaustive study of the Hiss-Chambers case in Professor Allen Weinstein's *Perjury*.

7. *Time* said that Avedon did not mean the photos to look like a police line-up and "never bothered to have them published, but a number of journalists knew of their existence. Among them was Charlotte Curtis, editor of the *Times* Op Ed page...." Avedon also took the picture of Orlando Letelier appearing on the Op Ed Page after his murder. (See Chapter III on the Far Left Lobby.)

NOTES TO CHAPTER X

1. "Labor in Viet Nam," Labor Division, Trade Union Branch, U.S. AID, 1970. "Labor Law and Practice in the Republic of Viet-Nam", U.S. Department of Labor, Bureau of Labor Statistics, 1968. "Labour's Love Gained," *Far Eastern Economic Review*, 8 May 1971. James L. Tyson, "Labor Unions in South Viet Nam," *Asian Affairs*, November-December 1974.

2. For a summary of this program see my article, "Land Reform in Viet Nam: A Progess Report," *Asian Affairs*, September-October 1973.

3. ILO Yearbooks for 1967 through 1972.

4. Statement to the author by the Labor Attache, U.S. Embassy, Saigon, October 1972.

5. An article on Vietnamese labor unions submitted to an American scholarly journal (not *Asian Affairs*) was rejected with the comment that it failed to describe the violent nature of internal labor politics in Viet Nam and that the attempts on Buu's life were part of this internal infighting. In fact I failed to find any evidence of such murderous infighting within labor or anti-Communist political groups in South Viet Nam, even in interviews with anti-Thieu and anti-Buu "Third Force" people.

6. See, for example, Hedrick Smith's description of Communist unions in *The Russians*, (New York, 1976), p. 224.

7. Adam B. Ulam, *The Bolsheviks* (New York, 1965), p. 178.

8. Ulam, p. 507. Lyman B. Kirkpatrick, *Soviet Espionage*, (New York: National Strategy Information Center, 1972), p. 8.

9. Frederick C. Barghoorn, "Soviet Foreign Propaganda," p. 258. Brian Crozier. "Strategy of Survival", p. 143.

10. Victor Riesel column, 30 December 1977.

11. Crozier, pp. 143-144.

12. Riesel column 28 January 1976, etc.

13. Riesel, 6 February 1976. See, for example, the Dudman article on "CIAid" quoted in the previous chapter.

14. Riesel, 3 July 1975; *The Economist*, 1 October 1977; William Safire, "Empty Triumphalism," *New York Times*, 7 June 1976, *New York Times*, 2 November 1977.

15. *New York Times*, 12 February 1980 and 19 February 1980.

16. For further details see the chapters on the Far Left Lobby and the CIA.

17. Quoted by *AIM Report*, June 1980, Part II.

18. Transcript of *On Company Business* broadcast as Non-Fiction Television via PBS under auspices of the TV Laboratory at WNET/Thirteen, New York City.

19. See for example, *AIM Report*, June 1980, Part II and *The Pink Sheet on the Left*, June 16, 1980.

20. Jose Julian Marti is a Cuban national hero, generally considered the Father of the Cuban movement for independence from Spain. He was a journalist and poet, imprisoned and exiled for his efforts for independence. He founded the Cuban Revolutionary Party in New York City in 1892 and was killed while leading an expedition to Cuba in 1895. An admirer of American democracy, he wrote many articles about American culture. (Cuba gained its independence after the U.S. War with Spain in 1898.)

NOTES TO CHAPTER XI

1. This chapter was written in cooperation with Charles Wiley, Executive Director of the National Committee for Responsible Patriotism. Wiley has been a student of Communist propaganda and a military correspondent for more than 25 years. He has been a reporter for several magazines and broadcasting chains, covering eight wars, including Viet Nam and Angola, visiting more than 100 countries, the most recent of which was China, where he was one of the first Americans to tour the Chinese-Soviet border.

I also received valuable suggestions from the late Dr. Donald Brennan, Director of National Security Studies, Hudson Institute. Dr. Brennan served as a consultant to the Departments of State and Defense, the Arms Control and Disarmament Agency, the Department of Energy, the Atomic Energy Commission, and the Executive Office of the President.

"Neutron bomb" is not an accurate description for this device, but since it has been so widely employed by the press, it will be used throughout this chapter. Actually the present weapon is not a bomb, being designed for use in a rocket missile or an artillery shell. It is more accurately described as an "Enhanced Radiation Reduced Blast" weapon. This was the term used in most official U.S. communications to Europe, and is one reason the NATO governments were so surprised and mystified when the furor over the "neutron bomb" first started in the American press. Many of their officials had never heard of a "neutron bomb."

2. *Documents on Disarmament*, Arms Control and Disarmament Agency, Washington, D.C., pp. 281-2.

3. Same, pp. 342-3.

4. *New York Times*, several issues during this period. Eugene Methvin, *The Riot Makers*, New Rochelle, N.Y., 1970, pp. 217-222.

5. *N.Y. Times*, and Methvin.

6. *N.Y. Times*, August 7, 1962.

7. Methvin, p. 219.

8. *N.Y. Times*, July 27 through August 7, 1962. Further notes by Charles Wiley, who was a correspondent at this festival.

9. For more technical details on the relative characteristics of the neutron bomb and other atomic weapons see Dr. Donald Brennan, "The Neutron Bomb Controversy", Hudson Institute Paper, 3 April 1978.

10. Quoted by Brennan, p. 13.

11. Accuracy in Media, "National Defense — Watching or Dogging?" Tape of April 22, 1978 session, Washington, D.C.

12. See the *Washington Post* from 7 June 1977 to 27 June 1977.

13. Ibid.

14. Cotter's letter to the *Washington Post*, July 20, 1977.

15. *Current Digest of the Soviet Press. Foreign Broadcast Information Service.* CIA Study of Soviet Propaganda Activities Abroad, Appendix R in *The CIA and the Media*, Hearings Before the Permanent Select Committee on Intelligence, House of Representatives, 27 December 1977 through 20 April 1978, p. 553.

16. Ibid.

17. CIA Study. pp. 563-565.

18. CIA Study. For further details and sources, see above, Chapter II and the chart of Communist propaganda organizations.

19. CIA Study. *Current Digest of the Soviet Press* and *Foreign Broadcast Information Service* during this entire period.

20. *Far Eastern Economic Review*, November 10, 1978.

21. Quoted in CIA Study, p. 555.

22. "To Preserve and Not to Destroy," National Council of Churches Statements

on Disarmament, 10 November 1977, p. 15. NARMIC (National Action Research on the Military Industrial Complex), a sub-unit of the AFSC, has published voluminous materials against the neutron bomb in cooperation with the Coalition for a New Foreign and Military Policy, located in the Maryland Avenue house with other Far Left Lobby groups.

23. "Religious Leaders Call for N-Bomb to be Outlawed," *Soviet News*, Soviet Embassy, London, 1 January 1978. "Patriarch Pimen's Message to Pope Paul", *Soviet News*, 3 January 1978.

24. *Soviet News*, 20 December 1977; 3 and 10 January 1978.

25. CIA Study.

26. "International Forum: The Amsterdam Appeal," published by "International Forum Bureau of the 'Stop de Neutronenbom' Initiative Group," Amsterdam, 19 March 1978.

27. *FBIS*, 5 October and 16 November 1977. 23 January 1978.

28. For more details on the links between these groups and the WPC, see chapter III. Their activities in cooperating with the WPC to attack the neutron bomb are described in some detail in *Congressional Record*, 15 May 1978, Remarks by Congressman Larry McDonald of Georgia. The Women's International League for Peace and Freedom publishes a monthly, *Peace and Freedom*. WSP publishes the monthly *Legislative Alert*. Both print regular attacks on the neutron bomb.

29. On the CIA and FBI, 23 June 1973. On the armaments industry, 15 January 1974, etc.

30. William Colby, *Honorable Men*, New York, 1978. *The CIA and Watergate*, by Walter Pincus, from proceedings of the CNSS conference on "The CIA and Covert Activities", September 12 and 13, 1974.

31. Scoville is on the Board of Advisors of the Center for Defense Information, one of the Maryland Avenue group described above. He has had numerous articles in their "Defense Monitor" and other periodicals attacking the neutron bomb. His articles are regularly quoted by Soviet media. e.g. an article in "Defense Monitor" of February 1977 was quoted in *New World Review*, and Radio Moscow quoted his memo to Congress of March 8, 1978 saying the defense budget could be cut by $10 billion. Similar article on April 15 and May 27, 1976.

32. "People Killer", *Nation*, July 9, 1977. "Ultimate Weapon", *Progressive*, August 1977. Also February 1978.

33. *Vanderbilt TV News Archives*. June-December 1977.

34. *Times*. 31 July 1977.

35. *Times*. 18 April 1978. See the April 26 letter from Dr. Donald Brennan contradicting Scoville's technical points and defending the *Times* editorial.

36. Both are prominent organizations in the Far Left Lobby. For more details on their activities see Chapter III.

37. *Times*. April 4 through 20, 1977. *Time* April 17.

38. William Safire columns, *New York Times*, 16 May 1978 and 4 October 1979. Richard Burt, "Brzezinski's Deputy, Source of Growing Influence," *Times*, 28 March 1979. John Rees, "Infiltration of the Media by the KGB and Its Friends," tape from Accuracy in Media Conference, 28 April 1978.

39. *FBIS*, Moscow Radio, 5-20 April 1978. *Soviet News*, 18 April 1978.

40. *Time*, April 24, May 1. *Atlas*, June 1978.

41. *Soviet News*, 2 May 1978. *FBIS*, Radio Moscow, 19-30 April 1978, etc.

42. Quoted in the CIA Study, "Soviet Covert Action and Propaganda", presented to the Oversight Subcommittee on Intelligence, February 6, 1980.

NOTES TO CHAPTER XII

1. "The Soviet and Communist Bloc Defamation Campaign," CIA Report submitted by Congressman Melvin Price, *Congressional Record*, 28 September 1965.

2. Allen W. Dulles, *The Craft of Intelligence*, (New York, 1963), p. 189.

3. Church League of America, *Protecting Traitors*, p. 45.

4. *Information Digest*, 15 June 1979.

5. "The Center for Constitutional Rights" by Congressman Larry McDonald, *Congressional Record* 10 September 1975.

6. Dom Bonafede, "Uncle Sam: The Flimflam Man?", *Washington Journalism Review*, April/May 1978.

7. See William Colby, *Honorable Men: My Life in the CIA*, (New York, 1978), and David A. Phillips, *The Night Watch*, (New York, 1977).

8. Quoted in *Protecting Traitors*, p. 28.

9. This statement was made to me by a prominent member of the Cuban refugee community in the U.S. with close ties to Latin American intelligence sources.

10. *The CIA File*, edited by Borosage and Marks (New York, 1976), p. 79.

11. Victor Riesel, "Americans Need Not Be Ashamed of ITT vs. Marxism", by Victor Riesel, *Human Events*, 20 June 1973.

12. The Senate Intelligence Committee later cleared the CIA of any direct role in the Allende overthrow (*New York Times*, 5 December 1975), but not before this issue had become a major weapon of the anti-intelligence forces in blackening the CIA's reputation and leading to later restrictions on all covert operations. Three members of the Senate Committee staff had close ties with the Far Left Lobby. William Miller (formerly on the Advisory Board of CIP), Karl Inderfurth, and Gregory Treverton presented reports at the hearing on Chile based on an "in depth inquiry done by the committee and staff over the past 8 months," supporting most of the allegations against the CIA and attacking the need for covert action in general. (Hearings of the Senate Intelligence Committee, 4 December 1975.) John Rees of *Information Digest* later said that he had interviewed these men, who said they received most of their information on Chile from: (1) Letelier; (2) Professor Richard Fagan of the University of California, who is closely associated with Trotskyite and Castroite groups and had travelled to Cuba in 1969 with an SDS party; and (3) Tad Szulc. (John Rees, "Infiltration of the Media by the KGB and Its Friends," AIM Conference, 20 April 1978.) Their reports were presented at this open hearing before being submitted to the Committee as a whole. Senator Goldwater protested angrily that the Republican members had not seen them.

13. This and subsequent data on TV coverage of intelligence subjects are from Ernest W. Lefever and Roy Godson, *The CIA and the American Ethic* (Ethics & Public Policy Center, Georgetown University, 1979). Lefever's center carried out a detailed analysis of TV evening news coverage of intelligence matters from 1974 through 1978 based on the Vanderbilt TV News Archives.

14. p. 230. Rositzke is a liberal who is quite critical of the CIA in some parts of his book (the introduction is by Arthur Schlesinger Jr.), and it seems unlikely he would give the CIA the benefit of the doubt on this incident.

15. Colby, *Honorable Men*, pp. 409-411. Daniel Schorr, *Clearing the Air* (Boston, 1977), pp. 144-152.

16. *Clearing the Air*, pp. 7-11, 263.

17. "Alleged Assassination Reports Involving Foreign Leaders," Select Committee to Study Governmental Operations, 20 November 1975.

18. Tom Wicker, *On Press* (New York, 1978), pp. 214-220.

19. *Protecting Traitors*, p. 35.

20. Colby, p. 417.

21. See for example transcript of "The Sub, the CIA, and the Press," from *Behind the Lines*, Educational Broadcasting Corporation broadcast on Channel 13, 26 March 1975 with Harrison Salisbury, Jack Anderson, Ben Bradlee of the *Washington Post*, Jack Nelson, *Los Angeles Times* Washington Bureau Chief, and John Oakes of the *New York Times*. Only Oakes defended the idea of witholding publication for reasons of national security. Bradlee claimed the facts were known already by "the godless Commies" (one of his favorite phrases). Salisbury called the whole important exercise "the submarine caper." See also Anthony Lewis, "The Secrecy Disease," *New York Times*, 31 December 1977. All the far left points against the project are summarized in a book published by Random House (the perennial publisher of anti-CIA tracts) in 1978: *A Matter of Risk* by Roy Varner and Wayne Collier.

22. See Clyde W. Burleson, *The Jennifer Project* (Prentice-Hall, 1977). This and the Varner Collier book are reviewed in *Naval Institute Proceedings*, June 1979, by Commander Robert E. Bublitz, U.S.N. (ret.).

23. Quoted in *AIM Report*, July 1975.

24. As late as May 1980 this never-used dart gun was the lead-off sequence of a three hour, three part series, *On Company Business*, of the Public Broadcasting

Service, a highly biased attack on the CIA for which the Special Consultant was Philip Agee, the CIA defector.

25. Schorr, p. 191-207.

26. Same, p. 7, 8.

27. *FBIS*, Radio Moscow, 28 April – 30 May 1976. *Digest of the Soviet Press*, May 1976.

28. *Protecting Traitors*, p. 30.

29. *New York Times*, 14 September, 1980. The Wise review is quoted in *Pink Sheet on the Left*, 14 July 1980. Donner was identified as a Communist by three former Communists testifying before HUAC on 13 December 1955, 14 December 1955, and 1 March 1956. See also HUAC Report, "Communist Legal Subversion," 16 February 1959. He invoked the First and Fifth Amendments when asked about party membership by HUAC on 28 June 1956. For additional details see Church League of America, *National Layman's Digest*, 1 October 1980. In his book Donner acknowledges the help of the Stern Foundation, Field Foundation, and the Rabinowitz Foundation.

30. HUAC: Annual Reports, 1960, 1962; "Report and Testimony of Robert C. Ronstadt, 10 October 1962.

31. "The CIA and the American Ethic", Ernest W. Lefever and Roy Godson, (Washington, 1979), p. 74, 78. *Protecting Traitors*, p. 18.

32. *Protecting Traitors*, p. 17.

33. John H. Maury, "The Media and the Intelligence Community," AIM Conference, November 2, 1979. Maury added that the first Admiral Turner learned that Stockwell had any criticisms to offer of CIA policies was when he read Stockwell's "letter of resignation" in *The Washington Post*.

34. See for example, Snepp interview on CBS, 11 November 1977; Gloria Emerson, "The Spy Who Rang My Doorbell," *New York*, 23 January 1978; favorable review by Morton Halperin in *Nation*, 29 April 1978; Snepp, "On CIA Secrecy, News, Leaks and Censorship," *New York Times* Op-Ed page, 3 March 1978; Tom Wicker, "Three Vital Appeals", *New York Times*, 11 July 1978.

35. Quoted in an Evans & Novak column reproduced in the *AIM Report*, March 1977, Part I. This was the second Evans & Novak column reporting on the Letelier Papers. It was suppressed by the *Washington Post* but did run in several other papers.

36. *New York Times*, 9 February 1976, 12 September 1977, 25 December – 28 1977. The final House hearings were reported in "The CIA and the Media", Subcommittee on Oversight, 27 December 1977 through 20 April 1978. The ubiquitous Morton Halperin appeared at this hearing. This report also contains the valuable document prepared by the CIA at the request of Representative John Ashbrook on "The Soviet Use of the Media" (in foreign countries). This is virtually the only place where the KGB is mentioned in the hearings or the report.

37. Listed by Daniel Tsang, research librarian on the Alternatives Acquisitions Project, Temple University Libraries, Philadelphia, in "Anti-Surveillance Periodicals," Library Journal, 1 December 1979.

38. Lefever & Godson, pp. 96-117.

39. From the tape of the session on "The Media and the Intelligence Community", Accuracy in Media Conference, 2 and 3 November 1979. For more details on Hersh's down-playing of the KGB threat, see the Appendix.

40. An array of the parallels between the proposed charter and the recommendations of Halperin's group was submitted to the Senate Intelligence Committee by Congressman Larry McDonald in a letter of 3 February 1978. This aroused indignant comments from Senators Hart and Huddleston against the charge that the Committee had been influenced by the ACLU, NLG, etc. But the parallels are plain to see. This letter and McDonald's testimony before the Committee also outlined some of the Communist connections of members of Halperin's group. Hearings Before the Select Committee on Intelligence, 27 and 30 January 1978.

41. *Times*, 6 May 1980. William Schaap wrote an article for the Op-Ed Page of the Times of 2 January 1980 attacking the bill prohibiting the naming of intelligence personnel. As is so often the case, the *Times* gave a completely inadequate identification of Schaap, saying only that he is editor of the *Covert Action Information Bulletin*. The paper did not say that this bulletin is the major offender on

revealing the names of CIA personnel overseas, or that Schaap is the associate of the CIA turncoat, Philip Agee, or that he is a former law partner of the Lubell brothers, two identified Communists.

NOTES ON CHAPTER XIII
1. New York, 1975.
2. Robert Morris, *Self Destruct—Dismantling America's Internal Security* (New Rochelle, 1979), p. 106.
3. These include: Committee for Scientific Truth in the Public Interest, 1511 Denniston Avenue, Pittsbugh, Pa. 15217. Scientists for Accuracy in Media, 1034 La Brea, Pocatello, Idaho 83201. Americans for Rational Energy Alternatives, Box 11802, Albuquerque, New Mexico 87192.
4. The addresses of these and similar organizations are: Chrsitian Anti-Communist Crusade, Box 809, Long Beach, Calif. 90801. Eastern European Bible Mission, Box 73, Walnut Creek, Calif. 94596. Evangelize China Fellowship, 3 The Brae, Groomsport, Bangor, County Down, U.K. Christian and Missionary Alliance, Nyack, N.Y. Open Doors, Box 6, Standlake, Witney, Oxon, U.K. Research Center for Religion and Human Rights in Closed Societies, Room 448, 475 Riverside Drive, New York, N.Y. 10027 .Others are described by P. J. Johnstone, in *Operation World, A Handbook for World Intercession*, STL Publications, (Bromley, England: STL Publications).
5. "Communist Bloc Intelligence Activities in the United States", Hearings Before the Senate Internal Security Subcommtitee, U.S. Senate, 18 November 1975, p. 25.

NOTES TO THE APPENDIX
1. *Tactics* magazine, 2 February 1970.
2. Ibid, page 8. For further details on Philip Stern, James Boyd, and these funds, see Chapter II on the Far Left Lobby.
3. Tape of conference available from AIM, 777 14th St., N.W. Washington, D.C. 20000.
4. These details on Landau's early career are from *Headquarters for Destruction: The Behind the Scenes Story of the North American Congress on Latin America* (Church League of America, 1972).
5. *Time*, 16 December 1966, p. 82.
6. These descriptions of Landau's films are from the IPS Catalogue for Fall 1979.

CHART II

FACTS VS. ALLEGATIONS ON ASSASSINATION ATTEMPTS

Leader	Facts	Comments
Castro	Several attempts, all unsuccessful.	Weight of evidence shows CIA launched attempts only on orders from very high authority, most probably with knowledge of Kennedys. Should be judged in light of conditions at that time. Castro was first breach in containment policy, a Communist dictatorship within 90 miles of U.S. During period of these attempts he was allowing Soviets to prepare to install nuclear missiles, a major threat to U.S., leading to "Missile Crisis". He was later quoted as criticizing Soviets for backing down and withdrawing missiles.
Lumumba	In 1960 CIA officers were ordered to devise plot to assassinate Lumumba, evidently with knowledge of Eisenhower and Allen Dulles. Attempt never materialized and Lumumba was later shot by Congolese rivals, with no CIA involvement.	
Trujillo	U.S. cooperated with dissidents in Dominican Republic. Supplied them with arms, but had no direct involvement in assassination.	Trujillo was one of the most brutal dictators in Latin American history. CIA and U.S. government cannot be criticized for encouraging his overthrow.
Diem	U.S. Government and CIA were privy to plot by South Vietnamese military to overthrow Diem, and gave it cautious support, but did not cooperate with or approve of assassination.	Assassination was evidently unauthorized even by the South Vietnamese coup leaders, but was carried out by junior officers. U.S. not involved.
General Schneider (Chile)	Killed by plotters who had been in contact with CIA. But CIA had specifically disapproved assassination and no U.S. weapons were used.	

INDEX

276

Rockefeller Commission 184, 186, 196
Rockford Institute 34, 253
Rogers, William 82
Rogovin, Mitchell 193
Rolling Stone 33, 202
Roraback, Catherine 36, 38
Rosen, Pauline 15, 163
Rosenthal, A. M. 185, 186, 191
Rosen, Pauline 120
Rositzke, Harry 184
Ross, Thomas 176, 177
Rovere, Richard 165
Royal Government of National
   Union (Grunk) 85, 90, 124n
Rubber Workers Union 71
Rubin Foundation 37, 40, 57, 201
Rubin, Reed 40
Rubin, Samuel 40, 57
Rudovsky, David 36, 38, 194
Russell, Philip 53
Russell, Richard 80
Russian Orthodox Church 163
Russo, Anthony 56, 174

S.A.N.E. 60, 113
Sadlowski, Ed 44
Safire, William 104, 119, 148
St. Louis Post Dispatch 42, 96
Sakharov, Andrei 213
Sale, Kirkpatrick 174
Salisbury, Harrison 266
Salper, Roberta 45
SALT I 1, 2
SALT II 3
Samuels, Dorothy 39
Sargeant, Howland H. 254
"Say No to the F.B.I." (pamphlet) 38
Schaap, William 38, 175
Schanberg, Sidney 92n, 125
Schell, Orville Jr. 192
Schlesinger, Arthur Jr. 44, 122
Schlesinger, James 160, 183
Schmidt, Helmut 167
Schneider, Rene 178, 187
Schorr, Daniel 186, 196
Schuman, Tomas (See Yuri
   Besmenoff)
Schurmann, Franz H. 46, 107

Schwartz, Dr. Fred 219
Scientific American 37, 51, 59, 165
Scoville, Herbert 51, 164
Scribner, David 38
Seixas, Angela 153
Senate Armed Service Committee
   3, 82, 185
Senate Committee on Multi-
   nationals 179
Senate Foreign Relations
   Committee 81, 130
Senate Committee on the Judiciary 227
Senate Select Committee on
   Intelligence 50, 166, 184, 206
Senate Select Committee to Study
   Governmental Operations with
   Respect to Intelligence Activities
   (Church Committee) 187, 193
Senate Subcommittee on Criminal
   Laws and Procedures 4
Senate Subcommittee on Internal
   Security 4, 35, 218, 255
Senkuttuvan, Arun 70
Shaplen, Robert 148
Shattan, Joseph 257
Shattuck, John 201
Shawcross, William 95, 129
Sheehan, Neil 193
Shelepin, Alexander 150
Sideshow 95
Siegel, Danny 46
Siemen-Netto, Uwe 261
Sihanouk, Samdech Norodom
   77n, 110, 119, 126, 231
Singapore 102, 132, 214
Singapore, University of,
   Students Union 69
Singapore Polytechnic
   Students Union 69
Singlaub, John 254
Sirik Matak 89
Sitnikov, Vassily 171
Smith, Benjamin E. 38
Snyder, Edward 50
Sobell, Martin 36
Social Democrats U.S.A. 60
Socialist International 69, 132
Socialist Workers Party 199, 239

Treverton, Gregory 206, 266
Tri-Continental Information Center in
   New York 56
Trieres, James J. 51
*The Trojan Horse: the Strange
   Politics of Foreign Aid* 53
Truehaft, Robert 36
Trumbo, Dalton 29, 204, 255
Trujillo, Rafael 187
Tyson, Brady 52
The U-2 Affair 176

Ulam, Adam B. 254
Umbricht, Victor 110
Union Theological Seminary 115, 127
UNESCO 61n, 75
United Nations (UN) 52, 110n,
   126, 127, 207, 217
United Auto Workers 151
U.N. Commission on Human Rights 71
U.N. Office of Refugees 110
United Press (UP) 35, 109, 113
U.S. Peace Council 15, 120
U.S. Information Agency (U.S.I.A.)
   See International Communications
   Agency
United Steel Workers 43
Uruguay 137n, 151

Van Houten, Margaret 56, 174
Vance, Cyrus 50, 166, 207
Vashee, Basker 48
Venceremos Brigade 27, 52
Viet Cong 56, 103, 111, 142, 145
Vietnam 49, 66, 101, 129, 145n,
   197, 200, 232
Viet Nam, an American Journey 118
Vietnam War 23, 26, 31, 193
Village Voice 197
Villastrigo, Edith 58
Vinh Son Church 104
Voice of America 223
Volunteers in Service to
   America (VISTA) 43, 56

Walker, Doris B. 36
Wall Street Journal 130, 257
Wannall, Ray 14, 26, 255

Waples, Douglas 255
War Without Winners 50
Warnke, Paul 51
Washington Post 25, 35, 54, 83, 96, 97,
   112, 113, 120, 126, 131, 160, 182,
   211, 259, 266
Waskow, Arthur 41, 44, 256
Watson, Francis 34, 255
Weather Underground 27, 35, 36, 37,
   46, 52, 138, 201
Weber, Susan 45, 50
Webster, William 4
Weiss, Cora 40, 57, 116
Weiss, Peter 37, 38, 40n, 201
Weissman, Steve 53
Welch, Richard S. 174, 195
Wexler, Haskell 201, 240
What Is To Be Done? 17, 18, 20
Wheaton, Rev. Philip 174
Wheeler, Earl 81
Whitten, Les 192
Wicker, Tom 82, 94, 97, 191, 192, 208
Wiley, Charles 250, 253, 254
Wilkins, Roger 54
Wilkinson, Allen 21
Wilkinson, Frank 37, 199
Willens, Harold 51
Williamson, Bill 147
Wise, David 51, 59, 176, 177, 199
Wolfe, Alan 57
Women Strike for Peace 15, 39, 40,
   42, 48, 58, 155n, 199, 214
Women's International Democratic
   Federation 14, 15, 58, 162
Women's International League for
   Peace and Freedom 39, 42, 48,
   58, 120, 164, 199
World Convention Against Atomic
   and Hydrogen Bombs (Tokyo) 157
World Council of Churches 224
World Federation of Democratic
   Youth 15
World Federation of Scientific
   Workers 162
World Federation of Trade Unions
   14, 149, 162
World Peace Assembly 43
World Peace Council 14, 15, 37, 47, 48,